AF412929

VERBAL CONTROL
WITH
MICROCOMPUTERS

No. 1468
$18.95

VERBAL CONTROL
WITH
MICROCOMPUTERS

BY MIKE RIGSBY

FIRST EDITION

FIRST PRINTING

Copyright © 1982 by TAB BOOKS Inc.

Printed in the United States of America

Library of Congress Cataloging in Publication Data

Rigsby, Mike.
    Verbal control with microcomputers.

    Includes index.
    1. Automatic speech recognition. 2. TRS-80 (Computer)
I. Title.
TK7895.S65R53   001.64'42   82-7039
ISBN 0-8306-2468-6   AACR2
ISBN 0-8306-1468-0 (pbk.)

Contents

Introduction

Machines can listen and respond to our spoken commands. Voice-actuated typewriters, sound-controlled toys, and interactive video games can all be built today without great expense. Imagine a battery-powered computer that can distinguish words; imagine building it for less than one hundred dollars! Consider using a TRS-80 computer to recognize words without any extra hardware or modifications. These are all possible and are explained here.

This book is composed of various practical applications of voice recognition technology. From the high school student seeking a science project, to the handicapped person, to the computer hobbyist, to the serious experimenter, there is information here for all.

You should approach this book from your own vantage point. Chapter 1 is a general overview of speech and the problems it presents to machine recognition. Chapter 2 describes devices that are commercially available for attachment to microcomputers. This chapter is good for the nontechnical person seeking off-the-shelf equipment to recognize verbal commands. Chapter 3 details two simple sound control projects, neither of which requires great electrical knowledge. Chapters 4 through 10 are programs (software) for the TRS-80 Model I, Level II, computer with a 16K memory. The programs accept sound input through the cassette recorder and require no external hardware (though a hand-held microphone would be useful). These programs could easily be adapted to any microcomputer that allows BASIC access to input data from the cassette port.

Chapter 4 provides a visual display of a spoken word. The TRS-80 Model III, Level II, 16K computer is slightly different from the Model I, but can use the software in Chapters 4 through 10 if the expression "=255" is changed to "> 200" every single time it appears in a program listing. Chapter 5 is a demonstration that allows the computer to recognize a word from a vocabulary of five. Chapter 6 allows for hands-off operation of a printer. A severely handicapped person could produce printed copy using this program, a computer, and a printer. Chapter 7 provides a simple method for voice control of external devices using a standard microcomputer no difficult wiring is required. Chapter 8 provides an example of fast speech recognition. Chapter 9 is an educational program aimed at about a fourth grade level; it draws a map and asks questions about the directional relationships of the states. Chapter 10 is an animated game with sound output and voice control. Chapter 11 provides software for a voice-operated printer, though it requires the use of the Voxbox peripheral unit.

Chapters 12 through 16 are more technical and deal with construction of a complete computer system, the Recognizer, which has been built and tested. Chapter 12 is an elementary refresher course in practical electronics and electrical construction. Chapter 13 explains the operation of the 1802 microprocessor and its instruction set. Chapter 14 details the construction of the Recognizer. Chapter 15 explains in great detail one program which works with the Recognizer, and Chapter 16 explains an even better program.

All the information in this book (except Chapter 2, for which I thank the manufacturers) was generated in my house with limited equipment.

I would like to thank my wife Annelle for her patience and support (and also for pulling our infant daughter Ember off the computer innumerable times).

Chapter 1
Spoken Words

Speech and noise are often difficult to separate. On a street, in the office, or at a party, people frequently find it troublesome to distinguish spoken words from background sounds. Volume is sometimes the characteristic used to separate desired speech from undesired noise. Consider the case of four people in an automobile, two in the front seat and two in back. Each pair can carry on a conversation while ignoring the talk between the others. Volume is the primary means of separation. A similar situation exists when communicating in a sporting arena; the nearest person produces loud sounds most of the time, but noise is clearly competitive with the sounds of interest.

REMOVING NOISE

Mechanical control of these variables is possible, but each method has limitations. The simplest and most often chosen method uses an insensitive microphone. It must be placed very close to the mouth of the person whose speech is to be recognized. The insensitive microphone will tend to ignore sounds more than a few feet away, thus cancelling out distant noise. The extremely close proximity of this pickup to the lips (the instructions for many units specify that the microphone should "almost touch the lips") provides good separation between noise and the desired sound to be distinguished by the computer. However, holding the microphone near the mouth defeats one of the desired characteristics of voice control—hands-off capability. Although a headset can be used to free your hands, such constraints do not allow you to enter a room and talk to the computer from any position.

Another method of separating noise from speech involves the use of an amplifier with automatic level control. The automatic level control can use a threshold value below which all sounds will be ignored and above which all sounds will be amplified. This will eliminate the noise until speech is uttered (or some other sound breaks the threshold level). If you do not use an automatic level control, the noise will be present when the amplifier is on, and it will cloud the information available for deciphering the spoken word. Automatic level control systems can also use filters to eliminate low-frequency or high-frequency components from the sounds being amplified. Using such a system complicates the input mechanism considerably, and leaves the designer with many variables that may be difficult to anticipate and deal with. Building a device for use in a home, for example, would require knowledge of expected noises. The smooth, even sound of a forced-air heating system would be more easily ignored than the sudden popping of a pine log in a fireplace. Clearly, automatic level control alone is not sufficient to separate voice from noise.

Yet another possibility involves the use of a computer to eliminate random, non-regular noise while passing sounds of regular frequencies and volume levels. Software to accomplish such goals would be complex, and many assumptions would be necessary.

VOLUME AND SPEECH

Inflection, the emphasis placed on certain syllables, is another tool available for use in volume considerations of sound. Any dictionary will show the proper place for emphasis on a given word. However, people do not always follow these rules. The emphasis on any given syllable will vary not only from person to person, but also from time to time in the speech of a single person.

If the first syllable in a word were always given strong emphasis, it would be easy to tell where one word stops and another begins. Detecting inflection is possible and is a good task for a computer. Inflection, being a stronger emphasis on one part of a word than others, is easier to detect by ear than by machine. The Recognizer designed for this book cannot distinguish syllables from one another; thus it cannot look at al the syllables and quantify the loudest one as the point of inflection. It must also be recalled that more than one spot in a word may receive emphasis.

The difference between the non-emphasized portion of speech and the rest of the word is rather small on a quantitative basis. The waveform of a word is so rugged that odd spikes may appear seemingly at random throughout the considered specimen. To view such differences and put them into terms that can be handled by electrical apparatus requires equipment such as that illustrated in Fig. 1-1. The speech considered must be viewed as an alternating current waveform, the power of which is to be measured on an average—but continuing—basis. The electrical wave representing the sound must be passed through a full-wave rectifier bridge (to convert it to a rough form of direct current) and a capacitor must be placed across it to smooth the wave out. This smoothing prevents one spike of high magnitude but short duration from outranking several spikes which are less high, though higher than average. The value of the capacitor cannot be chosen without knowledge of how

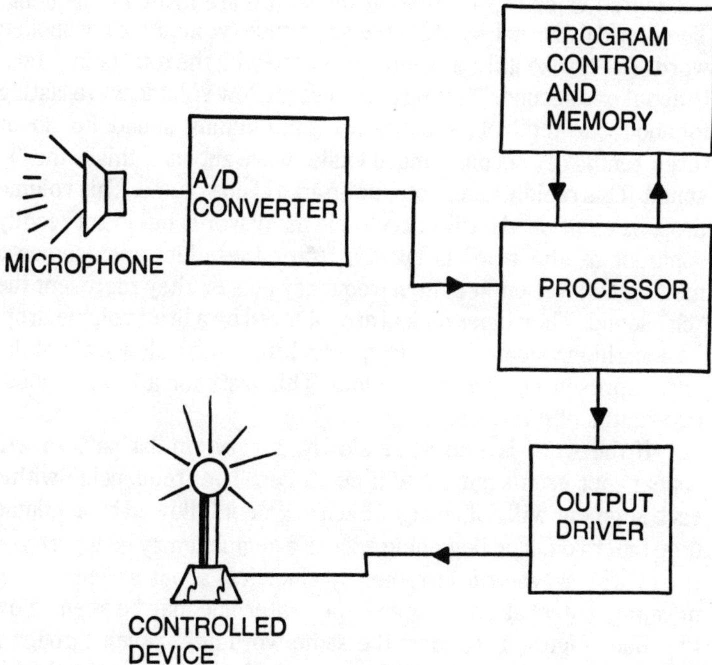

Fig. 1-1. Block diagram of speech recognizer.

much power is delivered from the amplifier, and how much smoothing out is desired.

Once the smooth waveform is obtained, it must be placed into a form that a computer can recognize, that is a digital format. A device know as an analog-to-digital converter is required to accomplish this task. Such devices are moderately complex. They are also expensive.

Volume drop is another phenomenon that makes voice recognition difficult. Just as certain portions of a word are stressed, other portions are left unstressed or nearly silent. When the word "microcomputer" is spoken, there is a trailing off and near pause after the "micro-" and before the "-computer". This volume drop trails off into the area of noise, giving a recognizer the problem of deciding whether the word has ended or not. Volume alone fails as a criteria for use by the sophisticated recognizer because it is not sufficient to determine word ending.

Figure 1-2 is a view of the electrical waveform generated by an amplifier when the word "Michael" is spoken. "Michael" will be used often when representations of a word are made in this book. The vertical axis in Fig. 1-2 is the magnitude (volume) of the spoken word. The horizontal axis represents time with the total being equal to about one second. Starting at the left is a low volume wave lasting for about one-tenth of a second; this is the "mmm" sound. For about three-tenths of a second a much louder wave appears; this is the "i" sound. This rapidly tapers off into an area of no volume. This volume drop, as mentioned earlier, occurs in many words but is not readily apparent as the word is spoken. After the silent spot comes a medium volume burst of high frequency pulses; they represent the "ch" sound. They taper off and are followed by a brief volume drop. Last is a high volume, lower frequency brust with a slow taper at the end, representing the "ael" sound. This lasts for a total of about two-tenths of one second.

If the word is said more slowly, a very similar pattern will appear, but each segment will be longer. The frequencies within each segment will not change. Each segment followed by a volume drop tapers off. The beginning edge of a segment may be tapered or sharp. The waveform is rather symmetrical about a center line, meaning that what occurs above the center line may be seen below that line. Figure 1-3 shows the same word after going through a bridge rectifier, but before being smoothed with a capacitor. At this point the volume levels are more apparent, and the frequency characteristic is still visible. Figure 1-4 shows the waveform after

4

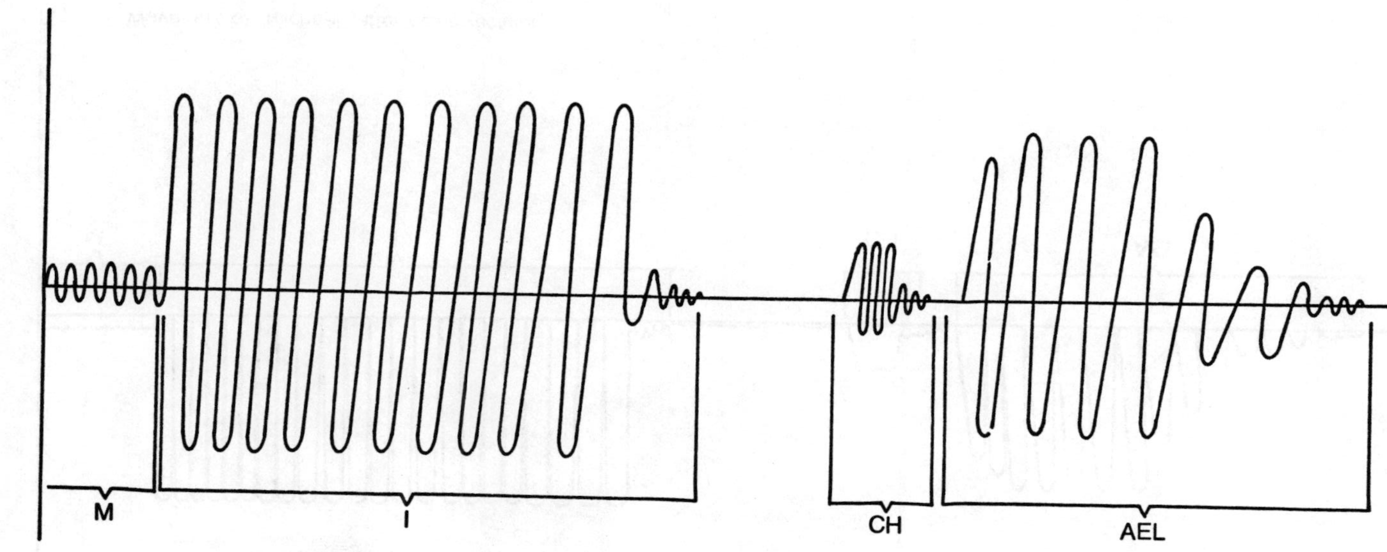

Fig. 1-2. Waveform of the word "Michael."

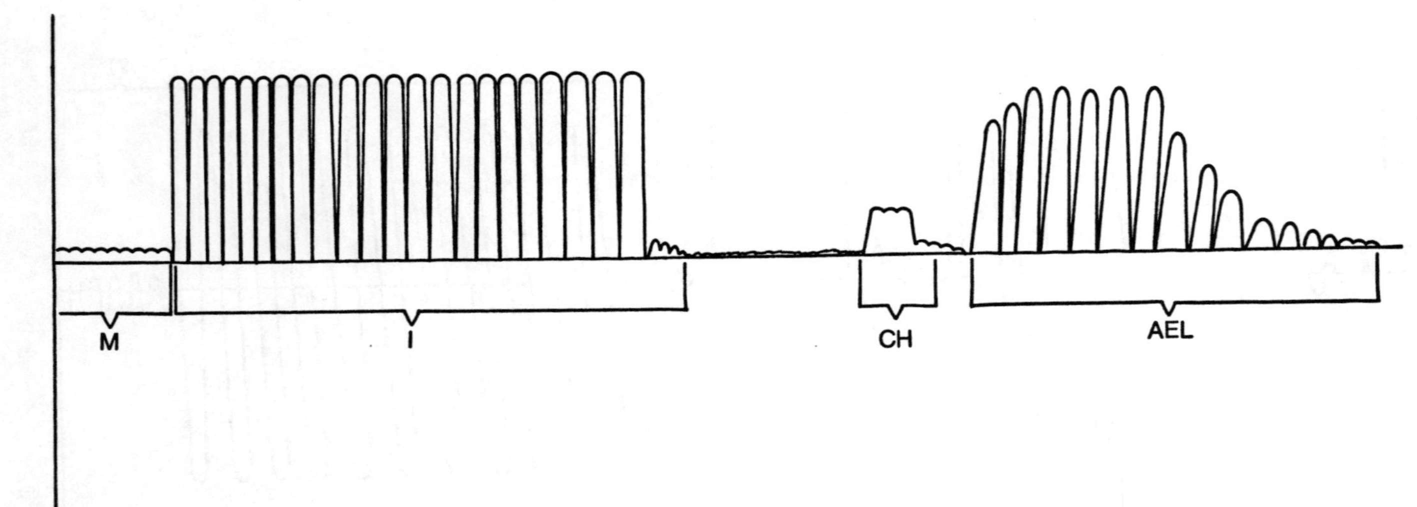

Fig. 1-3. Waveform of "Michael" after being rectified.

6

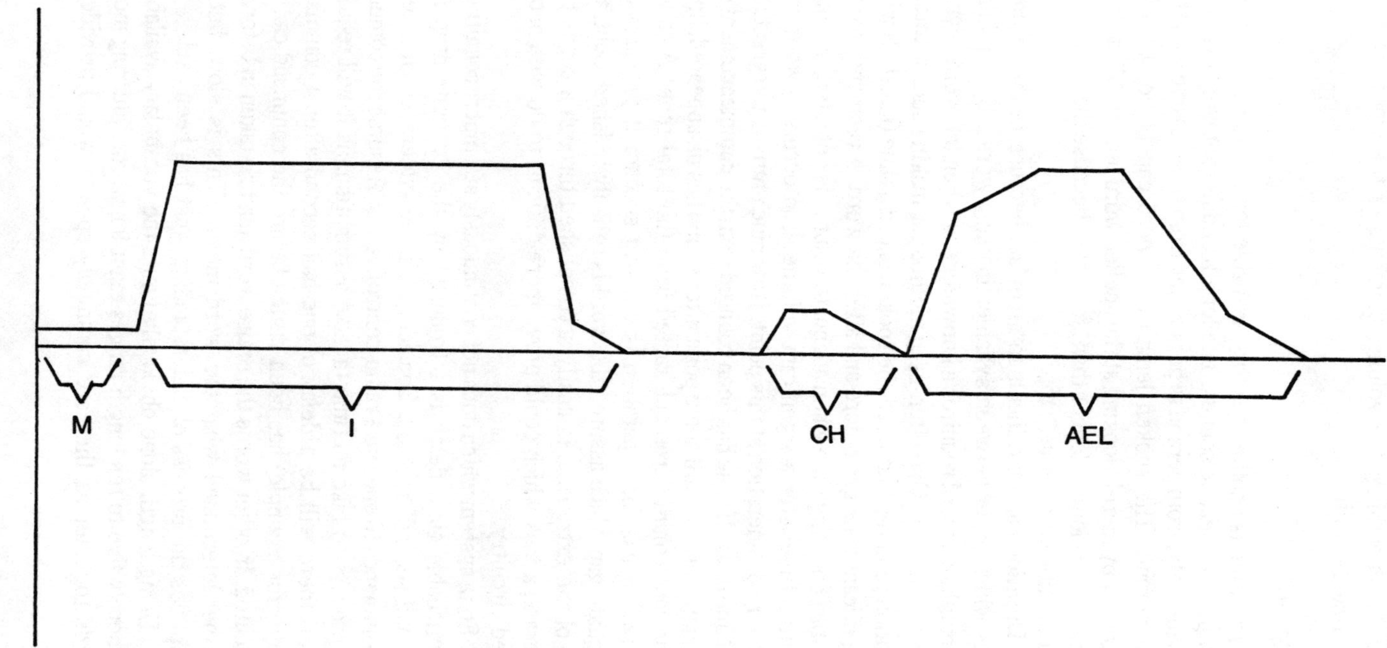

Fig. 1-4. Waveform of "Michael" after being rectified and smoothed by a capacitor.

capacitor smoothing; the volume elements of the word are now more readily visible.

DURATION

Duration is another quantity available for consideration when attempting to decode sounds. The length of different words varies, unfortunately, from person to person and from time to time with the same person. The spoken length of a word cannot be obtained intuitively by merely looking at the spelled word length. "Stop," for example, is as long or longer than "forward," because the "o" is held for a significant time in "stop."

Duration can be difficult to ascertain because of the volume drops which occur between syllables in many words. Determining the length of a word requires a knowledge of when the word begins and when it ends. One often-used method for making such a determination requires that words be spoken one at a time (isolated) with a significant time gap before and after the word. A recognition unit can start counting time when adequate volume is detected, and quit counting time after a significant volume drop occurs. Two items arise for consideration at this point. How much time is too great for a volume drop? If time has been counted from the commencement of adequate volume until some point after sound has disappeared, how is the last volume drop subtracted from the total time? A rough number to use for separation is one-half second; it provides an adequate gap which assures the word is reliably finished. Subtraction of the extra time is easily accomplished through a computer program, a task which could prove more difficult to do with hard-wired circuitry.

For a system which does not continuously attempt recognition, a noticeable time delay is introduced by the "volume drop for one-half second" method. Consider a simple system which listens to commands to operate a radio-controlled toy. Assume the computing process to take no time (a false assumption, as it will require time); there will be a delay of one-half second after a command (stop," for example) has been issued before the command can be executed. In other words the entire word must be taken in before it can be determined what the word means. This is slow, but it simplifies the process of understanding what has been said.

Using length alone obviously limits the vocabulary available, as merely five to ten length ranges exist for words. Slurring more words together as they are commonly spoken would provide a greater capability, but effective verbal control with a 25-word slurred sentence would be impractical.

Length can be used in sophisticated systems to aid in noise elimination. If a sound exists at a consistent volume level for too long a period of time, then it must be some form of noise. This noise can be stored and subtracted from any potential word being heard. A key problem here is the same one faced before—just how much time a steady sound must exist to be considered not part of a word.

LENGTH AND VOLUME COMBINED

Length and volume together can be used to create a simple, though somewhat limited, recognition system. Taking a sound and amplifying it are necessary for any system. The system roughed out in Fig. 1-5 could be used to control a television or lights in a room. It would have a command recognition involving only two responses, but would be relatively free from false operations. The amplifier must be adjusted so that ordinary talking and room sounds will not exceed the threshold required for recognition attempts. To operate the system requires raising your voice, at which point the timer will start. If the sound coming from the amplifier is sufficiently loud, it will go through the rectifier and be converted into rippled direct current; then it will be smoothed by the capacitor (chosen to hold the signal up for short word drops) and operate the timer. If the sound is too short, the timer will reset and nothing will happen. If it is of fair length (the word "on," for example), and it goes away, then the first output will be activated. If it is longer (for example, the words "turn off" slurred together), then the second output will be activated. The advantages of such a system include simplicity (no computer) and microphone independence. Noise is separated from the desired commands by the requirement that the user shout. This

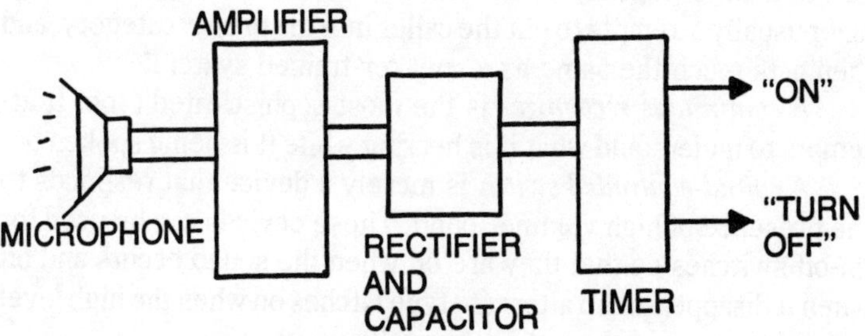

Fig. 1-5. Block diagram of two response sound control system.

forces the separation. The microphone need not be close to the user and can be placed in any convenient location.

SYSTEM DEFINITIONS

A speaker-trained, voice-dependent, isolated-word recognizer sounds more involved than it actually is. A device that is *speaker-trained* must be taught by the person who is to use it. *Voice dependence* is another way of saying that the machine should only respond to one person's voice. Before running off to purchase one of these devices to use as a key for your front door, note that this is not the purpose of being voice dependent. Voice-dependent systems are more easily designed than voice-independent systems; they will work for the person who trains them, and they may also work for someone else who has a similar sounding voice. A voice-dependent system to open your front door could be built with a high degree of selectivity, but a sore throat could leave you locked out until spring! *Isolated-word systems* can respond to only one word at a time, and that word must be preceded and followed by a period of silence, in order that the recognizer may know what it is trying to recognize.

A *speaker-independent*, word-isolated system still requires that the word under consideration be preceded and followed by a period of silence, but it does not require training and it should respond to the voice of any person. Such systems in use now usually have a small vocabulary and operate over a phone line (you call them up and speak a number in response to a question). They have several "templates" of different voice characteristics in their memory system and they attempt to fit the caller into a category as fast as possible so they can then recognize what is uttered. Different categories are needed because the duration of speech and frequency response of a Southern male may be significantly different from the duration and frequency of a Northern female. This type of recognizer usually attempts to put the caller into the proper category, and then acts much the same as a speaker-trained system.

A *continuous recognizer* is the most sophisticated type. It attempts to understand what it is hearing while it is being spoken to.

A *sound-controlled switch* is merely a device that responds to the presence of high volume sound. These devices can be used for on-off switches so that they are on when the sound occurs and off when it disappears. An alternate type latches on when the high level sound occurs, and it must be manually reset.

A sound-controlled switch with *logic* is merely a simple switch that can be used for some form of sequential control. The logic can be nothing more than a stepping relay. For example, a four-step sound-controlled switch could cause a toy to go forward, then right, then left, then stop. Each sound would cause the toy to perform the next step in the sequence.

A *limited recognition* sound-controlled switch utilizes some technique other than volume (usually length) to provide greater selectivity than a sound controlled switch. Such a device can distinguish a few commands, such as "go" and "stop," based solely on length and volume. The selectivity is not exclusive; such a switch will enter the "go" mode if "a" is pronounced, or the "stop" mode if "help" is pronounced. In other words, any sound which is loud enough and of the proper length will cause the device to operate.

A limited recognition sound-controlled switch with logic allows for more deliberate and unlimited control. Using two variable length commands and a stepping switch to advance from point to point, you can obtain precise control. Consider a case where the two commands are "go" and "activate;" the "go" command could be used to advance a stepping relay and illuminate an indicator light that shows what you want the toy to do. The command "activate" could then be used to cause the selected function to be performed. For example, a toy might have four lights, indicating forward, right, left, and stop. The command "go" could cause the lights to move sequentially from forward to right to left to stop. When the light indicating what you want the toy to do is illuminated, you could then speak the command "activate." This will cause the toy to perform the action that you have selected.

Numerous devices are available commercially that adapt to various microcomputers for the purpose of recognizing speech. In Chapter 2 these units will be described, their features listed, and suppliers given.

FREQUENCY

Because many frequencies are found in speech, a method can be used to detect frequencies and their presence or absence. A filter in an electrical circuit is much the same as a filter in an air conditioning system; it allows some things to go through while stopping others. There are several types of filters available; two major categories are active and passive. *Active filters* use electronic components such as integrated circuits or transistors, and they require the application of power in order to perform their duty. *Passive filters* are composed of elements such as capacitors and inductors, and they work without an external power source. Active filters are more easily designed to pass desired frequencies and block undesired frequencies than are passive filters. They are also more economical.

The type of filter which will be of concern to the recognition builder is the *bandpass* filter. Several criteria must be assigned when a filter is designed. There must be a center frequency known as the pass frequency. The bandwidth determines what other frequencies will be allowed to go through. Important as bandwidth is the attenuation level outside the bandwidth. Theoretically, all frequencies will be passed; some will meet with more resistance than others. This resistance must be set to a particular value so that electronic components beyond the filter will ignore frequencies outside the approved bandwidth. Decisions must be made regarding the number of frequencies of interest, and the bandwidth of each. The narrower the bandwidth, the more difficult the filter is to build. The more filters you use, the more information your machine has available to make recognition decisions.

Frequencies readily available are those from 500 to 3,000 hertz. Frequency is measured in a quantity known as *hertz*. One hertz is one cycle per second. One cycle per second is a way of describing the phenomenon that occurs when a voltage starting at zero goes positive, then back to zero, then negative, and then back to zero. This occurrence (zero to positive to zero to negative to zero) is known as a *cycle*. If this cycle occurred one time during a second it would be said to have a frequency of one hertz. If it occurred 500 times during one second, then it would have a frequency of 500 hertz. This cycle does not have to occur five hundred times to have a frequency of five hundred hertz; it must merely occur fast enough so that if it lasted for one second, 500 cycles would occur.

Inexpensive microphones and amplifiers do not have excellent frequency pass characteristics. To expand the range would require costly equipment; the merit of this is doubtful, at least until the information in the available band is fully utilized. Telephone lines do not significantly exceed this range and would therefore not provide any better information to a unit which could handle more.

DIGITAL VOICE

Voice produces an alternating waveform that is well balanced. Although this wave is fairly symmetrical about a center line, it varies in amplitude (volume) and shape of pulse (Fig. 1-6).

To handle this wave using digital electronics, it must be digitized. A Schmitt trigger circuit will do this by rendering a positive

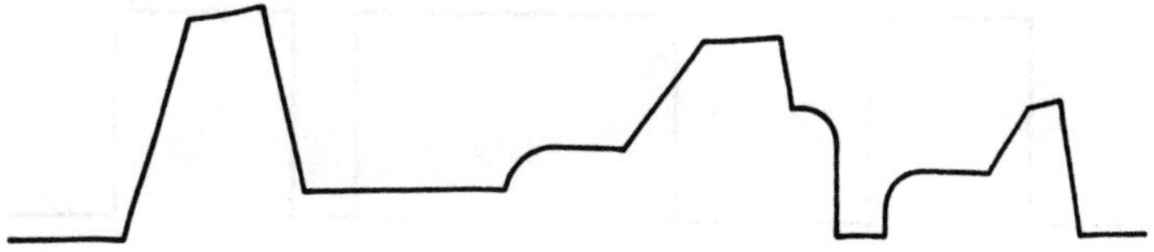
Fig. 1-6. Diagram of a rectified smoothed wave.

output when the input exceeds an arbitrary level and rendering a ground (negative) output when it falls below the trigger level (Fig. 1-7).

The places where a wave goes from high to low or low to high through the center line are called *zero crossings*. Zero crossings may be counted, inasmuch as they provide another clue to the information stored within the spoken word. The total number of zero crossings are related to frequencies involved and duration of speech.

SLURRING, A TASK FOR CONTINUOUS SYSTEMS

Slurring is a common attribute of speech. People in general conversation do not leave space between words, but slur all words and sentences together. Some people speak very rapidly and leave less space between words than they do between syllables. This slurring effect makes it difficult to pick a single word out of spoken conversation for detection.

Continuous recognition is the process whereby words not spoken by themselves are processed. An effective continuous system must take the individual sounds of words, *phonemes*, and recognize them while words are being spoken. These phonemes must be put together and pieced into words. Possibly this could be done by one microprocessor with sophisticated software or by several—one gathering and holding the information while the others examine it, not concerned about getting a little behind or having to stop processing to listen. Key words may be used by a recognizer to help understand what filler words were used but poorly understood. For example, we might even hear someone say, "I went ta town and drove my card, which needed gasulane." Given the previous sentence, it would not be difficult to surmise that the proper statement would be "I went to town and drove my car, which needed gasoline."

ALGORITHMS

How right is right? When comparing an unknown word against test samples, how good must the comparison be? As it gets close to

13

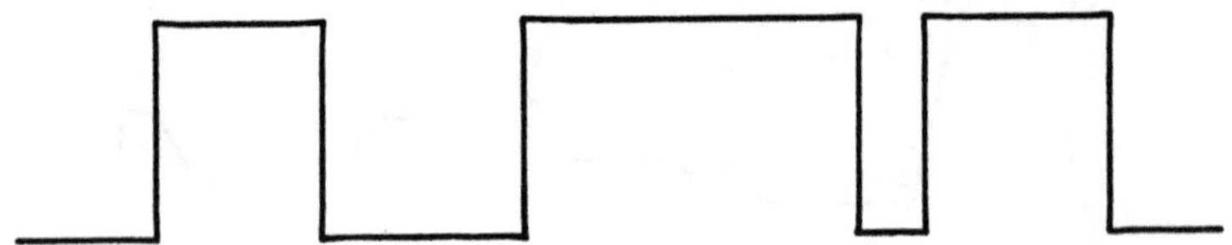

Fig. 1-7. Digital version of wave in Fig. 1-6.

being perfect, there will be more correct answers. Matches will occur less frequently. If the acceptable range is lowered, a word will be identified more often, but the wrong words will be identified more often also.

Any recognition system requires an algorithm upon which to base its operation. An *algorithm* is a method or "game plan" upon which decisions are made. Some compromise between complexity of hardware and software is usually made, though a designer with a particular skill in one area might base his system primarily upon the fundamentals with which he felt the most comfortable. Obviously one could utilize volume, duration, frequency, zero crossings, pauses, context, and various human samples to establish a system. Each of these variables contains variables and decisions which can be made. Only the more elemental systems will be detailed here; moving beyond that is beyond the scope of the concepts presented here.

Chapter 2
Commercial Recognizers

Among the devices commercially available to attach to microcomputers is the Voxbox recognizer for the TRS-80 microcomputer. This unit, sold by Radio Shack, allows words or phrases to operate the computer. It attaches to the expansion interface or to the card edge connector at the rear of a Model I machine. It can accept up to 32 words or phrases, each with a length less than one and two-tenths seconds. The device is an isolated-word, speaker-trained device. To operate the system, you need a Model I TRS-80 with Level II BASIC and at least 16K of RAM. The Voxbox recognizer includes a push-to-talk microphone that must be held almost at the lips for recognition to occur. Each word or phrase must begin with at least one-tenth of a second of continuous speech. The end of the word is indicated by the first silence of at least one-tenth of a second. The unit operates from its own power supply, included. It is recommended for use primarily as entertainment. Physically the box is about the size of a paperback book and is colored the same as the computer. At the rear of the Voxbox is a card edge connector which is pin for pin identical to the one at the rear of the keyboard unit. With a printer attached at this connector and with the proper software, it is possible to type by talking (see Chapter 11).

The Voxbox recognizer works best in a quiet room where background noise is not present. Like most recognizers, this one can be fooled easily. The goal is to achieve understanding. It will recognize and do so with an accuracy of better than 90 percent, with reasonable effort on the part of the user.

Software is included in the purchase, along with instructions to aid in individually written programs. A machine-language driver must first be loaded, and this must occur after the question MEMORY SIZE is requested by the computer. The memory size must be set in order that the driver program will be loaded into the highest part of the RAM memory, away from the area in RAM where most BASIC programs are stored. After the driver is loaded, a program written in BASIC may be loaded into the computer. Three programs are included: Inventory Demonstration, Lunar Lander, and Voice Plotter. The Inventory Demonstration program allows you to enter and correct data numbers by verbal command. Nothing happens with these numbers other than appearing on the video display, but it is an interesting way of indicating the device potential. The Lunar Lander program is a game wherein data for a space craft landing is entered and altered by voice command. The game lacks sophistication, but the effect of verbal entry makes it fascinating. The Voice Plotter program gives a graphic representation of the frequencies and energy in any spoken word. This word picture visibly demonstrates how very differently the same word is pronounced by different people, or by the same person twice.

In all of these programs there is a training mode and an operating mode. In the training mode, each desired word must be pronounced one or more times. The 32 word vocabulary allows for 32 entries; that can be 32 different words or 16 words twice or four words eight times or any other combination totaling no more than 32. The advantage of training more than once on each word is that such training increases the probability of a correct match in the operating mode. The words spoken may be in any language (they don't even have to be words), but they must be repeatable. The operate mode takes whatever sounds are input and compares them with the learned patterns in memory. If there is an acceptable comparison, the computer declares a match. A recognition parameter is available in the driver software and it may be changed to increase or decrease the flexibility of the match. It should be noted that the Voxbox recognizer is speaker-trained and for that reason will usually not respond to the same words spoken by another person. Complete details are provided in the documentation to enable you to write your own programs.

DIGITAL SPEECH PROCESSOR

The lowest priced recognition unit I have found is the Digital Speech Processor by Design Solution, Inc. This unit works with any

Model I Level II TRS-80 system, though a Level II with disk drive is recommended to "reduce voice image loading times." To quote from Design Solution's literature:

"Experiment with Digital Speech Synthesis and recognition using a BASIC editor program provided with this system. Speech is entered, digitized, and stored in memory or on disk files. Vocabulary files are constructed using Digital core images of your voice. Labeled and indexed sounds, words, and phrases are then available for use in your basic programs. Different vocabulary files can be loaded for different BASIC programs, etc. . . . Experiment with data compression from BASIC by increasing and decreasing sample rates. Develop your own voice recognition programs. Simulate low pass, bandpass, and high pass filters. This is truly a software man's dream come true. Enter a string of numeric data and let your TRS-80 repeat it to you. Let your TRS-80 dictate data files for error checking, etc.

"The Digital Speech Processor lends itself totally to music synthesis. Its internal D/A [digital-to-analog] converter and your software can create almost any imaginable waveform. Modify timbre, attack/decay, and pitch, all from software.

"The Digital Speech Processor has a self-contained condensor microphone for voice or music input. The DSP also features a 2-inch speaker and amplifier for output of speech and music. Extended features include input active and modulation level prompting indicators and an auxiliary output for your external amplifier, stereo, tape recorder, etc. . . ."

A 40-conductor cable is required but not supplied for connection to the TRS-80. This is available from Radio Shack in the form of a 40-conductor ribbon cable (part #278-771) and two edge connectors (part #276-1558).

COGNIVOX

The Cognivox recognizer produced by Voicetek, is another unit available at the low end of the cost spectrum. It is also an isolated-word, speaker-trained system. Cognivox can handle a 32-word vocabulary and can provide voice response as well as recognition. Each word must be spoken by the user three times in the training mode. Word length must be greater than 150 milliseconds and less than three seconds. Software is provided on a cassette tape rather than as a listing. Software available includes two sophisticated speech-operated video games, as well as utilities—such as a talking calculator, vocal memory dump, and so forth. This unit can be used to generate or study music. It works on the TRS-80 without the expansion interface. The producer states that is uses a "novel speech processing technique based on the time domain signal and proprietary non-linear pattern matching techniques."

Cognivox can be purchased for many systems, including Rockwell's AIM-65, the PET/CBM, the Apple II, Exidy's Sorcerer, and the TRS-80. A version is also available for any Z-80 central processing unit with a parallel I/O port available for interfacing.

VET-2

Scott Instruments produces a voice entry terminal, the VET-2 which is designed for data entry where keyboard entry proves inefficient. Available for the Apple II or TRS-80, this unit interfaces with off-the-shelf software or programs written in BASIC, Integer-BASIC, Applesoft BASIC, or machine code. With the Apple II computer only, the VET-2 may be used in "parallel" with the keyboard—a key may be pressed or the name for that key may be spoken. This Keyvet feature enables the user to run existing software under voice control without modifying the software. It should be noted that some programs may have memory conflicts with the VET-2; also, the Keyvet feature does slow execution time (normally not noticeable). Therefore, every application may not work. This unit along with an Apple II computer would enable a severely handicapped programmer to return to work and use his voice, instead of the keyboard. It could also be used with off-the-shelf Apple peripherals to aid handicapped people in performing tasks which used to require human assistance.

The VET-2 handles a 40-word vocabulary, though it has a provision for adding additional multiples of 40 on disk, and these can be linked to provide a larger vocabulary. Memory space utilized for the 40-word vocabulary is about 4,600 bytes, while the control software uses about 6,000 bytes—for a total of about 10.6K bytes of memory utilized within the microcomputer. Like the other units, this one has a training mode and a run mode, though there is great flexibility in the training mode (words can be changed or retrained at any time without losing the resident program). With a properly chosen vocabulary and certain prompting features, this unit can be used by several people with high accuracy. VET-2 utilizes frequency, zero crossings, and amplitude as quantities to consider in recognizing voice.

Three outstanding people shared their expertise in speech sciences, electronics, and computing to develop this device. Dr.

Brian Scott, president of Scott Instruments, obtained his Doctorate degree under the advisory of Dr. Ronald A. Cole at the University of Waterloo, Canada, specializing in the theory and application of speech perception. R. Gary Goodman received his Ph.D. in Computer Science from Stanford University. Among his accomplishments was the design of the language used by HARPY, the first 1,000-word continuous speech recognition system. Lee Hardesty obtained his Bachelor's degree in Mathematics at North Texas State University. He pursued interests which led to skill in electronics and establishment of a business that provided hardware and consultation for research and commercial enterprises. This combination of talents enables the VET-2 to respond in a manner similar to the way the human mind functions.

This device is the most expensive considered here, but it is much less costly than most commercial units and has been committed to serious purposes, such as aids for the severely handicapped.

AIDS FOR HANDICAPPED PEOPLE

One promising area for these machines is in the field of aids for handicapped people. Voice control can allow persons to program or operate computers with all the skill of non-disabled people. People with severe lack of motor control can use voice control. (However, physical control is necessary to turn on computers and load the software necessary for voice control.) The ability to link the voice software to other software is needed if the recognizer is to perform any useful task. Output control is needed to operate real-world equipment.

An example of such a system might be an electrically controlled wheelchair being driven by a quadriple amputee. With a headset he could give verbal commands which would then be sent by radio to a nearby microcomputer. The microcomputer could process the command and execute the appropriate output, perhaps sending a radio command to the wheelchair ordering motion in some specific direction. The fallibility of any such system and all of its components must be considered before undertaking such a task. Such a wheelchair would need to move very slowly in order that time would be available to process commands and try again should an error occur. Electrical interference of the drive motors could affect the radio transmissions or the local logic decoding controls. This interference (caused by brushes on the motors) could cause numerous problems in the electronic circuits if control and motor circuits are served from the same battery source. Electrical interference from the computer itself is significant, and could affect the radio transmissions. The wheelchair would have to have backup failsafe devices, such as bumper switches to stop operation in the event of object contact. Failure of the operator to maintain voice control is a distinct possibility, a cough or excitement could change the voice pattern and render such recognition devices temporarily useless.

Although several cautions have been noted, control of many devices is feasible. A TRS-80 Model I, Level II, with 16K of memory and the additions of a Voxbox and an output controller (available from Radio Shack) would be capable of controlling appliances, lights, or any number of electrical items. (See SOURCES for robot arm suppliers.)

UNINTERRUPTIBLE POWER SUPPLY

When committing a recognizer to serious applications, the problem of maintaining a reliable power supply becomes significant. In business and industry there are many computer applications that are considered to be so critical that computer failures cannot be tolerated. Computers that handle airline reservations, for example, cause chaos if they lose their memory or foul transactions in progress. Electric utilities are not in a position to provide the absolutely reliable service so essential to these operations. Although the local power company does not wish to drop a computer that is controlling a wheelchair, they have miles of power lines that can be faulted by car accidents, squirrel misjudgements, falling trees, lightning, and a host of other uncontrollables. The only solution is to install a UPS, or *uninterruptible power supply*. A UPS unit is basically an inverter that takes direct current electricity and converts it into alternating current of the proper frequency and voltage. UPS systems have a battery to provide the energy when power lines fail. Such systems must be sized to handle the computer and all necessary peripherals for the desired period of outage time. The greater the power supplied and the longer it must be provided, the more the unit will cost. The units are measured in watts, an electrical quantity which is the same as the product of amps and volts. One supplier of these units is Sun Research, Inc. (Box 210; New Durham, NH 03855; phone (603) 859-7110. (For commercial recognizers; see Sources.)

Chapter 3

Easily Constructed Sound Controls

A simple hardware device is the voice-operated switch. Such a switch merely causes some action to occur when it detects sound. A simple switch, latching a relay on, is shown in Fig. 3-1. The microphone takes sounds and converts them to a weak electrical signal. This signal is amplified by the Darlington transistor, Q1. The transistor is normally turned off and will turn on when positive voltage is applied to the base. When the transistor is off, no voltage is developed across R1. When a sufficiently loud sound occurs, a small wave of energy leaves the microphone, and during positive portions of the wave cycle it turns the transistor on. When the transistor is on, voltage is developed across the potentiometer. This positive voltage goes to the gate lead of the SCR, or silicon-controlled rectifier. The reason for the potentiometer is that the full six volts of the battery (minus a small loss in the transistor) appears across the resistor, and this high voltage would damage the SCR if applied to the gate lead. When the SCR gate lead is made more positive than the cathode by about 1.5 volts, it goes into conduction and passes current. It will continue to pass current (whether voltage is present at the gate or not) until the current path is somehow broken externally. When the SCR is passing current, the relay coil will energize and its normally open contact will close, allowing some item to be controlled (a light, for example). To turn the light off will require opening S1, which will open the current path through the SCR and allow it to cease conducting. When the switch is closed,

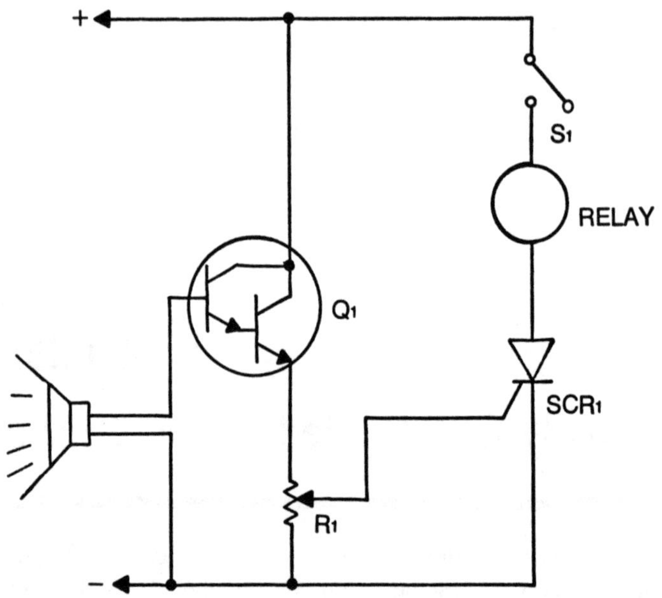

Fig. 3-1. Voice-operated switch schematic.

the device will be prepared to operate again upon the next sufficient sound.

The usefulness of a one-time latched switch is limited. It could be used to turn on lights at the sound of a car horn, or lights in a building upon the clapping of hands or the sound of a shrill whistle. The requirement of physical involvement to manually reset the sound recognizer severely restrains the useful applications.

Adding logic to the sound switch makes it more useful. To keep the concept simple, relay logic is used instead of electronics. The logic system will allow the sound switch to operate four lights in sequence. The first loud sound will illuminate lamp number one. The next sound will operate lamp two, then three, then four. The fifth sound will reset the system and the sixth wound will start over again by lighting lamp number one.

It is first necessary to understand the diagrams before explaining the system. Figure 3-2 shows the coil and contact symbols. The round circle represents a relay coil, the number or letter inside that circle is used to represent that relay. If proper voltage is applied across that coil, it is assumed that the relay will pick up. Contacts

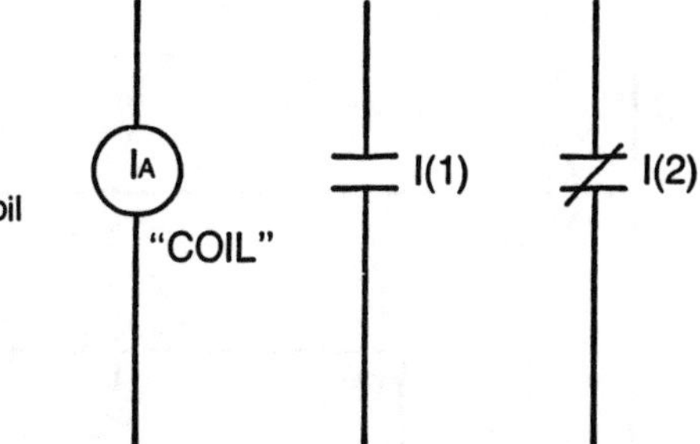

Fig. 3-2. Illustration of relay coil and contact symbols.

are drawn in the position they would be found if their relay coil were de-energized. The labeling I (1) indicates the relay coil and contact used. The part of the label outside the parenthesis defines the relay coil controlling the contact. The label component within parenthesis tells which contact is being used and is primarily intended to show how many contacts are utilized.

Our simple sound-controlled switch perceived sound only one time, and then latched its relay in the energized position, requiring the physical operation of a switch to return to the ready position. To circumvent this seal-up characteristic, two relays have been used (see Fig. 3-3), IA and I. A contact of IA, IA(1) closes upon energization of coil IA. This causes relay coil I to be energized and its normally closed contact I(1) opens, resetting the electronics of the sound switch and de-energizing coil IA, which in turn drops coil I. Contact I(2), normally open, will briefly close and then open during this operation. Contact I(2) is the initiating contact used by the logic counter circuit shown in Fig. 3-4.

Consider the diagram in Fig. 3-4. Starting in the reset position, all relay coils are de-energized. Upon receipt of an appropriate sound, the sound-switch causes contact I(2) to close. I(2) of course

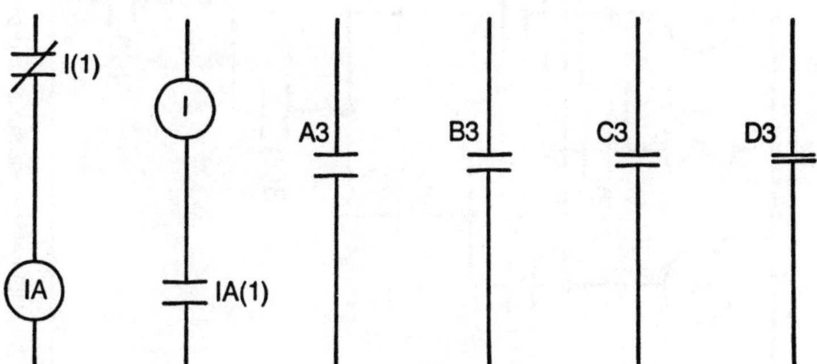

Fig. 3-3. Anti-seal-up system and relay logic output.

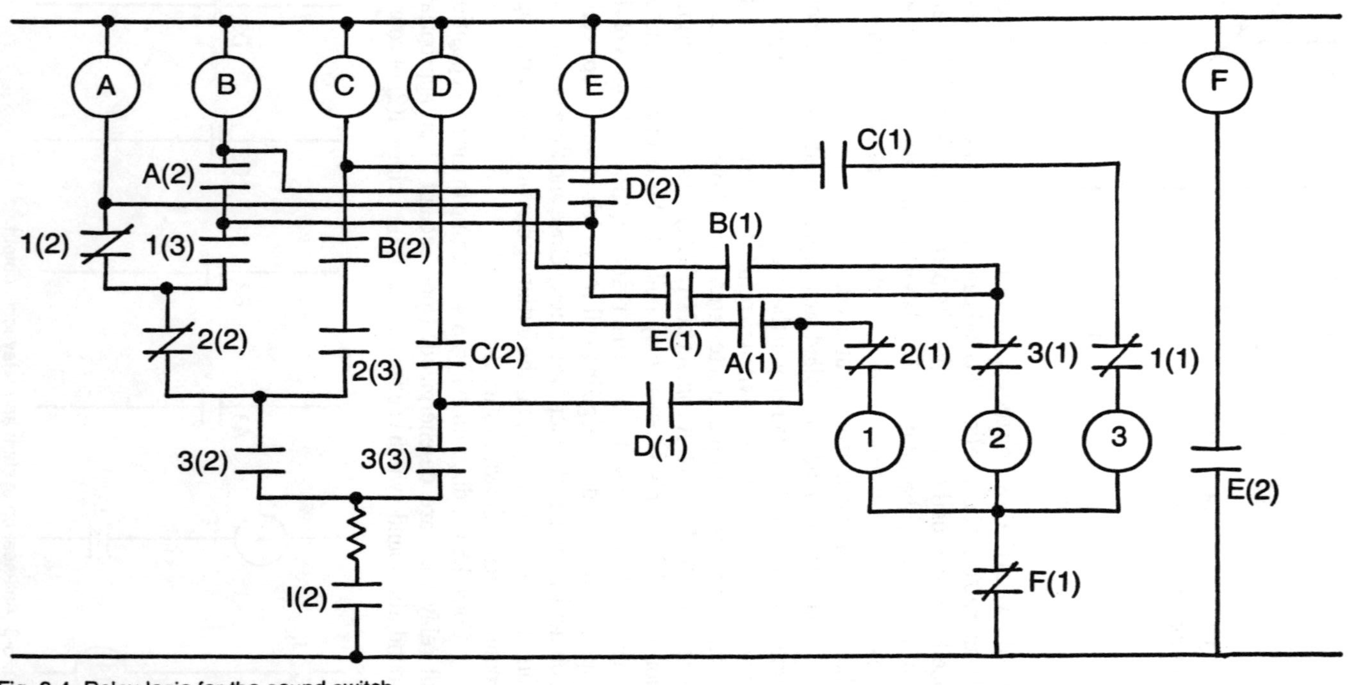

Fig. 3-4. Relay logic for the sound switch.

will quickly open, but the situation needs to be studied in slow motion. Current will flow upward through I(2), 3(2), 2(2), 1(2), and A, energizing relay A. Remember that relay coil A has been energized; that causes contact A(3) to make up and allows light number one to come on (see Fig. 3-3). A(1) makes up, providing another path from positive to the coil of relay A. Contact F(1), coil 1, contact 2(1), and A(1) provide an alternate voltage path for current to the coil of A. Relay coil 1 will not be energized until contact I(2) drops out, for I(2) is shorting out coil 1. When contact I(2) opens up, coil A will continue to be energized through the F(1), 1, 2(1), A(1) path. The two six volt coils, 1 and A are in series with a 12-volt supply, thus they both receive the necessary energy to operate. Lamp number one will stay lit until the next operation of I(2).

Upon the next closure of I(2), a path is established from I(2) through 3(2), 2(2), 1(3), and A(2) to coil B. B energizes, lighting lamp number two and creating the path F(1), 2, 3(1), and B(1) to coil B. When I(2) opens, coil 2 energizes and drops coil 1 by opening contact 2(1) which in turn drops relay coil A, turning off light number one. The process continues.

Upon the next closure of I(2), a path is established from I(2) through 3(2), 2(3), and B(2) to coil C. This illuminates lamp number three and sets up the C coil holding path F(1), 3, 1(1), C(1), C. When I(2) opens, coil 2 is dropped by 3(1) and this also drops B which turns lamp number two off. Lamp number three is now sealed on.

Upon the next closure of I(2), a path is established from I(2) through 3(3), and C(2) to coil D. D(3) closes and lamp number four lights. A path is established through F(1), 1, 2(1), and D(1) to hold D energized. Upon the opening of I(2), relay 1 is energized, dropping coil C and light number three.

Upon the closure of I(2) a path is created through I(2), 3(2), 2(2), 1(3), and D(2) to coil E. E(2) energizes coil F which causes F(1) to open, dropping coils 1, D, and E. If I(2) remains closed very long, coil A will be energized and the sequence will restart. If I(2) drops out promptly, no coils will be energized and the circuit will be ready to commence counting at the next sound.

Chapter 4
Sound Plot

It is not necessary to buy or build complex peripheral devices for the purpose of experimenting with voice recognition. An ordinary TRS-80 Model I can be used if a tape recorder and the proper software are available. Any computer which allows software control of the cassette input port can operate as a voice recognizer.

A cassette recorder will function as an amplifier if it is in the record mode and if the amplifier output is taken through the earphone jack. For TRS-80 users this means removing the plugs from the aux and mic jacks and depressing the small lever in the left rear of the tape compartment while depressing the record and play buttons. Of course one could place a cassette in the recorder rather than depress the lever in the rear of the tape compartment, but there is no purpose served by recording on the tape and most recorders will stop when the tape reaches the end.

All the programs from here through Chapter 10 have been written BASIC for a TRS-80 with no external equipment (besides a tape recorder). For the "80" computer the port is latched and it must be reset each time the data value is high. The entire operation is so slow in BASIC that no more than 30 or 40 bits of information can be input per second, and this information is nothing more than volume or absence of volume data. Surprisingly, much can be done with such limited information. As with most systems, the closer one tets to the microphone, the better the results will be.

The Sound Plot program that follows takes a spoken word and

displays its representation in bar graph form on the video screen. It first asks for a word, then displays the representation along with an indicator line (so that the graph can be accurately transferred to paper, if desired). Next there is a time delay followed by a question requiring the depression of the Enter key. Without this required depression, it would be easy to make a noise and erase the existing plot before it had been adequately considered. This program is useful for "grooming" a recognition vocabulary; it allows you to see how closely two similar words appear. With this knowledge, it is possible to select a vocabulary that will be most easily distinguished by the machine. This is also a useful tool for examining speech patterns and considering algorithms that would enhance speaker-independent recognition.

Following the operation of this program, line 10 clears the video screen. Line 20 clears space for an array named SND with dimensions of six rows by 30 columns. This numbering system is slightly deceptive, for the computer starts counting at zero instead of one. This program does not need so large an array; it is a carryover from earlier development attempts. Line 25 moves program control to line 1000. Lines 1000 through 1020 print instructions on the video screen. Line 1030 moves program control to line 30 and line 32 sets the variable Y equal to zero. Line 40 causes X to equal the value found at input port number 255. Input port number 255 is the cassette input; if you are using a computer other than the TRS-80 model I, this statement would have to be changed to match the reality of that system. Line 50 tests to see if sound was found at the input port; if sound was greater than the threshold value, the number input will be 255, otherwise it will be 127. If sound is found, the program jumps to line 65; otherwise it goes to line 60 and loops until sound is detected. Line 65 clears the video screen again. Line 70 resets the input port—without this statement the program would go to 255 upon the first detection of sound and remain at that value. Line 80 causes row 1 column 0 to be filled with the value of X, which happens to be 255 on the first pass. Each future time this statement is passed, the row will continue to be 1 but the column will assume whatever value Y has taken on. Line 90 examines the cassette port again, assigning the value received to X. Line 100 advances the count of Y. Line 110 tests to see if Y is equal to 31, a number beyond the range allowed for at the time when the array was set up. If Y is equal to 31, then the program jumps to line 200; otherwise, it advances to line 120, which jumps back to line 70 and continues the loop.

Lines 210 and 211 set variables equal to zero. Line 220 pulls the value found in row 1 column 0 out of the array and lets it equal to the variable C. Lines 230 and 240 test the value of C. Since C must be either 255 or 127, those are the numbers tested. If 255 is found, D is made to equal nine. D will be set on the video screen in a later step, and it must be noted that nine will produce a trace higher on the screen than will ten; therefore nine corresponds to 255, the number input representing a higher volume sound. Line 250 increments the

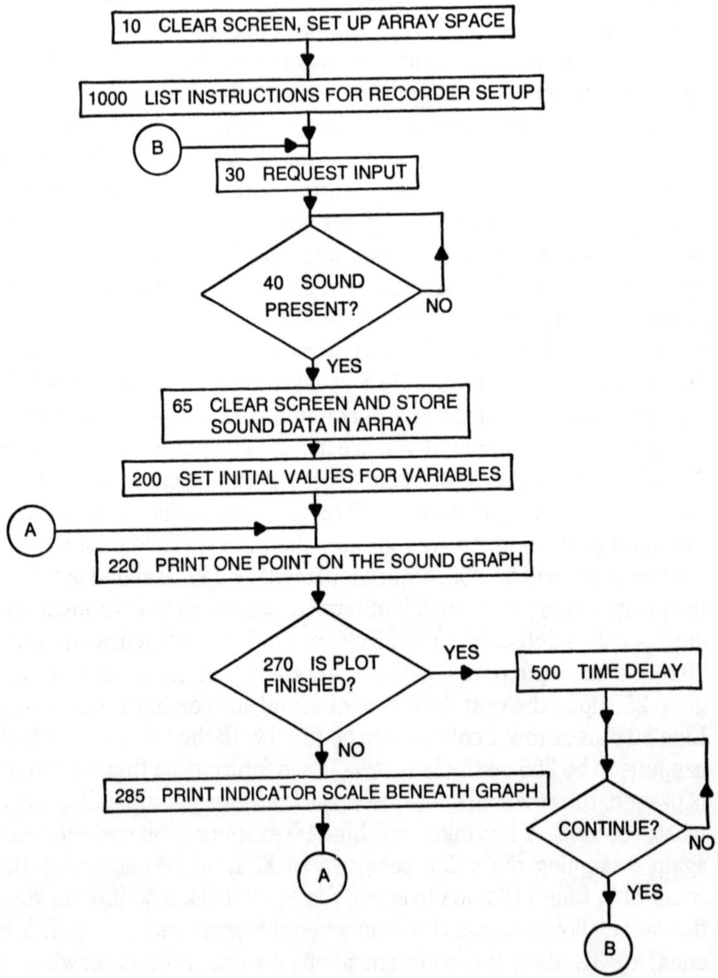

Fig. 4-1. Flowchart for Sound Plot program.

value of B for the next pass of this loop. Line 260 places a small square on the screen, one position of the bar graph. Line 270 increments F, the variable which determines which position is to be printed on the video screen. Line 280 causes the program to escape this loop when the array values are nearly exhausted. Lines 285, 286, 287, 600, and 610 are used to print a broken line beneath the graph which may be used for visual examination of the exact spacing of high and low sounds found in the word tested. Line 290 jumps to 220 and causes the loop to continue. Lines 500 and 510 generate a time delay. Line 515 requires depression of the Enter key to continue. Line 520 returns control to line 30 and the process is completed.

A flowchart for this program is given in Fig. 4-1.

SOUND PLOT PROGRAM LISTING

```
10 CLS
20 DIMSND(6,30)
25 GOTO 1000
30 PRINT"SAY A WORD"
32 Y=0
40 X=INP(255)
50 IF X=255 THEN 65
60 GOTO 40
65 CLS
70 OUT255,00
80 SND(1,Y)=X
90 X=INP(255)
100 Y=Y+1
110 IF Y=31 THEN 200
120 GOTO 70
200 PRINT
210 B=0
211 F=0
220 C=SND(1,B)
230 IF C=255 THEN D=9
240 IF C=127 THEN D=10
250 B=B+1
260 SET(F,D)
270 F=F+1
280 IF F=30 THEN 500
285 G=G+1
286 IF G=2 THEN 600
287 SET(F,12)
290 GOTO 220
500 FOR X=1 TO 1000
510 NEXT X
515 INPUT"CONTINUE";A
520 GOTO 30
600 G=0
610 GOTO 290
1000 PRINT"REMOVE 'AUX' AND  'MIC' PLUGS FROM TAPE RECORDER"
1010 PRINT"PUSH LITTLE BUTTON IN TAPE COMPARTMENT AT LEFT REAR"
1020 PRINT"OR INSERT TAPE AND DEPRESS 'PLAY' AND 'RECORD' BUTTONS"
1030 GOTO 30
```

Chapter 5

Sound

Sound represents a true example of speaker-dependent voice recognition. In this program five words are learned by the computer. The five words are: "goodbye," "hello," "Michael," "go," and "Annabelle." Figure 5-1 illustrates these five words in my voice. As in the previous program, input is through the cassette recorder. This program will not work well unless the lips of the operator are almost touching the microphone of the recorder. The program first exhibits a learning mode during which it will ask for each word to be spoken (one at a time). Next it will request that one of the learned words be spoken. The program will determine which word was spoken. When in the running mode (recognizing spoken words), there will be a gap of several seconds between speaking and recognition. This time delay is a result of the numerous comparisons and decisions being made by manipulations in the BASIC language.

It would not be difficult to expand the vocabulary or the number of passes on each word, but the recognition time will increase significantly with each addition. It is not necessary to use the words provided. For example, "adios" could be spoken in place of "goodbye," but the word "goodbye" would be displayed on the screen when "adios" was spoken. To change the word list, each word must be changed in two places as follows:

goodbye	lines 30 and 470
hello	lines 80 and 480
Michael	lines 140 and 490

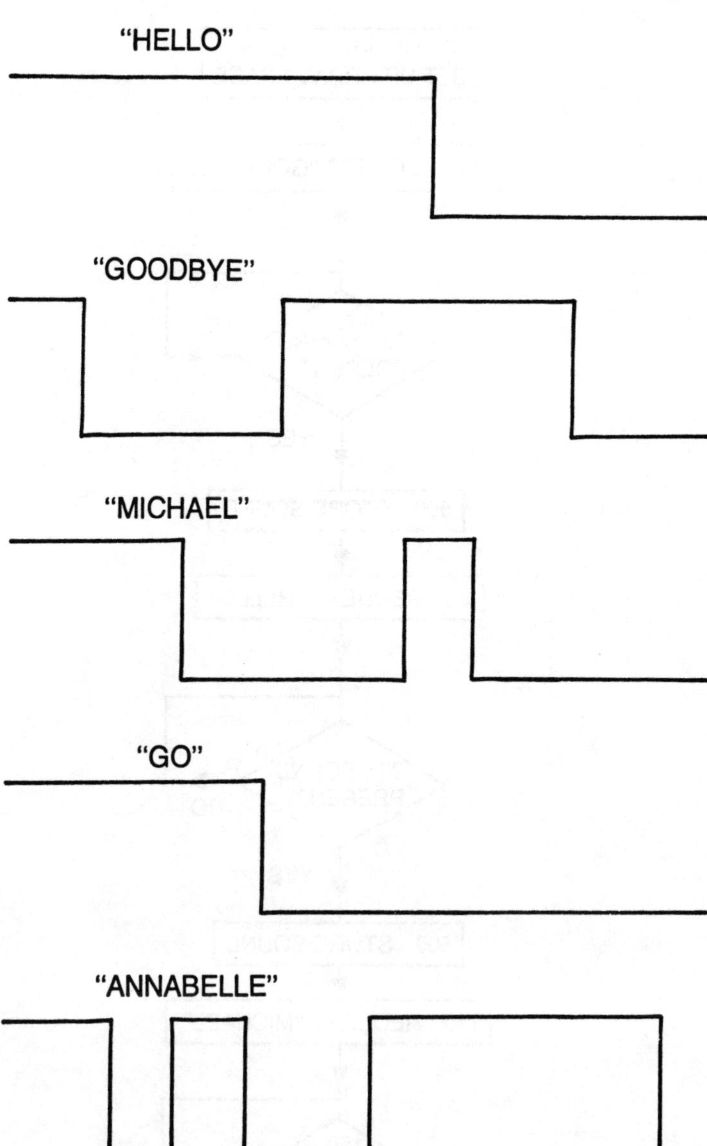

Fig. 5-1. Plot of five selected words.

go   lines 200 and 495
Annabelle   lines 260 and 497

Remember when changing vocabulary that similar sounding words are difficult to distinguish. Even excellent recognizers have

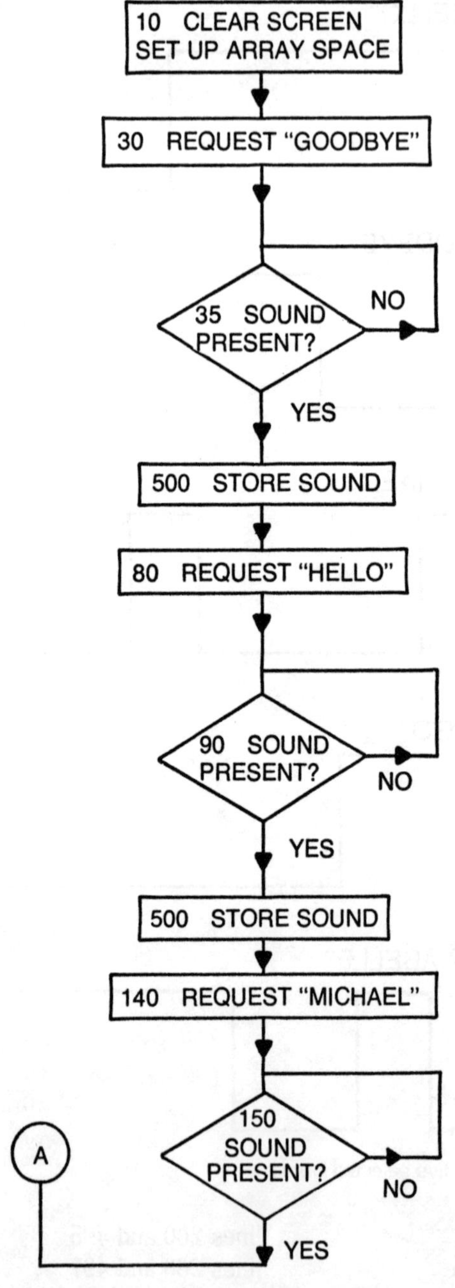

Fig. 5-2. Flowchart of Sound program.

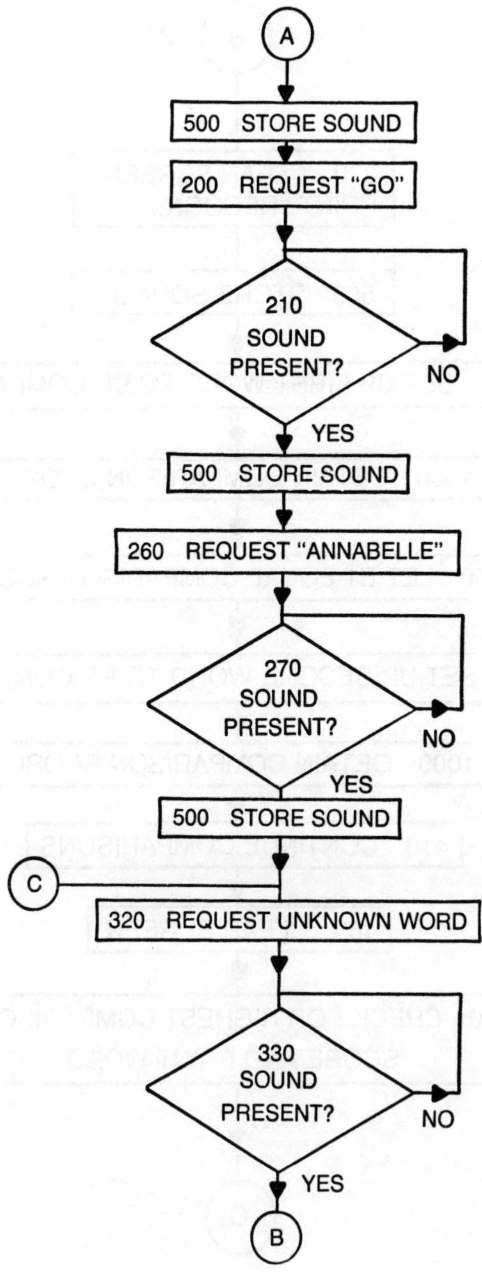

Fig. 5-2. Continued from page 32.

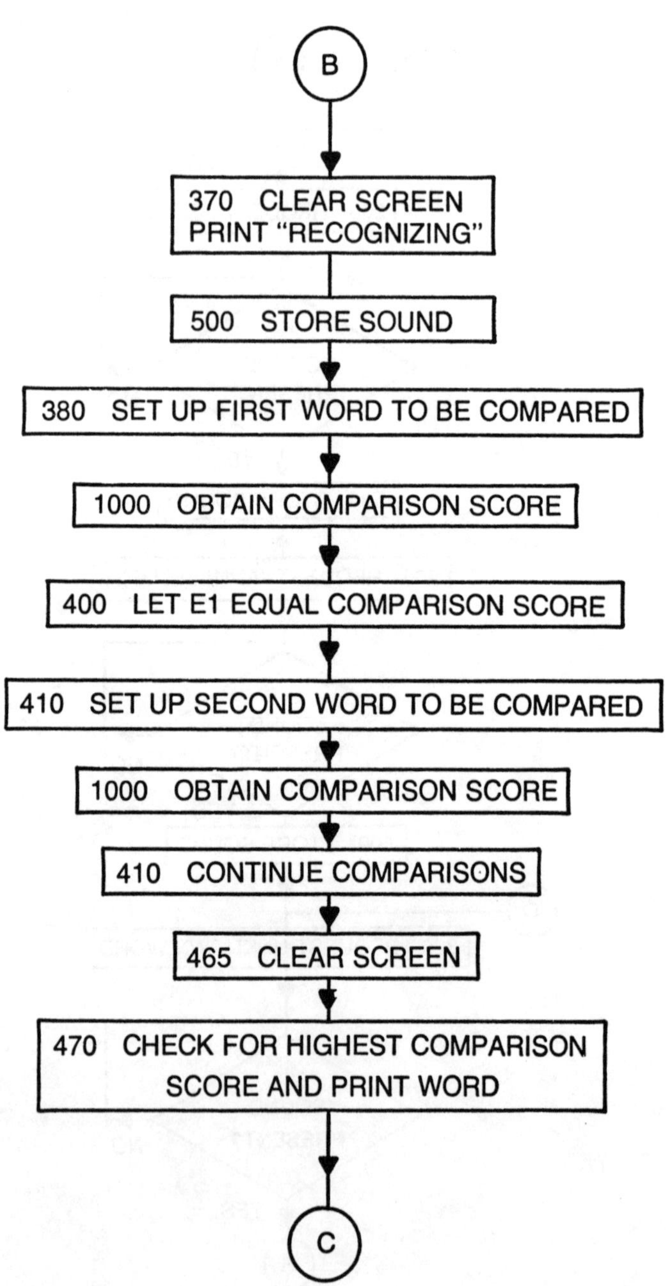

Fig. 5-2. Continued from page 33.

difficulty with words like "bog" and "dog." Although the manipulations in this program consume considerable time, the program itself does not occupy much memory. Because this program is small, it would be easy to adapt to games or other programs.

Figure 5-2 is a flowchart of the program.

SOUND PROGRAM LISTING

```
10  CLS
20  DIMSND(6,30)
30  PRINT"SAY    GOODBYE"
35  P=1
40  X=INP(255)
50  IF X=255 THEN  70
60  GOTO 40
70  GOSUB 500
80  PRINT"  SAY  HELLO"
90  P=2
100  X=INP(255)
110  IF X=255 THEN 130
120  GOTO 100
130  GOSUB 500
140  PRINT "SAY MICHAEL"
150  P=3
160  X=INP(255)
170  IF X=255 THEN 190
180  GOTO 160
190  GOSUB 500
200  PRINT"  SAY   GO"
210  P=4
220  X=INP(255)
230  IF X=255 THEN 250
240  GOTO 220
250  GOSUB 500
260  PRINT" SAY    ANNABELLE"
270  P=5
280  X=INP(255)
290  IF X=255 THEN 310
300  GOTO 280
310  GOSUB 500
320  PRINT"SAY ONE OF THE TRAINED, BUT DESIRED WORDS"
330  P=6
340  X=INP(255)
350  IF X=255 THEN 370
360  GOTO 340
370  CLS
371  PRINT"RECOGNIZING"
372  GOSUB 500
380  B=1
390  GOSUB 1000
400  E1=E
410  B=2
420  GOSUB 1000
430  E2=2
```

```
440 B=3:GOSUB1000:E3=E
450 B=4:GOSUB1000:E4=E
460 B=5:GOSUB1000:E5=E
465 CLS
470 IFE1.E2ANDE1.E3ANDE1.E4ANDE1.E5 PRINT"GOODBYE"
480 IFE2.E1ANDE2.E3ANDE2.E4ANDE2.E5 PRINT"HELLO"
490 IFE3.E1ANDE3.E2ANDE3.E4ANDE3.E5 PRINT"MICHAEL"
495 IFE4.E1ANDE4.E2ANDE4.E3ANDE4.E5 PRINT"GO"
497 IFE5.E1ANDE5.E2ANDE5.E3ANDE5.E4 PRINT"ANNABELLE"
498 GOTO 1510
500 Y=0
510 SND(P,Y)=X
520 Y=Y+1
530 OUT255,00
540 IFY=31 THEN RETURN
550 X=INP(255)
560 GOTO510
1000  Y=0
1005 E=0
1010 IF SND(6,Y)=SND(B,Y) THEN E=E+1
1020 Y=Y+1
1030 IF Y=31 RETURN
1040 GOTO 1010
1510 GOTO 320
```

Chapter 6

Listening Typewriter

The Listening Typewriter program enables you to control a printer (or interfaced typewriter) by voice. The program is very reliable, easy to operate, and does not require a microphone close to the speaker. It can be used by a severely physically disabled person who can see and utter sound under intelligent control.

The program must be loaded and put into the RUN mode, the same as any BASIC program. Your cassette recorder must be set up to receive sound, as explained in the instructions which the program displays. After getting through the instructions (which require depressing the Enter key) the program operates entirely by voice. The letters of the alphabet are sequentially flashed at the top of the screen. After Z comes the words "SPACE" and "PRINT." When a desired letter appears, the operator must make a sound ("now," "stop," "go," or any utterance) and the letter (or space) will be added to the message line at the bottom of the screen. As soon as the letter appears on the message line, this request will appear in the center of the screen: "DO YOU WISH TO CANCEL THIS LETTER?" If the character added to the message line is not desired, make a sound and it will disappear; otherwise it will become a permanent path of the message in a few seconds. The letters will continue to cycle until another repeats this cycle.

If the cycle is stopped when "PRINT" is at the top of the screen, the message "LET'S PRINT" will appear at the very bottom of the display while "SAY STOP TO CANCEL THE PRINT OP-

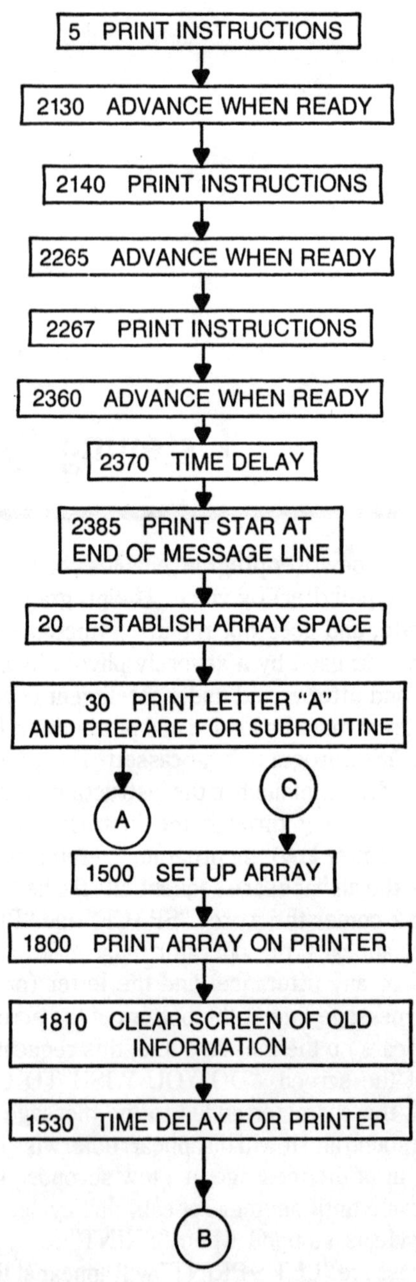

Fig. 6-1. Flowchart of Listening Typewriter program.

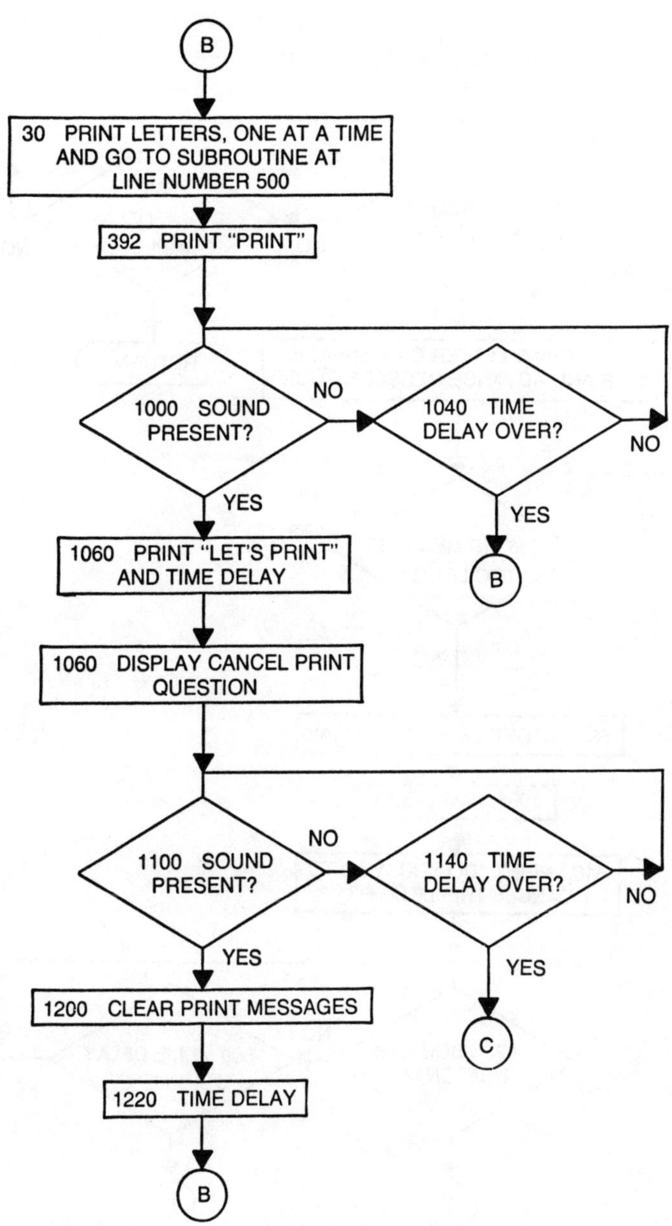

Fig. 6-1. Continued from page 38.

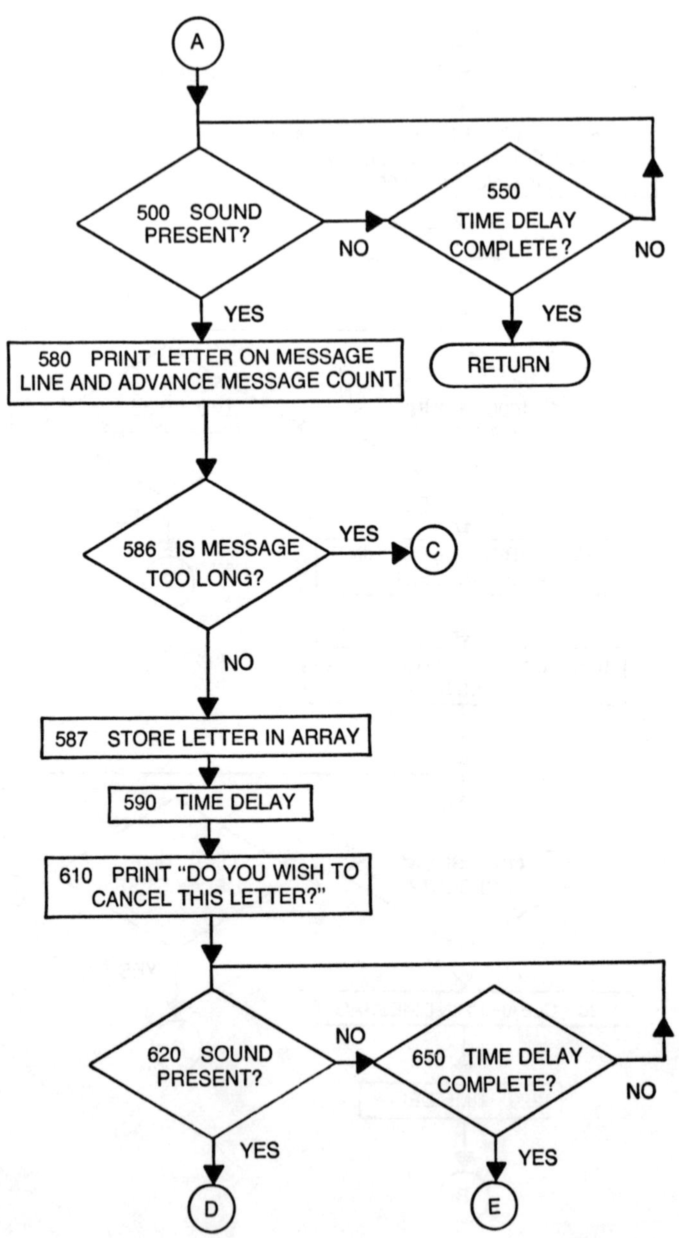

Fig. 6-1. Continued from page 39.

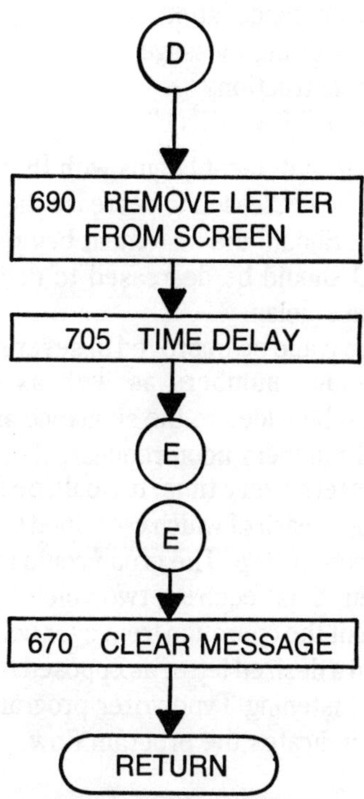

Fig. 6-1. Continued from page 40.

ERATION" will appear in the center. If another noise is uttered, the print operation will be cancelled and the cycle will continue. If not cancelled, the message line will be printed and cleared off the video screen in preparation for the next line of information. Before the characters cycle again there will be a delay of about eight seconds; this is to allow any printer noises to subside before the program begins "listening" again.

It will be noticed that a star exists at the right end of the message line. When the message reaches that point, it will be printed wheter a print command is issued or not.

It is possible to obtain excellent results using this program, but it is rather tedious and can become frustrating. After practice, the time delays could be shortened considerably to decrease the tedium. The delay locations are:

Delay between letters	line 550
Delay for letter cancellation	line 660
Delay after "PRINT"	line 1040

Delay for print cancellation	line 1150
Delay after printing message	line 1530
Delay after instructions	line 2370
Delay after "LET'S PRINT"	line 1070

Where the program statement begins with IF, the number after the equal sign should be decreased to decrease the delay and increased to increase delay. Should the statement begin with FOR, then the number after TO should be decreased to decrease delay and increased to increase delay.

This program could be improved in several ways, one of which would be to include numbers as well as letters. The word "NUMBER" could be added to the sequence and it could trigger a mini-sequence of numbers upon request. Rather than sequencing through all the letters every time, it would be feasible to sequence through five groups (each of which contained five or six letters) and command the group to stop. The group could then sequence until a letter was chosen, thus requiring two voice commands per letter. This would prevent the operation from ever being more than eleven spaces away from a desired letter as opposed to the maximum of 28 spaces with the Listening Typewriter program.

Figure 6-1 indicates the program flow.

LISTENING TYPEWRITER PROGRAM LISTING

```
5 D=832
10 CLS
11 GOTO 2000
15 PRINT@894,"X"
20 DIMP$(100)
30 PRINT@90,"A     "
40 A$="A"
50 GOSUB500
60 PRINT@90,"B"
70 A$="B"
80 GOSUB500
90 PRINT@90,"C"
100 A$="C"
110 GOSUB500
120 A$="D"
130 PRINT@90,"D"
140 GOSUB500
150 A$="E"
160 PRINT@90,"E"
170 GOSUB500
180 A$="F"
190 PRINT@90,"F"
200 GOSUB500
203 A$="G"
206 PRINT@90,"G"
209 GOSUB500
212 A$="H"
215 PRINT@90,"H"
218 GOSUB500
221 A$="I"
224 PRINT@90,"I"
227 GOSUB500
```

```
230 A$="J"
233 PRINT@90,"J"
236 GOSUB500
239 A$="K"
242 PRINT@90,"K"
245 GOSUB500
248 A$="L"
251 PRINT@90,"L"
254 GOSUB500
257 A$="M"
260 PRINT@90,"M"
263 GOSUB500
266 A$="N"
269 PRINT@90,"N"
272 GOSUB500
275 A$="O"
278 PRINT@90,"O"
281 GOSUB500
284 A$="P"
287 PRINT@90,"P"
290 GOSUB500
293 A$="Q"
296 PRINT@90,"Q"
299 GOSUB500
302 A$="R"
305 PRINT@90,"R"
308 GOSUB500
311 A$="S"
314 RINT@90,"S"
317 GOSUB500
320 A$="T"
323 PRINT@90,"T"
326 GOSUB500
329 A$="U"
332 PRINT@90,"U"
335 GOSUB500
338 A$="V"
341 PRINT@90,"V"
344 GOSUB500
347 A$="W"
350 PRINT@90,"W"
353 GOSUB500
356 A$="X"
359 PRINT@90,"X"
362 GOSUB500
365 A$="Y"
368 PRINT@90,"Y"
371 GOSUB500
374 A$="Z"
377 PRINT@90,"Z"
380 GOSUB500
383 A$=" "
386 PRINT@90,"SPACE"
389 GOSUB500
392 PRINT@90,"PRINT    "
395 GOSUB1000
398 GOTO 30

500 Y=0
510 OUT255,00
520 Y=Y+1
530 S=INP(255)
540 IF S=255 THEN580
550 IF Y=20THEN RETURN
560 GOTO 520
580 PRINT@D,A$
585 D=D+1
586 IF D=894THEN 1500
587 N=N+1
588 P$(N)=A$
590 FORY=1TO200
600 NEXT Y
610 PRINT@576,"DO YOU WISH TO CANCEL THIS LETTER?"
620 Y=0
625 OUT255,00
```

```
630 S=INP(255)
640 IFS=255 THEN 690
650 Y=Y+1
660 IFY=100 THEN 670
665 GOTO 630
670 PRINT@576,"
675 RETURN
690 PRINT@(D-1)," "
695 P$(N)=" "
700 D=D-1
702 N=N-1
705 FOR Y=1TO100
706 NEXT Y
710 GOTO 670
1000 Y=0
1010 OUT255,00
1020 S=INP(255)
1025 Y=Y+1
1030 IF S=255 THEN 1060
1040 IF Y=25 THEN RETURN
1050 GOTO 1020
1060 PRINT@905,"LET'S PRINT"
1070 FORY=1 TO 200
1080 NEXT Y
1090 PRINT@576,"SAY STOP TO CANCEL THE PRINT OPERATION"
1100 Y=0
1110 OUT255,00
1120 S=INP(255)
1130 IF S=255 THEN 1200
1140 Y=Y+1
1150 IF Y=100 THEN 1500
1160 GOTO 1120
1200 PRINT@576,"                                        "
1210 PRINT@905,"              "
1220 FORY=1 TO 100
1230 NEXT Y
1240 RETURN
1500 GOTO 1600
1510 D=832
1520 PRINT@832,"
                "
1525 PRINT@576,"                                        "
1530 FOR Y=1 TO 800
1540 NEXT Y
1550 RETURN
1600 B$=P$(1)
1603 C$=P$(2)
1606 D$=P$(3)
1609 E$=P$(4)
1612 F$=P$(5)
1615 G$=P$(6)
1618 H$=P$(7)
1621 I$=P$(8)
1624 J$=P$(9)
1627 K$=P$(10)
1630 L$=P$(11)
1633 M$=P$(12)
1636 N$=P$(13)
1639 O$=P$(14)
1642 O$=P$(15)
1645 R$=P$(16)
1648 S$=P$(17)
1651 T$=P$(18)
1654 U$=P$(19)
1657 V$=P$(20)
1660 W$=P$(21)
1663 X$=P$(22)
1666 Y$=P$(23)
1669 Z$=P$(24)
1672 A1$=P$(25)
1675 B1$=P$(26)
1678 C1$=P$(27)
1681 D1$=P$(28)
1684 E1$=P$(29)
1687 F1$=P$(30)
```

```
1690 G1$=P$(31)
1693 H1$=P$(32)
1696 I1$=P$(33)
1699 J1$=P$(34)
1702 K1$=P$(35)
1705 L1$=P$(36)
1708 M1$=P$(37)
1711 N1$=P$(38)
1714 O1$=P$(39)
1717 P1$=P$(40)
1720 Q1$=P$(41)
1723 R1$=P$(42)
1726 S1$=P$(43)
1729 T1$=P$(44)
1732 U1$=P$(45)
1735 V1$=P$(46)
1738 W1$=P$(47)
1741 X1$=P$(48)
1744 Y1$=P$(49)
1747 Z1$=P$(50)
1750 A2$=P$(51)
1753 B2$=P$(52)
1756 C2$=P$(53)
1759 D2$=P$(54)
1762 E2$=P$(55)
1765 F2$=P$(56)
1768 G2$=P$(57)
1771 H2$=P$(58)
1774 I2$=P$(59)
1777 J2$=P$(60)
1780 K2$=P$(61)
1783 L2$=P$(62)
1786 M2$=P$(63)
1800 LPRINTB$;C$;D$;E$;F$;G$;H$;I$;J$;K$;L$;M$;N$;O$;O$;R$;S$;
T$;U$;V$;W$;X$;Y$;Z$;A1$;B1$;C1$;D1$;E1$;F1$;G1$;H1$;I1$;J1$;K1
$;L1$;M1$;N1$;O1$;P1$;O1$;R1$;S1$;T1$;U1$;V1$;W1$;X1$;Y1$;Z1$;A2
$;B2$;C2$;D2$;E2$;F2$;G2$;H2$;I2$;J2$;K2$;L2$;M2$
1803 FOR QR=1 TO 63
1804 P$(QR)=""
1805 NEXT QR
1810 GOTO 1510
2000 PRINT"THIS VOICE CONTROLLED PRINTER PROGRAM REQUIRES THAT"
2010 PRINT"YOUR PRINTER BE ON NOW."
2020 PRINT
2030 PRINT"REMOVE ANY TAPE FROM THE CASSETTE."
2040 PRINT"REMOVE THE 'AUX' AND 'MIC' PLUGS FROM THE RECORDER."
2050 PRINT
2060 PRINT"PUSH THE LITTLE CATCH AT THE LEFT REAR OF THE TAPE"
2070 PRINT"COMPARTMENT WHILE DEPRESSING THE 'PLAY' AND 'RECORD'"
2080 PRINT"BUTTONS."
2090 PRINT
2100 PRINT"WHEN THIS HAS BEEN COMPLETED, THE RECORD MECHANISM"
2110 PRINT"SHOULD BE RUNNING WITH ONLY ONE PLUG (EAR) INSERTED."
2120 PRINT
2130 INPUT"PRESS ENTER FOR THE REST OF THE INSTRUCTIONS";AR
2140 CLS
2150 PRINT"LETTERS WILL FLASH IN ALPHABETICAL SEQUENCE AT THE"
2160 PRINT"UPPER CENTER OF THE SCREEN.  WHEN YOU SEE A LETTER"
2170 PRINT"THAT YOU DESIRE TO HAVE PRINTED, SAY 'GO'."
2180 PRINT
2190 PRINT"THAT LETTER WILL BE DISPLAYED ON A MESSAGE LINE AT"
2200 PRINT"THE BOTTOM OF THE SCREEN. A MESSAGE WILL THEN APPEAR"
2210 PRINT"NEAR THE CENTER OF THE SCREEN. THE MESSAGE READS, 'DO
2220 PRINT"YOU WISH TO CANCEL THIS LETTER?'  IF YOU REPLY, 'YES'"
2230 PRINT"THE LETTER WILL BE REMOVED AND THE SEQUENCE CONTINUE."
2240 PRINT"REMAIN SILENT AND THE LETTER WILL BECOME PART OF THE"
2250 PRINT"LINE TO BE PRINTED."
2260 PRINT
2265 INPUT"DEPRESS ENTER TO SEE THE REST OF THE INSTRUCTIONS";RT
2267 CLS
2270 PRINT"AFTER 'Z' IS DISPLAYED COME THE WORDS 'SPACE' AND"
2280 PRINT"'PRINT'.  'SPACE' IS USED TO INSERT A SPACE AND"
2290 PRINT"'PRINT' CAUSES THE LINE TO BE TRANSFERRED TO THE PRINTER"
2300 PRINT
```

```
2310 PRINT"THERE WILL BE A STAR AT THE END OF THE MESSAGE LINE."
2320 PRINT"IF YOU ATTEMPT TO SET A LETTER IN PLACE OF THE STAR,"
2330 PRINT"THE LINE WILL AUTOMATICALLY BE PRINTED."
2340 PRINT
2350 PRINT"DEPRESS ENTER, WAIT ABOUT TEN SECONDS AND THE"
2360 INPUT"PROGRAM WILL BEGIN";RT
2370 FOR Y=1TO3500
2380 NEXT Y
2385 CLS
2390 GOTO 15
```

Chapter 7

Radio Control

The Radio Control program is designed to provide sound control of a simple radio-operated toy. A small quantity of hardware must be constructed and modified to utilize this piece of software.

The most economical radio-controlled toys have a controller with one button. When that button is depressed, the toy ceases forward motion and some kind of pointer turns indicating the direction of motion in which the toy is prepared to go. When this directional indicator reaches the desired point, the button is released and the toy starts to travel in that direction. This program allows the cassette recorder to function as the input device through

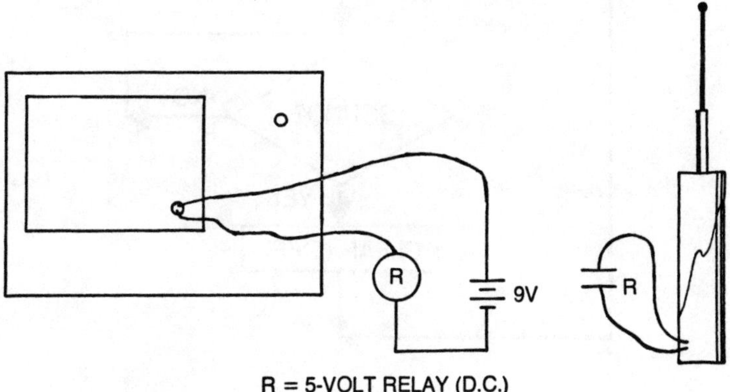

Fig. 7-1. Output controller via video display.

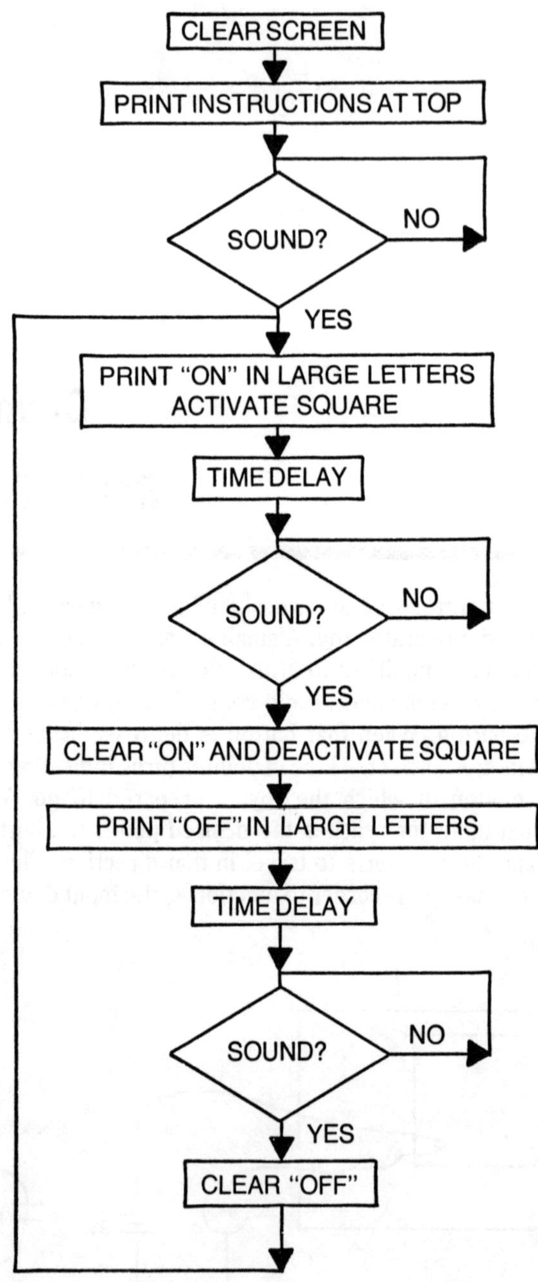

Fig. 7-2. Flowchart of Radio Control program.

which sounds are taken and utilized for control of the toy. When a sound of sufficient volume is detected, the word "ON" appears in giant letters across the screen and the pushbutton on the toy controller is pressed by the computer. When another sound is detected, the word "OFF" appears and the button is released.

The question which immediately comes to mind is, "How does the computer push the button?" There lies the significant value of this system; there is an easy method by which output control may be gained from the video monitor of any computer. A simple photo-resistor (part #276-116, available at Radio Shack) in series with the coil of a relay (see Fig. 7-1) will cause the relay to operate when exposed to light and release when exposed to darkness. This photo-cell will control the relay when placed against the video monitor and exposed to light or darkness. The Radio Control program turns a square on and off to correspond with the words "ON" and "OFF." This square is located in the lower right-hand corner of the monitor. You can attach the photoresistor in any manner that seems feasible (such as tape) but it should not receive undue amounts of room light.

In the program you may notice that the square as well as the large words are generated using POKE statements. These provide for greater speed of display and less statement lines than would be necessary for the SET statement. When typing a program containing POKE statements, it is wise to save the listing on tape before running because errors could destroy the program. To put it another way, 30 minutes of typing can disappear when you run the program if something was POKED in the wrong place.

It is necessary to take the contacts of our relay and wire them in parallel with the contacts of the single pushbutton on the toy controller. This should prove to be simple, but a soldering iron will be required.

Of course, you could set up an entire row of photoresistors (or phototransistors) and control many squares. Controlling items in the real world is not limited to computers with costly output ports; anyone can gain physical control of the world in this manner.

Figure 7-2 is a flowchart of this simple program.

RADIO CONTROL PROGRAM LISTING

```
10 CLS
20 PRINT"ASSURE THAT YOUR VIDEO PICKUP UNIT IS IN PLACE."
30 PRINT"SET UP THE CASSETTE RECORDER TO RECEIVE SOUND."
40 PRINT"'ON' WILL FUNCTION LIKE 'BUTTON PUSHED'."
50 PRINT"'OFF' WILL FUNCTION LIKE 'BUTTON RELEASED'."
60 OUT255,00
```

```
70  X=INP(255)
80  IFX=255 THEN  100
90  GOTO 60
100  FORY=16248 TO 16255
110  POKE Y,191
120  NEXT Y
130  FOR Y=16312 TO 16319
140  POKEY,191
150  NEXT Y
160  FOR Y=16376 TO 16383
170  POKEY,191
180  NEXT Y
190  POKE15700,191
200  FOR Y=15701 TO 15704
210  POKEY,131
220  NEXT Y
230  POKE15705,191
240  POKE15708,191
250  POKE15709,140
260  POKE15710,176
270  POKE15713,191
280  POKE15764,191
290  POKE15769,191
300  POKE15772,191
310  POKE15775,191
320  POKE15777,191
330  POKE15828,191
340  POKE15833,191
350  POKE15836,191
360  POKE15841,191
370  POKE15892,191
380  FORY=15893 TO  15896
390  POKEY,176
400  NEXTY
410  POKE15839,191
420  POKE15897,191
430  POKE15900,191
440  POKE15903,131
450  POKE15904,140
460  POKE15905,191
470  FORY=1 TO 100
480  NEXT Y
490  OUT255,00
500  X=INP(255)
510  IF X=255 THEN 530
520  GOTO 490
530  CLS
540  POKE15700,191
550  FOR Y=15701 TO 15704
560  POKEY,131
570  NEXT Y
580  POKE15705,191
590  POKE15708,191
600  FOR Y=15709 TO 15713
610  POKEY,131
620  NEXT Y
630  POKE15716,191
640  FOR Y=15717 TO 15722
650  POKEY,131
660  NEXT Y
670  POKE 15764,191
680  POKE 15769,191
690  POKE15772,191
700  FOR Y=15773 TO 15776
```

```
710 POKE Y,176
720 NEXT Y
730 POKE 15780,191
740 FOR Y=15781 TO 15784
750 POKEY,176
760 NEXT Y
770 POKE15828,191
780 POKE15833,191
790 POKE15836,191
800 POKE15844,191
810 POKE15892,191
820 FOR Y=15893 TO 15896
830 POKEY,176
835 NEXT Y
840 POKE15897,191
850 POKE15900,191
860 POKE15908,191
870 FOR   Y=1 TO 100
880 NEXT Y
890 OUT255,00
900 X=INP(255)
910 IF X = 255 THEN 930
920 GOTO 900
930 CLS
940 GOTO 100
```

Chapter 8

High-Speed-Recognition

To some people the time delay for recognition proves to be objectionable; for others, the problem of speaker-dependence is unacceptable. If there are but a few commands in need of recognition, it is possible (easy even) to move away from speaker dependence and toward high-speed recognition.

The first step toward such recognition software is to reduce the commands to the least possible number. Voice recognition must be acknowledged as the most sensitive program function; therefore the vocabulary must be built around it, not the reverse. Use the Sound Plot program to select words that are distinctly (and repeatably) different. Speak each potential word several times and record the results on paper. A sample group of words may be viewed in Fig. 8-1. Notice that there are differences for each word spoken by the same person.

Search for similarities and differences. An algorithm must be built around these qualities. For the sample program of this chapter, words "up," "down," and "fire" were selected. "Attack" was too different from the other three. The recognition software awaits sound; if that sound lasts for less than seven units of time, the word is declared to be "up." If it lasts longer than seven units but less than 14, the word is declared to be "down." If it lasts longer than 14 units of time, the word is declared to be "fire."

To summarize the process: select a vocabulary. Be flexible; "up" could be "raise," "lift," "pull up," "move higher," or many

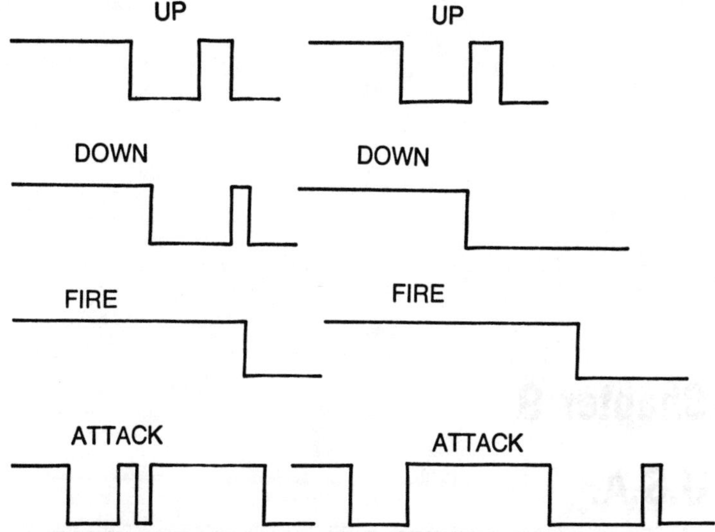

Fig. 8-1. Plot of several test words.

other statements. Use the Sound Plot program to determine which choices are best. Compare the chosen words and find easily distinguished differences. Keep the algorithm simple so that recognition will be rapid.

Following is a program listing for a high speed recognition program. Remember that programs need not be long and complex to perform interesting tasks.

HIGH-SPEED RECOGNITION PROGRAM LISTING

```
10  CLS                      100  PRINT"FIRE"
20  Q=0                      110  FOR W=1 TO 80
25  OUT 255,00               120  NEXT W
26  Z=INP(255)              130  GOTO 20
27  IF Z>200 THEN 30        500  Q=Q+1
28  GOTO 26                 510  GOTO 70
30  FOR D=1 TO 30          1000  PRINT"UP"
40  OUT255,00              1010  GOTO 110
50  X=INP(255)             1500  PRINT"DOWN"
60  IF X>200 THEN 500      1510  GOTO 110
70  NEXT D
80  IF Q>7 GOTO 1000
90  IF Q>14 GOTO 1500
95  PRINTQ
```

Chapter 9

U.S.A.

U.S.A. is a fully sound-controlled game. Designed primarily for teaching directional skills to students at about the fourth grade level, the game can defeat most adults at the difficult level. The easy version of the game displays a map of the continental United States with each state's initials placed on the map. Questions are asked about the relative position of one state to another (north, south, east, or west) and an answer must be given before the next question is displayed. The computer keeps score and displays that score after each question. If an erroneous answer is given, the correct response will be displayed. No question requires difficult decisions, and the positions involved are clear; nothing is "northeast" or southwest."

The difficult version of the game is like the simple one, except that the names of the states are not given on the map. After all the questions have been answered, a reward phrase of some type will be displayed, depending upon the number of correct answers and the version of the game played.

After the game has been loaded and the cassette recorder has been set to receive sounds, type RUN and then depress Enter. The keyboard will not be used again. Instructions will be presented; making any sound will cause the program to advance. A training mode will be entered and the words requested will be "north-bound," "southward," "east," and "go west." More instructions will be given; to advance, you must utter any sound. A question will be

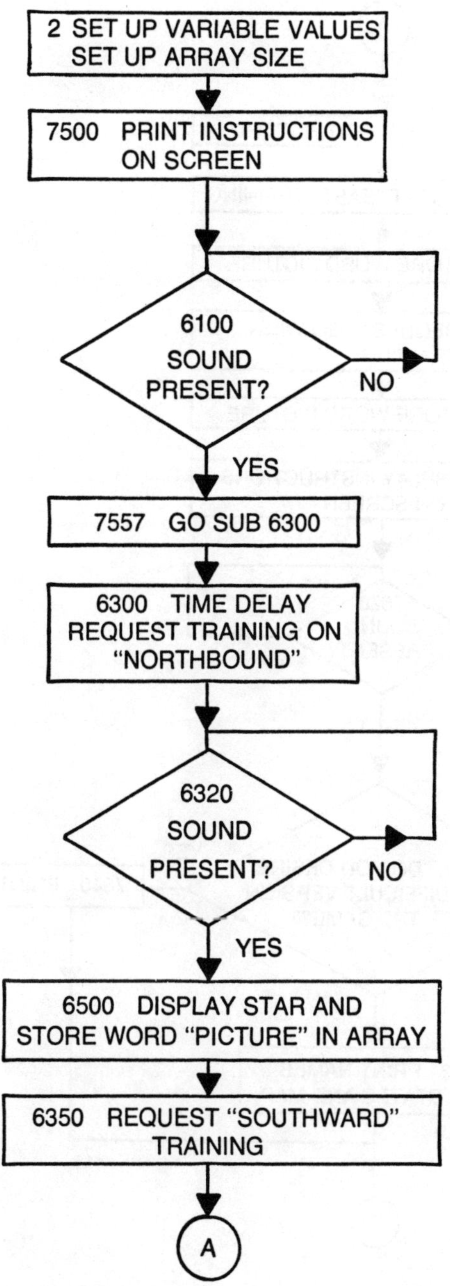

Fig. 9-1. Flow diagram of U.S.A. program.

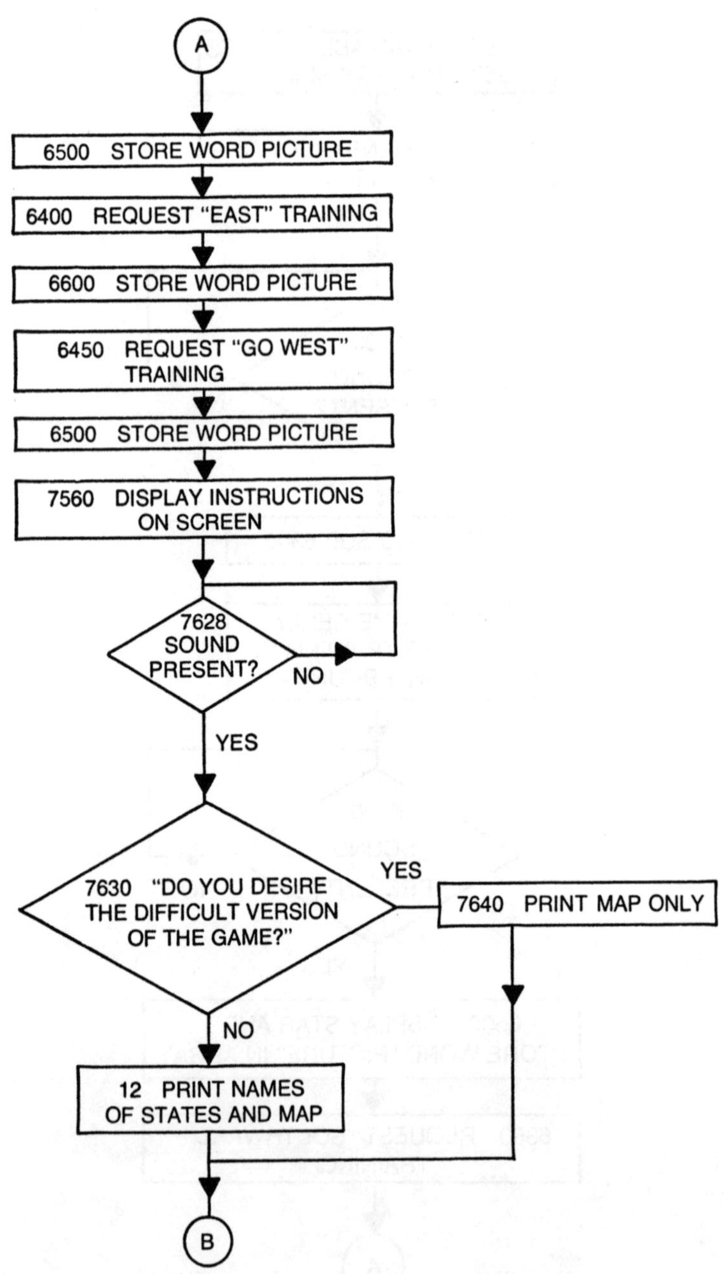

Fig. 9-1. Continued from page 55.

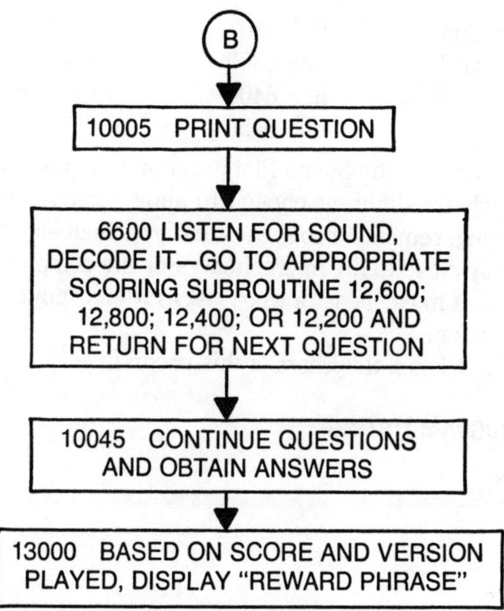

Fig. 9-1. Continued from page 56.

asked about playing the difficult or easy version of the game. Remaining silent for a few seconds will result in the easy version; talking will cause the program to jump to the difficult version. Then the map will be displayed and a question will be asked at the bottom of the screen. The answer should be one of the trained phrases. A star will be displayed to indicate that recognition is in progress (it takes several seconds to perform this manipulation in the BASIC language). When the computer has determined what was said, it will print a letter, "N," "S," "E," or "W"—for north, south, east, or west. Do not rest at this point, if the letter that comes up is not the one requested, say "no" and that answer will be cancelled. The computer will await your response and try again. Do not make a sound when the letter appears if it is the answer desired; otherwise, the computer will erase it, and you will have to answer again. When the answer has been recognized and accepted, it will be checked for accuracy. If it is wrong, the correct answer will be displayed followed by the present score. If correct, the present score will be displayed. Then the next question will be asked. There are about 25 questions.

It is quite probable that a better selection of directional words can be found than the ones given; if so, the lines which should be changed are:

Northbound	line 6307
Southward	line 6350
East	line 6400
Go West	line 6450

When you use the Sound Plot program it is possible to select words which are different enough to allow for easy recognition. When training, remember to speak clearly without abnormal inflection and stay close to the microphone. For the computer to recognize a word, it must "hear" a word just as it was spoken during the training section.

Figure 9-1 is a flowchart of this program.

U.S.A. PROGRAM LISTING

```
2 A$="HUMAN"
3 DIMSND(5,30)
4 D$="N"
5 GOTO7500
10   CLS
11 GOTO 15
12 CLS
13 GOSUB8000
15   GOTO 180
20   FOR L=0 TO A
30   SET(X+L,Y)
40 NEXTL
50   RETURN
60   FOR L=0 TO A
70   SET(X,Y+L)
80   NEXT L
90   RETURN
100   FOR L=0 TO A
110   SET(X+L,Y+L)
120   NEXT L
130   RETURN
140   FOR L=0 TO A
150   SET(X-L,Y+L)
160   NEXT L
170   RETURN
180 Y=1
190   SET(6,Y)
200   SET(7,Y)
210   X=10
220   A=6
230   GOSUB20
240   Y=2
250   SET(5,Y):SET(8,Y):SET(9,Y)
280   X=17
290   A=10
295   GOSUB20
300   X=118
310   A=3
315   GOSUB 20
320   Y=3:X=5:A=2:GOSUB60
360   SET(21,Y):SET(23,Y):X=28:A=11:GOSUB20
410   X=65:A=1:GOSUB20
440   SET(117,Y)
450   SET(122,Y)
460   Y=4:SET(6,Y):X=20:A=4:GOSUB60
510   SET(23,Y)
520   X=40:A=24:GOSUB20
550   SET(67,Y)
560   X=117
570   A=3
580   GOSUB60
590   SET(123,Y)
600   SET(124,Y)
```

```
610   Y=5:SET(7,Y):SET(24,Y):X=47:A=5:GOSUB60
670   SET(61,Y)
680   X=68
690   A=5
700   GOSUB20
710   SET(116,Y)
720   SET(125,Y)
730   Y=6:SET(5,Y):X=8:A=12:GOSUB20
780   SET(24,Y):X=62:A=3:GOSUB60
820   SET(73,Y):X=78:A=6:GOSUB20
860   X=111
870   A=4
880   GOSUB20
890   X=121
900   A=3
910   GOSUB20
920   Y=7
930   SET(4,Y)
940   SET(25,Y)
950   X=71
960   A=6
970   GOSUB 20
980   SET(85,Y)
990   X=108
1000   A=2
1010   GOSUB20
1020   SET(112,Y)
1030   X=115
1040   A=2
1050   GOSUB 60
1060   SET(120,Y)
1070   Y=8
1080   SET(3,Y)
1090   X=18
1100   A=2
1110   GOSUB 20
1120   SET(26,Y)
1130   X=47
1140   A=8
1150   GOSUB 20
1160   SET(71,Y)
1170   X=78
1180   A=6
1190   GOSUB 20
1200   X=87
1210   A=4
1220   GOSUB 20
1230   SET(107,Y)
1240   SET(112,Y)
1250   SET(118,Y)
1260   SET(119,Y)
1270   Y=9
1280   SET(1,Y)
1290   SET(2,Y)
1300   SET(19,Y)
1310   X=27
1320   A=20
1330   GOSUB 20
1340   X=56
1350   A=6
1360   GOSUB 20
1370   SET(70,Y)
1380   X=82
1390   A=4
1400   GOSUB 60
1410   SET(85,Y)
1420 SET(86,8)
1430   SET(91,Y)
1432 X=101
1433 A=5
1434 GOSUB20
1440   SET(107,Y)
1450 SET(114,Y)
1455 SET(113,8)
1460   X=115
1470   A=5
1480   GOSUB20
1490   Y=10
1500   SET(1,Y)
1510   X=18
```

```
1520   A=2
1530   GOSUB 60
1540   X=31
1550   A=4
1560  GOSUB 60
1570   X=63
1580   A=4
1590   GOSUB 60
1600   SET(71,Y)
1610   SET(84,Y)
1620   X=91
1630   A=2
1640   GOSUB 20
1650   X=101
1660  A=0
1670   GOSUB 20
1680   X=114
1690   A=5
1700   GOSUB 60
1710   SET(119,Y)
1720   SET(120,Y)
1730   Y=11
1740   X=2
1750   A=9
1760   GOSUB 20
1762  X=100
1763  A=7
1764  GOSUB20
1770   X=46
1780   A=5
1790   GOSUB 60
1800   SET(72,Y)
1810   SET(73,Y)
1820   SET(85,Y)
1830   SET(94,Y)
1840   SET(101,Y)
1850   SET(108,Y)
1860   SET(109,Y)
1870   X=114
1880   A=4
1890   GOSUB 20
1900   SET(120,Y)
1910   Y=12
1920   SET(1,Y)
1930   SET(10,Y)
1940   X=12
1950   A=6
1960   GOSUB 20
1970  SET(63,12)
1971  SET(64,12)
1972  SET(65,12)
1973  SET(66,11)
1974  SET(67,11)
1975  SET(68,11)
1976  SET(69,11)
1977  SET(70,11)
1978  X=71
1980  A=3
1990   GOSUB 20
2000   X=86
2010   A=2
2020   GOSUB 60
2030   SET(94,Y)
2040   X=99
2050  A=1
2060   GOSUB 20
2070   X=110
2080   A=4
2090   GOSUB 20
2100   SET(117,Y)
2110   SET(119,Y)
2120   Y=13
2130   X=0
2140   A=2
2150   GOSUB 60
2160   SET(10,Y)
2170   X=19
2180   A=12
2190   GOSUB 20
2200   X=46
2210   A=17
```

```
2220   GOSUB 20
2230   X=75
2240   A=7
2250   GOSUB 20
2260   SET(86,Y)
2270   SET(93,Y)
2280   X=97
2290   A=2
2300   GOSUB 20
2310   SET(111,Y)
2320   SET(115,Y)
2330   SET(116,Y)
2340   Y=14
2350   SET(0,Y)
2360   SET(9,Y)
2370   SET(24,Y)
2380   SET(76,Y)
2390   X=83
2400   A=9
2410   GOSUB 20
2420   X=94
2430   A=2
2440   GOSUB 20
2450   SET(112,Y)
2460   Y=15
2470   SET(0,Y)
2480   SET(8,Y)
2490   X=23
2500   A=2
2510   GOSUB 60
2520   X=32
2530   A=7
2540   GOSUB 20
2550   SET(64,Y)
2560   X=75
2570   A=3
2580   GOSUB 60
2590   SET(83,Y)
2600   X=90
2610 A=2
2620   GOSUB 60
2630   X=106
2640   A=6
2650   GOSUB 20
2660   Y=16
2670   SET(1,Y)
2680   SET(9,Y)
2690   X=34
2700   A=5
2710   GOSUB 60
2720   X=40
2730   A=10
2740   GOSUB 20
2750   X=50
2760   A=5
2770   GOSUB 60
2780   X=64
2790   A=11
2800   GOSUB 20
2810 X=83
2820   A=3
2830   GOSUB 60
2840   X=98
2850   A=4
2860   GOSUB 20
2870   SET(105,Y)
2880   SET(106,Y)
2890   X=113
2900   A=2
2910   GOSUB 60
2920   Y=12
2930   X=99
2940   A=4
2950   GOSUB 60
2960   Y=17
2970   X=2
2980   A=3
2990   GOSUB 60
3000   SET(10,Y)
3010   X=50
```

```
3020    A=7
3030    GOSUB 20
3040    SET(66,Y)
3050    SET(97,Y)
3060    SET(103,Y)
3070    SET(104,Y)
3080    SET(107,Y)
3090    SET(108,Y)
3100    Y=18
3110    SET(11,Y)
3120    SET(12,Y)
3130    X=22
3140    A=2
3150    GOSUB 60
3160    X=58
3170    A=8
3180    GOSUB 20
3190    SET(76,Y)
3200 X=92
3210 A=4
3220    GOSUB 20
3230    SET(102,Y)
3240    X=109
3250    A=4
3260    GOSUB 20
3270    Y=19
3280    SET(13,Y)
3290    X=67
3300    A=3
3310    GOSUB 60
3320    SET(77,Y)
3330    SET(78,Y)
3340    X=84
3350 A=3
3352 SET(88,17)
3353 SET(89,17)
3354 SET(91,17)
3355 SET(87,18)
3360    GOSUB 20
3370    SET(97,Y)
3380 X=102
3390 A=0
3400    GOSUB 20
3410    SET(112,Y)
3420    Y=20
3430    SET(14,Y)
3440    SET(15,Y)
3450    SET(21,Y)
3460    SET(78,Y)
3470    SET(82,Y)
3480    SET(83,Y)
3490 X=92
3500 A=5
3502 SET (102,20)
3510    GOSUB 20
3520 X=108
3530 A=5
3540    GOSUB 20
3550    Y=21
3560    SET(3,Y)
3570    SET(16,Y)
3580    SET(21,Y)
3590    X=23
3600    A=16
3610    GOSUB 20
3620    X=48
3630    A=10
3640    GOSUB 20
3645 SET(107,21)
3650    SET(79,Y)
3660    SET(81,Y)
3670    X=85
3680 A=6
3690    GOSUB 20
3692 X=97
3693 A=9
3694 GOSUB20
3700    SET(113,Y)
3710    Y=22
3720    SET(4,Y)
```

```
3730  X=17
3740  A=3
3750  GOSUB 20
3760  X=32
3770  A=5
3780  GOSUB 60
3790   X=40
3800  A=7
3810  GOSUB 20
3820  X=47
3830  A=7
3840  GOSUB 60
3850  X=57
3860  A=11
3870  GOSUB 20
3880  X=68
3890  A=5
3900  GOSUB 60
3910  X=80
3920  A=4
3930  GOSUB 20
3940  X=97
3950  A=0
3960  GOSUB 20
3970  SET(112,Y)
3980  Y=23
3990  X=4
4000  A=3
4010  GOSUB 20
4011  X=54
4012  A=3
4013  GOSUB 60
4020  X=18
4030  A=4
4040  GOSUB 60
4050  X=47
4060  A=7
4070  GOSUB 20
4080  X=68
4090  A=11
4100  GOSUB 20
4120  X=97
4130  A=9
4140  GOSUB 20
4150 SET(112,Y)
4160 SET(110,24)
4165 SET(111,24)
4170  Y=24
4180  X=8
4190  A=2
4200  GOSUB 20
4210  X=79
4220  A=17
4230  GOSUB 20
4240  X-107
4250  A=2
4260  GOSUB 20
4270  Y=25
4280  SET(10,Y)
4290  SET(78,Y)
4300  X=84
4310  A=6
4320  GOSUB 60
4330  SET(91,Y)
4340  X=97
4350  A=2
4360  GOSUB 20
4370  SET(107,Y)
4380  Y=26
4390  X=11
4400  A=7
4410  GOSUB 20
4420  X=54
4430  A=5
4440  GOSUB 20
4450  SET(78,Y)
4460  SET(91,Y)
4470  SET(100,Y)
4480  SET(101,Y)
4490  SET(106,Y)
```

```
4500    Y=27
4510    X=17
4520    A=2
4530    GOSUB 20
4540    X=60
4550    A=9
4560    GOSUB 20
4570    X=77
4580    A=2
4590    GOSUB 60
4600    SET(92,Y)
4610    SET(102,Y)
4620    SET(104,Y)
4630    SET(105,Y)
4640    Y=28
4650    X=20
4660    A=3
4670    GOSUB 20
4680    SET(31,Y)
4690    X=69
4700    A=8
4710    GOSUB 20
4720    SET(92,Y)
4730    SET(103,Y)
4740    Y=29
4750    X=24
4760    A=23
4770    GOSUB 20
4780    SET(69,Y)
4790    SET(93,Y)
4800    SET(102,Y)
4810    Y=30
4820    SET(39,Y)
4830    SET(70,Y)
4840    X=71
4850    A=3
4860    GOSUB 60
4870 SET(77,Y)
4880    X=92
4890    A=9
4900    GOSUB20
4910    SET(103,Y)
4920    Y=31
4930    SET(40,Y)
4940    SET(41,Y)
4960    SET(77,Y)
4970    X=82
4980    A=2
4990    GOSUB 60
5000    A=9
5010    GOSUB 20
5020    X=104
5030    A=3
5040    GOSUB 100
5050    Y=32
5060    SET(42,Y)
5070    X=78
5080    A=2
5090    GOSUB 20
5100    X=92
5110    A=7
5120    GOSUB 20
5130 X=98
5140    A=4
5150    GOSUB 100
5160    Y=33
5170    SET(42,Y)
5180    SET(43,Y)
5190    X=47
5200    A=4
5210    GOSUB 20
5220    X=68
5230    A=8
5240    GOSUB 20
5250    SET(81,Y)
5260    SET(82,Y)
5270    Y=34
5280    X=44
5290    A=2
5300    GOSUB 20
```

```
5310    SET(52,Y)
5320    X=65
5330    A=2
5340    GOSUB 20
5350    X=77
5360    A=3
5370    GOSUB 20
5380    Y=35
5390    SET(53,Y)
5400    SET(54,Y)
5410    SET(63,Y)
5420    SET(64,Y)
5430    X=108
5440    A=2
5450    GOSUB 60
5460    Y=36
5470    X=55
5480    A=2
5490    GOSUB 100
5500    SET(62,Y)
5510    SET(103,Y)
5520    SET(104,Y)
5530    Y=37
5540    SET(61,Y)
5550    SET(105,Y)
5560    SET(106,Y)
5570    Y=38
5580    X=57
5590    A=5
5600    GOSUB 20
5610    SET(107,Y)
5611 GOTO 5800
5612 SET(109,5)
5613 SET(108,5)
5620 SET(110,5)
5626 SET(114,3)
5627 SET(114,4)
5628 SET(115,5)
5630 SET(121,9)
5632 SET(122,9)
5634 SET(123,9)
5640 SET(118,12)
5650 SET(121,11)
5652 SET(122,11)
5654 SET(123,11)
5660 SET(124,12)
5662 SET(125,13)
5664 SET(125,14)
5670 SET(115,15)
5672 SET(116,15)
5674 SET(117,15)
5680 SET(114,17)
5682 SET(115,17)
5684 SET(116,17)
5686 SET(117,18)
5700 RETURN
5800 IF Z$="Y" THEN5850
5810 IFZ$="YES" THEN 5850
5820 GOTO 5612
5850 RETURN
6000 CLS
6010 PRINT@249,"N"
6011 PRINT@313,"½"
6012 LETA2=375
6013 GOSUB6020
6014 GOSUB6030
6015 GOTO 7500
6019 LETA2=635
6020    PRINT@A2,"W½ ¢E"
6021 RETURN
6029 A5=701
6030    PRINT@A5,";"
6031 RETURN
6032 PRINT@505,"S"
6100 OUT255,00
6110 SN=INP(255)
6120 IF SN=255 RETURN
6130 GOTO 6110
6150 OUT255,00
6160 PQ=0
```

```
6170 FOR XZ=1 TO 30
6172 NEXT XZ
6180 CLS
6190 PRINT"IF YOU DESIRE THE DIFFICULT VERSION, SAY 'YES'"
6195 PRINT"IF NOT, PLEASE REMAIN SILENT"
6200 SN=INP(255)
6210 PQ=PQ+1
6220 IF PQ=35 RETURN
6230 IF SN=255 THEN Z$="Y"
6240 GOTO 6200
6300 FOR TQ=1TO500
6305 NEXTTQ
6306 OUT255,00
6307 PRINT"SAY 'NORTHBOUND'"
6310 P=1
6320 X=INP(255)
6330 IFX=255THEN6345
6340 GOTO 6320
6345 GOSUB6500
6350 PRINT"SAY SOUTHWARD"
6360 P=2
6370 X=INP(255)
6380 IFX=255THEN6395
6390 GOTO 6370
6395 GOSUB6500
6400 PRINT"SAY   EAST"
6410 P=3
6420 X=INP(255)
6430 IFX=255THEN6445
6440 GOTO6420
6445 GOSUB6500
6450 PRINT"SAY   GO WEST"
6460 P=4
6470 X=INP(255)
6480 IFX=255THEN6492
6490 GOTO6470
6492 GOSUB6500
6495 RETURN
6500 Y=0
6505 POKE16383,42
6510 SND(P,Y)=X
6520 Y=Y+1
6530 OUT255,00
6539 IFY=31POKE16383,32
6540 IFY=31THENRETURN
6550 X=INP(255)
6560 GOTO6510
6600 P=5
6610 OUT255,00
6620 X=INP(255)
6630 IFX=255 THEN6650
6640 GOTO6620
6650 GOSUB6500
6660 B9=1
6670 GOSUB6800
6680 E1=E
6690 B9=2:GOSUB6800:E2=E
6700 B9=3:GOSUB6800:E3=E
6710 B9=4:GOSUB6800:E4=E
6720 IFE1.E2ANDE1.E3ANDE1.E4THEND$="N"
6730 IFE2.E1ANDE2.E3ANDE2.E4THEND$="S"
6740 IFE3.E1ANDE3.E2ANDE3.E4THEND$="E"
6750 IFE4.E1ANDE4.E2ANDE4.E3THEND$="W"
6755 PRINT@958,D$
6757 GOTO20000
6760 IFG$="E"GOTO12600
6762 IFG$="W"GOTO12800
6766 IFG$="S"GOTO12400
6767 IFG$="N"GOTO12200
6800 Y=0
6810 E=0
6820 IFSND(5,Y)=SND(B9,Y)THENE=E+1
6830 Y=Y+1
6840 IFY=31RETURN
6850 GOTO6820
7500   CLS
7510   PRINT@128,"IN THIS GAME, A MAP OF THE STATES WILL BE"
7520 PRINT"BE DRAWN. QUESTIONS WILL BE ASKED AND I KEEP"
7530 PRINT"SCORE.  IF YOUR ANSWER IS CORRECT, YOU GET ONE"
7540   PRINT"POINT; IF NOT, I GET THE POINT.":PRINT
```

```
7550 PRINT"SAY 'CONTINUE' TO PROCEED"
7555 GOSUB6100
7557 GOSUB6300
7560 CLS:PRINT"TO ANSWER A QUESTION, SAY ONE OF THE FOLLOWING:"
7570 PRINT"NORTHBOUND, SOUTHWARD, EAST, GO WEST"
7600  PRINT
7620 PRINT"YOU WILL HAVE A CHOICE OF THE EASY OR HARD VERSION"
7622 PRINT"OF THIS GAME. IF YOU WISH TO PLAY THE EASY VERSION,"
7624 PRINT"THEN REMAIN SILENT UNTIL THE NEXT QUESTION DISAPPEARS."
7626 PRINT"  SAY 'GO' TO GET TO THE NEXT QUESTION"
7628 GOSUB 6100
7630 GOSUB6150
7635 IFZ$="Y"THEN 7640
7636 IF Z$="YES"THEN 7640
7637 GOSUB12
7638 GOTO 10005
7640  GOTO 10000
8000 PRINT@56,"NH"
8005 PRINT@70,"WA                                          VT     ME"
8010 PRINT@144,"MT           ND MN"
8020 PRINT@198,"OR   ID             SD            WI   MI
   NY      MA"
8030 PRINT@274,"WY                IA                  PA     CT"
8040 PRINT@327,"NV                    NE         IL IN  OH
   NJ RI"
8050 PRINT@386,"CA         UT     CO     KS      MO      KY   WV VA
   DE"
8060 PRINT@491,"  TN     NC     N"
8062 PRINT@573,"½"
8070 PRINT@524,"AZ    NM           OK    AR             SC"
8071 GOSUB6019
8080 PRINT @616,"MS AL   GA"
8081 GOSUB 6029
8090 PRINT@668,"TX       LA               "
8100 PRINT@755,"FL         S"
8110 RETURN
10000   GOSUB 10
10005   PRINT@829," ":PRINT"IF YOU MOVED FROM TENNESSEE (TN) TO NORTH"
10010 PRINT "CAROLINA (NC), YOU WOULD BE MOVING IN WHAT DIRECTION"
:G$="E":GOSUB6600
10045   PRINT@829," ":PRINT"IF I GO FROM GEORGIA (GA) TO FLORIDA (FL),"
10050 PRINT  "WHAT DIRECTION DO I GO":G$="S":GOSUB6600
10061 PRINT@829," ":PRINT"LEAVING MONTANA (MT) WHICH DIRECTION IS NEW"
10070 PRINT"MEXICO (NM)":G$="S":GOSUB6600
10090 PRINT@829," ":PRINT"TO GO FROM NORTH DAKOTA (ND) TO NEBRASKA
(NE) ONE"
10100 PRINT"MUST TRAVEL WHICH WAY":G$="S":GOSUB6600
10110 PRINT@829," ":PRINT"A TRUCK IN WISCONSIN (WI) CARRIED FREIGHT
TO NEW YORK (NY)."
10120 PRINT"WHICH DIRECTION DID THE TRUCK TRAVEL":G$="E":GOSUB6600
10140 PRINT@829," ":PRINT"A BOY IN PENNSYLVANIA (PA) HAD COUSINS
VISITING FROM"
10150 PRINT"SOUTH CAROLINA (SC).  WHICH WAY DID THE COUSINS TRAVEL":G$=
"N":GOSUB6600
10170 PRINT@829," ":PRINT"A MAN IN ILLINOIS (IL) DROVE TO INDIANA (IN)."
10180 PRINT"WHICH WAY DID HE DRIVE":G$="E":GOSUB6600
10200 PRINT@829," ":PRINT"LEAVING UTAH (UT) WHICH WAY"
10210 PRINT"IS NEVADA (NV)":G$="W":GOSUB6600
10230 PRINT @829," ":PRINT"IF YOU FLY FROM SOUTH CAROLINA (SC) TO ARKANSAS
(AR)"
10240 PRINT"WHICH WAY WILL YOU GO":G$="W":GOSUB6600
10260 PRINT@829," ":PRINT"TO GO FROM MISSOURI (MO) TO MINNESOTA
(MN) ONE MUST"
10270 PRINT"TRAVEL WHICH WAY":G$="N":GOSUB6600
10290 PRINT@829," ":PRINT"WHICH WAY IS RHODE ISLAND (RI) IF YOU ARE
IN"
10300 PRINT"MAINE (ME)":G$="S":GOSUB6600
10320 PRINT@829," ":PRINT"A MAN LEFT ARIZONA (AZ) TO VACATION IN IDAHO (I
D)"
10330 PRINT"WHICH WAY DID HE GO":G$="N":GOSUB6600
10350 PRINT@829," ":PRINT"IF YOU LIVED IN OHIO (OH) AND MAILED A PACKAGE
TO" .
10360 PRINT"DELAWARE (DE) WHICH DIRECTION WOULD THE PACKAGE GO":G$=
"E":GOSUB6600
10380 PRINT@829," ":PRINT"IF YOU FLY FROM CALIFORNIA (CA) TO WEST VIR
GINA (WV)"
10390 PRINT"WHICH WAY WILL YOU GO":G$="E":GOSUB6600
10410 PRINT@829," ":PRINT"A WOMAN LIVING IN VIRGINIA (VA) DROVE TO KENT
UCKY (KY)"
10420 PRINT"WHICH WAY DID SHE DRIVE":G$="W":GOSUB6600
```

```
10440 PRINT@829," ":PRINT"WHICH WAY IS IOWA (IA) IF YOU HAPPEN TO BE
IN"
10450 PRINT"NEW JERSEY (NJ)":G$="W":GOSUB6600
10470 PRINT@829," ":PRINT"TO MOVE FROM CONNECTICUT (CT) TO MASSACHU
SETTS (MA)"
10480 PRINT"REQUIRES TRAVEL IN WHAT DIRECTION":G$="N":GOSUB6600
10490 PRINT @829," ":PRINT"A DOG IN TEXAS (TX) WALKED FOR MONTHS
 TO REACH"
10500 PRINT"HIS HOME IN SOUTH DAKOTA (SD).  HE WALKED WHICH WAY"
:G$="N":GOSUB6600
10520 PRINT@829," ":PRINT"A FAMILY IN MICHIGAN (MI) TRAVELED TO THE
 BEACH"
10530 PRINT"IN ALABAMA (AL).  WHICH DIRECTION DID THEY TRAVEL":G$=
"S":GOSUB6600
10550 PRINT@829," ":PRINT"TO GO FROM NEW HAMPSHIRE (NH) TO VERMONT (VT)
10560 PRINT"REQUIRES TRAVEL IN WHICH DIRECTION":G$="W":GOSUB6600
10580 PRINT @ 829," ":PRINT"A GIRL IN WYOMING (WY) WANTED TO SKI I
N COLORADO (CO)"
10590 PRINT"WHAT WAY DID SHE WISH TO TRAVEL":G$="S":GOSUB6600
10610 PRINT@829," ":PRINT"A FARMER IN MISSISSIPPI (MS) WENT HUNTING IN"
10620 PRINT"LOUISIANA (LA).  WHICH WAY DID HE GO":G$="W":GOSUB6600
10640 PRINT@829," ":PRINT"TO MOVE FROM NEVADA (NV) TO KANSAS (KS)
 REQUIRES"
10650  PRINT"TRAVEL IN WHAT DIRECTION":G$="E":GOSUB6600
10670 PRINT@829," ":PRINT"TWO MEN IN OREGON (OR) SAILED A BOAT TO"
10680 PRINT"WASHINGTON (WA).  WHICH WAY DID THEY SAIL":G$="N":GOSUB6600
10710 PRINT@829," ":PRINT"LEAVING OKLAHOMA (OK)"
10720 PRINT"WHICH DIRECTION IS ARKANSAS":G$="E":GOSUB6600
10740 PRINT @829," ":PRINT"THE END IS HERE"
10750 GOTO 10750
12200 IFD$="N"THEN12280
12210  C=C+1
12220 IF C+B=25 THEN 13000
12230  PRINT@829," ":PRINT"THE CORRECT ANSWER IS NORTH."
12240  PRINT"COMPUTER  ";C;"     ";A$;"    ";B
12250 FOR X=1 TO 1500
12260  NEXT X
12270  RETURN
12280  B=B+1
12290 IF C+B=25 THEN 13000
12300  PRINT@829," ":PRINT"YOU ARE CORRECT."
12310  PRINT"COMPUTER   ";C;"     ";A$;"    ";B
12320 FOR X=1 TO 1500
12330  NEXT X
12340  RETURN
12400 IFD$="S"THEN 12480
12410  C=C+1
12420 IF C+B=25 THEN 13000
12430  PRINT@829," ":PRINT"THE CORRECT ANSWER IS SOUTH."
12440  PRINT"COMPUTER   ";C;"     ";A$;"    ";B
12450 FOR X=1 TO 1500
12460  NEXT X
12470  RETURN
12480  B=B+1
12490 IF C+B=25 THEN 13000
12500  PRINT@829," ":PRINT"YOU ARE CORRECT."
12510  PRINT"COMPUTER   ";C;"     ";A$;"    ";B
12520 FOR X=1 TO 1500
12530  NEXT X
12540  RETURN
12600 IFD$="E"THEN12680
12610  C=C+1
12620 IF C+B=25 THEN 13000
12630  PRINT@829," ":PRINT"THE CORRECT ANSWER IS EAST."
12640  PRINT"COMPUTER   ";C;"     ";A$;"    ";B
12650 FOR X=1 TO 1500
12660  NEXT X
12670  RETURN
12680  B=B+1
12690 IF C+B=25 THEN 13000
12700  PRINT@829," ":PRINT"YOU ARE CORRECT."
12710  PRINT"COMPUTER   ";C;"     ";A$;"    ";B
12720 FOR X=1 TO 1500
12730  NEXT X
12740  RETURN
12800 IFD$="W"THEN 12880
12810  C=C+1
12820 IF C+B=25 THEN 13000
12830  PRINT@829," ":PRINT"THE CORRECT ANSWER IS WEST."
12840  PRINT"COMPUTER   ";C;"     ";A$;"    ";B
```

```
12850 FOR X=1TO 1500
12860  NEXT X
12870  RETURN
12880  B=B+1
12890 IF C+B=25 THEN 13000
12900  PRINT@829," ":PRINT"YOU ARE CORRECT."
12910  PRINT"COMPUTER    ";C;"     ";A$;"    ";B
12920 FOR X=1 TO 1500
12930  NEXT X
12940  RETURN
13000 IFB=25 THEN 13500
13010 IFB.19 THEN 14000
13020 IFZ$="Y"THEN 13100
13030 IF Z$="YES"THEN 13100
13040 CLS
13050 PRINT@320," "
13055 GOSUB 15000

13060 PRINTA$", THAT WAS A GOOD TRY, I BET YOU CAN DO BETTER NEX
T TIME."
13070 END
13100 CLS
13105  GOSUB 15000
13110 PRINT@320," ":PRINTA$", PERHAPS YOU SHOULD TRY THE EASY VERSI
ON AGAIN."
13115 END
13500 IFZ$="Y"THEN 13600
13510 IF Z$="YES"THEN 13600
13515 CLS
13520 PRINT@320," ":PRINTA$", YOU MAY BE A GENIUS."
13525 PRINT"TRY TO BEAT ME AT THE HARD"
13530 PRINT"VERSION OF THE GAME."
13535 GOSUB 15000
13540 END
13600 CLS
13610 PRINT@320," ":PRINT"PERFECT SCORE"
13615 PRINTA$", YOU ARE A SUPER GENIUS.  YOU   WON----CONGRATULATI
ONS----"
13620 PRINTA$", WHAT NAME SHALL I CALL YOU OTHER THAN SUPER"
13621 INPUT"GENIUS";R$
13630 CLS
13640 PRINT@320," ":PRINTA$", ";R$", ";"----SUPER GENIUS----"
13650 END
14000 IFZ$="Y" THEN 14500
14010 IF Z$="YES" THEN 14500
14020 CLS
14030 PRINT@320," ":PRINTA$", THAT WAS A GOOD JOB.  TRY AGAIN A
ND SEE IF YOU CAN DO EVEN BETTER."
14035 GOSUB15000
14040 END
14500 CLS
14510 PRINT@320," ":PRINTA$", YOU ARE CLOSE TO BEING A GENIU
S. KEEP ON TRYING--GOOD LUCK"
14515 GOSUB 15000
14520 END
15000 PRINT"COMPUTER    ";C;"     ";A$;"    ";D
15001 RETURN
20000 OUT255,00
20005 ZR=0
20010 X=INP(255)
20015 ZR=ZR+1
20020 IF X=255 THEN 20050
20030 IFZR=50 THEN6760

20040 GOTO20010
20050 PRINT@958," "
20055 FORQP=1TO50
20056 NEXTQP
20060 GOTO6600
```

Chapter 10

Stomper

Stomper is a unique game program that utilizes voice-independent recognition, smooth animated graphics, and sound output. Only a standard TRS-80 Model I, Level II computer with 16K RAM, an amplifier for the sound output, and enough time to input the listing given in this chapter, is required.

The Stomper is a small man who begins his life at the upper right-hand corner of the video monitor. He stands there happily doing nothing, but life cannot be so simple. From the left side of the monitor come the monsters, one at a time, to complicate the situation. If a monster hits Stomper or if Stomper hits a monster, then life terminates. Fortunately, it is impossible for a monster to travel to the top of the screen. Stomper is safe there. Unfortunately, monsters who make it to the right edge of the screen are rewarded by decreasing the value of Stomper's life. Stomper starts with nothing. He is allowed a temporary dip in the flow of life, but should his vital signs sink below nine on a point scale, he is terminated. There is a way to exist, and even grow. Stomper will respond to voice commands. He can go up and down or he can stop and stomp. If he stomps a monster, the monster will cry and fall off the bottom of the screen; Stomper's life will be improved by one point.

The monsters are more evil than they look. Some have been known to exude a foul substance beneath their bodies, the odor of which is sufficient to kill a man even should he be a fair distance clear of their nasty, cavity ridden teeth. Monsters reaching the right edge of the screen are rather stupid. They simply pile up there until some of their carnivorous relatives come along to clear up the mess.

You, the great wizard outside the computer, control Stomper with your booming voice. When you talk, everybody stops to listen.

Moving from this fanciful game description into the mechanics of operation, Stomper becomes a learning aid for those who desire to combine some of the novel techniques available today in programming. The recognition mode used in this program utilizes the high-speed mode of recognition—that is, the meaning of the word is declared when you stop speaking into the microphone. The severely limited vocabulary (three words) was chosen based upon length differences found in the first voiced portion of each word or phrase. The choices "up," "down," and "stompem" for (stomp them) will be found to be of different lengths and these lengths will be fairly constant from person to person. The recognition factors are found in lines 9050 and 9060. The value found at line 9050 is the value of Q for which "up" will be recognized. The value found at line 9060 is the one for which "down" is detected. Anything greater than these values will be assumed to be the "stompem" request. Judicious logic enhances the recognition process. If the little man is at the upper limit of the screen and a sound shorter than "stompem" is heard, he will go down. A similar situation exists at the bottom of the screen. Put another way, if Stomper is at the top of the screen, he can't go up; the only choices to which he will respond are "down" and "stompem." If the request is anything except "stompem," he assumes it to mean "down."

As with the other recognition programs, the best results are obtained if the operator is very close to the microphone and no peripheral noises are presented. A cassette recorder operating in the record mode (with aux and mic plugs removed) can be used as the input device. An external microphone plugged into the mic jack works best, though the system will work with commands shouted into a built-in condensor microphone. The plug that normally goes into the aux jack can be placed into an amplifier (Radio Shack sells a battery-powered unit for under fifteen dollars) for the sound effect output. String variables such as A$ may be used to represent a graphic picture, such as that of a man. If this is done, one need only use a statement such as PRINT AT 10, A$ and the picture will be displayed in the upper left-hand corner starting at screen position 10. The speed of this operation is such that flicker-free animation becomes possible.

Towards the back of the Radio Shack manual is a page that lists

Graphics Characters and assigns them the numbers 128 through 191. These characters (along with control codes, number 0 through 31) may be used to represent any picture that can be drawn using a video display worksheet (Fig. 10-1). There is a limitation on the string variable of 255 characters. Any picture requiring more than 255 elements must be drawn using more than one string variable. Getting the graphic elements into the string variable is accomplished by means of READ and DATA statements, such as those beginning at line 1000. Towards the first part of the program, a CLEAR statement (see line number five) is normally needed to reserve adequate string storage space. Time is consumed reading the DATA statements, though it need be done only once during the operation of the program. It will be noticed that a time delay exists in Stomper while "STOMPER IS HUNTING HIS BOOTS." This delay occurs because the strings are being loaded with information via the READ statements.

Consider an example, the drawing of a man and his representation as A\$. Examine Fig. 10-2, the construction of A\$. In line 1000, A\$ is defined as nothing. Line 1010 determines exactly how many elements are used in this construction. Line 1020 causes a value to be read. Line 1030 tells what to do with that value. If the value in the

PRINT AT		0	1	2	3	4	5	TAB
0	0							
	1							
	2							
64	3							
	4							
	5							
	Y							

Fig. 10-1. Portion of video display worksheet for TRS-80.

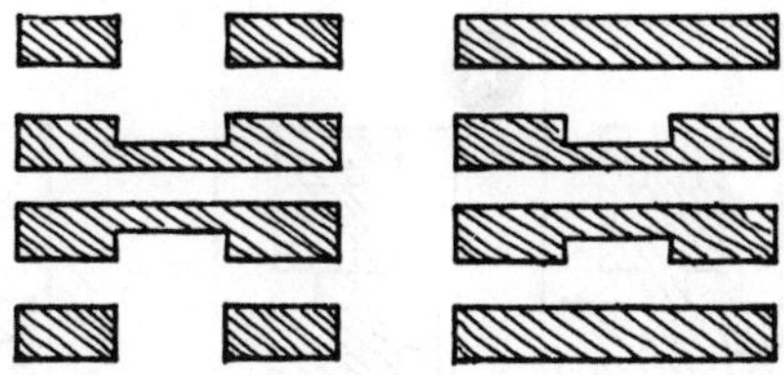

Fig. 10-2. Head and neck of Stomper, piecewise.

DATA statement is a positive number, A$ will accept a character unit. If the value in the DATA statement is negative, A$ will accept a control unit. The statement A$ = A$ + is a method of adding the new character or control unit to the ones set up on preceding passes of the FOR . . . NEXT loop which is being executed. The expression CHR$ (128+X) allows X to be a number between 0 and 63 (rather than 128 through 191), thus saving the continual typing of a third digit in the DATA statements. The expression CHR$ (26) is a downward linefeed for the video display; the expression STRING$ (ABS(X),8) causes the display to back up and erase the number of spaces defined by X. Line 1040 continues the loop. The next few lines are DATA statements representing the picture. Line 1090 is a RETURN from this subroutine that is done when all the reading is completed.

To summarize, you must create a picture first on some type of video worksheet. You must then break it into graphic characters. These characters have numbers which must be assigned to a string variable. At the end of each line of the drawing, it is necessary to return the imaginary cursor to the starting point of the next line; a control number (negative number in this example) is used for that purpose.

You can notice on Fig. 10-3 that space exists around the figures represented by the variables. These arbitrary blanks aid in the animation process. If you want to move the character represented by A$ down the screen, it could be accomplished by statements such as PRINT AT 0, A$:PRINT AT 64, A$. The top of the head left over from the first PRINT statement would be erased by the second statement. The A$ man cannot be used for upward movement on the screen because he will leave a trail of feet as the movement occurs. If you examine the video screen layout (see Fig. 10-1) it can be seen that the smallest PRINT motion in the horizontal plane covers two rectangles—location 0 and location 1 are two blocks apart. The smallest vertical motion covers three rectangles—location 0 and location 64 are three blocks apart. Smooth, slow animation therefore requires that three frames be drawn for vertical motion and two

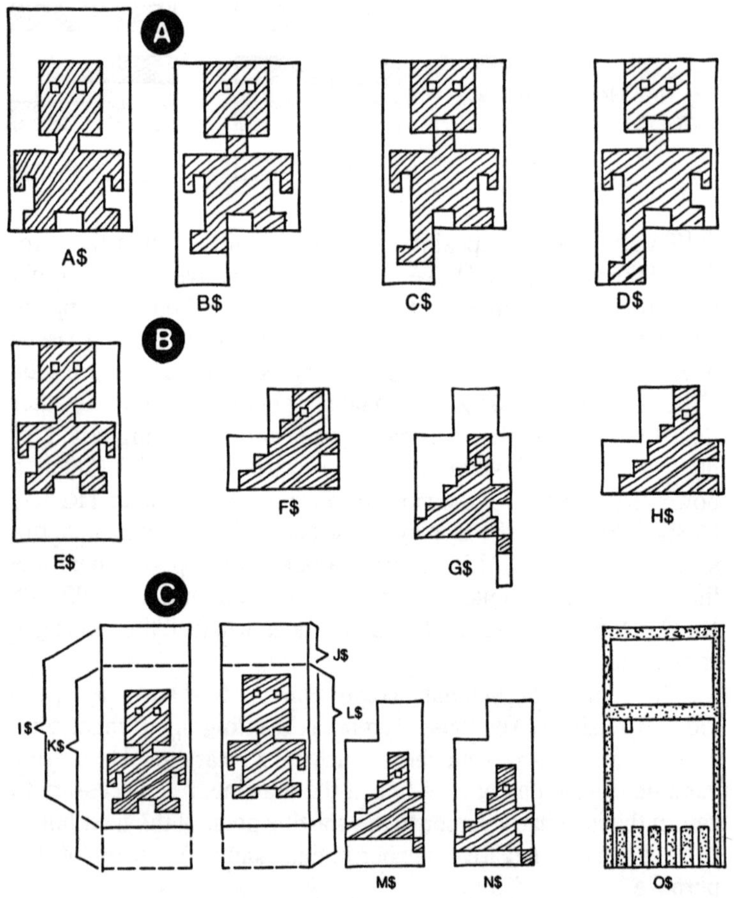

Fig. 10-3. Graphic elements of The Stomper.

for horizontal motion of the same figure. Erasure characteristics are different for up, down, left, and right motions; therefore many figures must be drawn and properly placed for animation.

All statements in a program require time to execute and time spent away from graphic action must be limited or the motion will be "jerky." This is why the program assumes the peculiar flow seen in Fig. 10-4, is a flowchart of this program. It would be possible to examine the little man's position, compare it to the monster's, check for sound input, generate sound output, perform whatever action was needed, and keep up with the score in a very straightforward manner. The comparisons and calculations consume too much time and would cause rough movement. The approach used here

Table 10-1. Variable List.

B	Mark of Beast
B1	(131 + (64*B)) Starting address for Beast
M	Mark of Man (Stomper)
M1	(((M-1)*64)+45) Address for man
DD	Code to action
	1—up
	2—down
	3—stomp
I	Loop variable
X	Data variable
B2	Present location of Beast
B3	B2-B1
D	Loop variable in sound area
Q	Counter in sound area
X1	Sound input variable
MF	Man's future
SC	Score

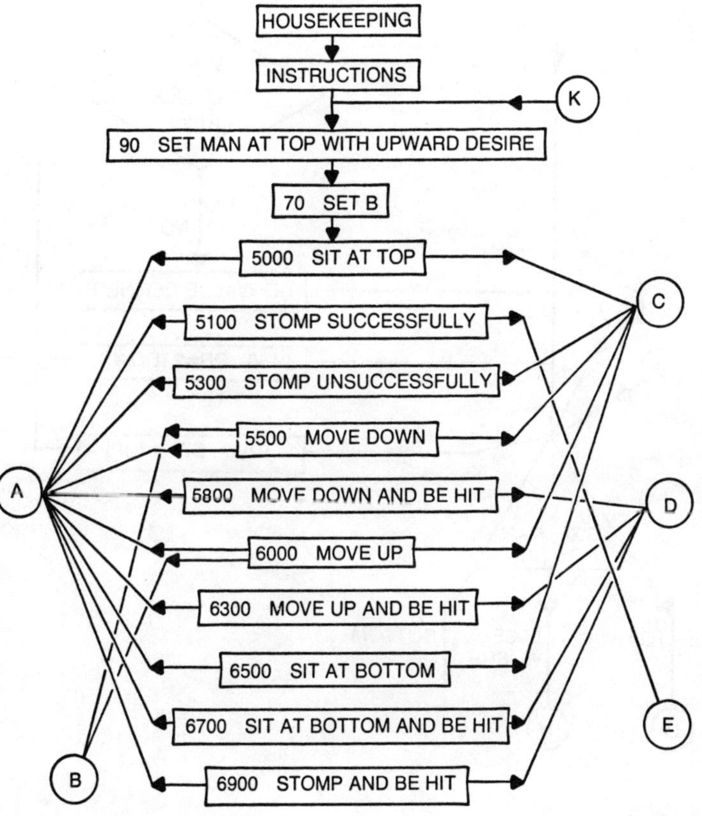

Fig. 10-4. Flowchart of The Stomper program.

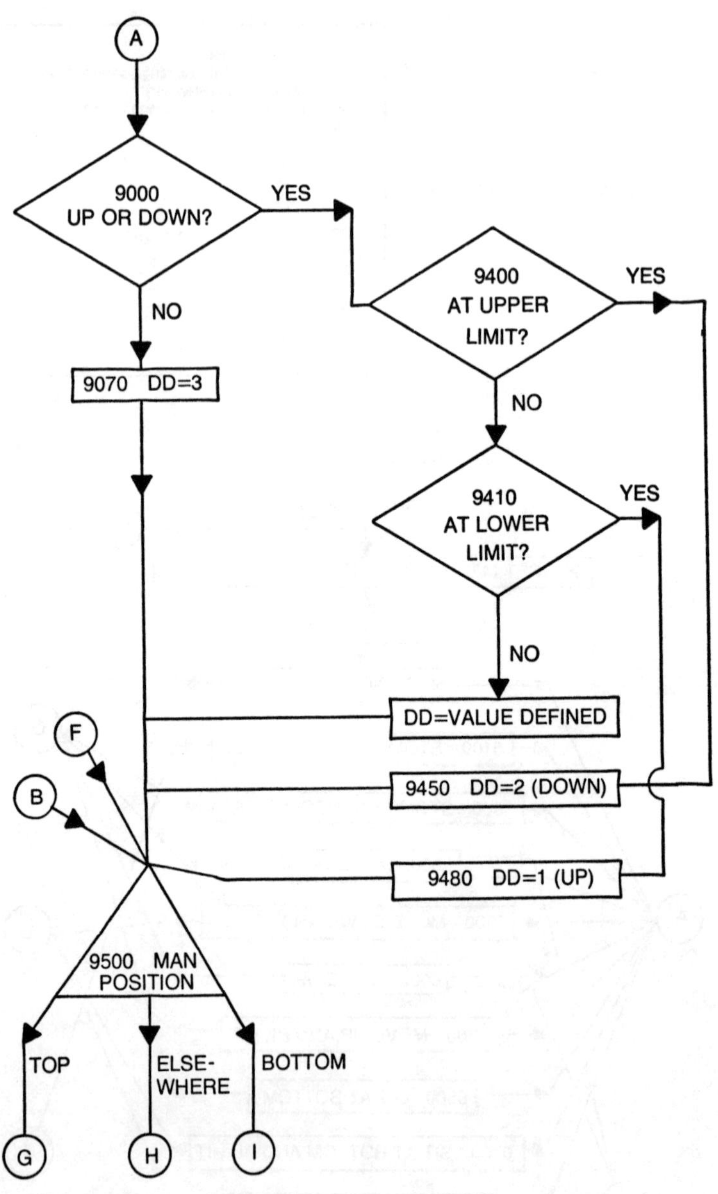

Fig. 10-4. Continued from page 75.

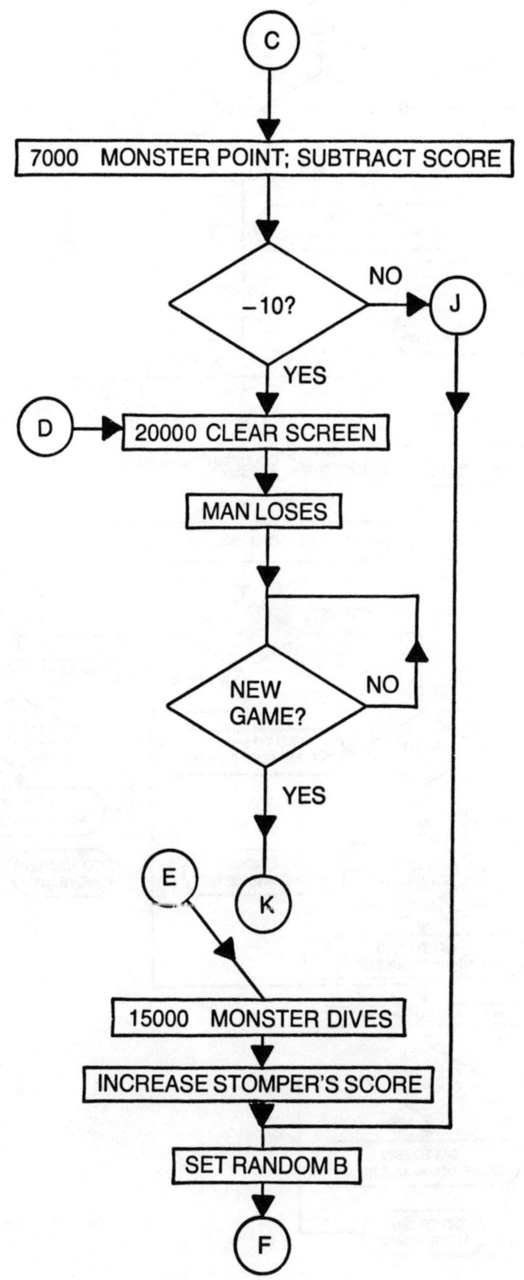

Fig. 10-4. Continued from page 76.

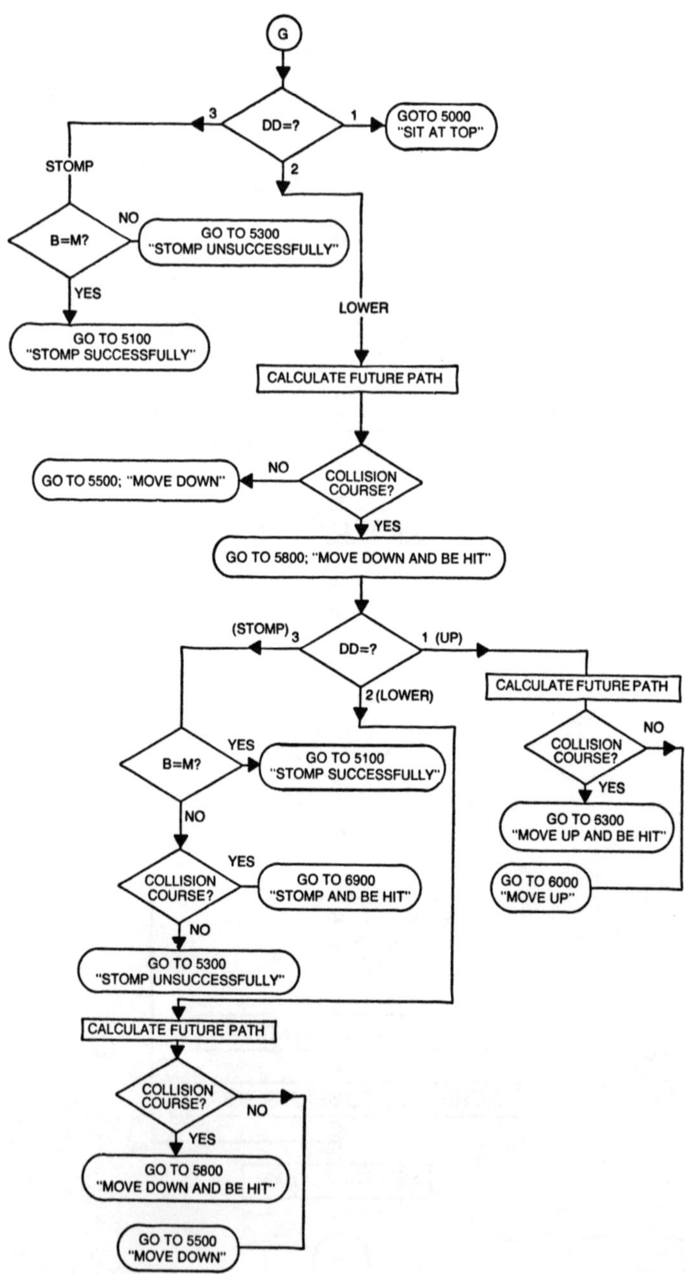

Fig. 10-4. Continued from page 77.

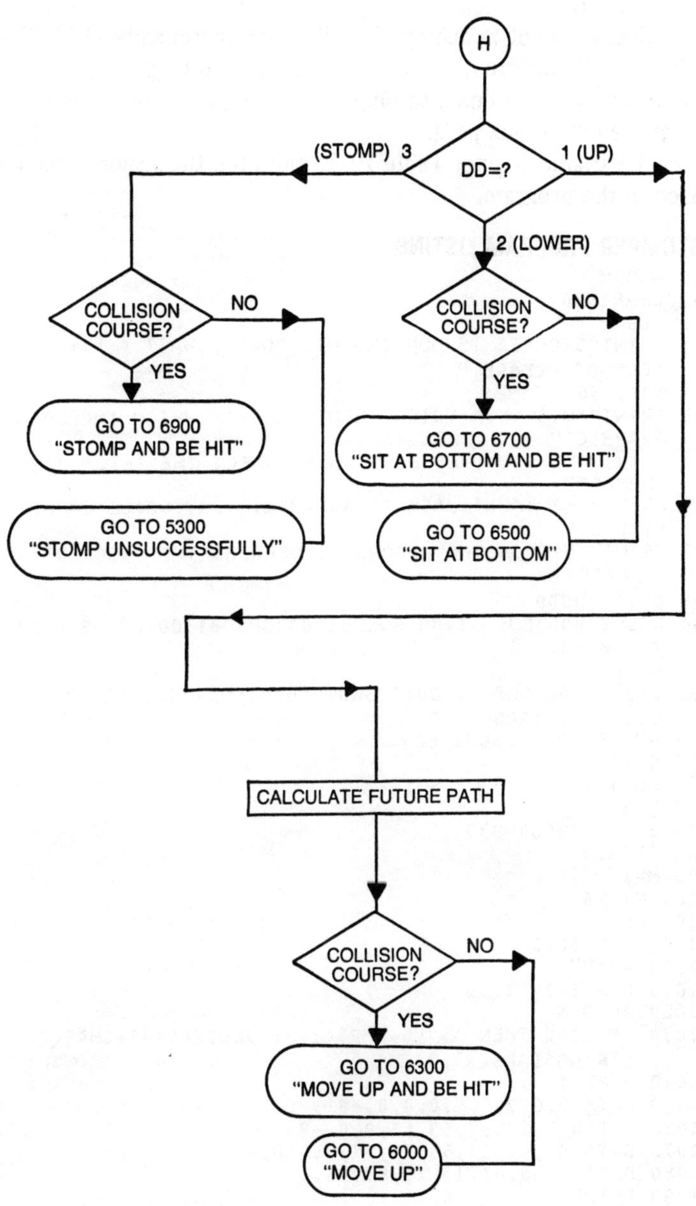

Fig. 10-4. Continued from page 78.

allows the animation to proceed checking only for one position and sound input.

Sound output is achieved easily. The statements OUT 255, 02:OUT 255, 00 will cause one square pulse to be generated. The more times this is done, the higher the frequency of sound taken from the output aux plug.

A variable listing, Table 10-1, indicates the major variables used in the program.

STOMPER PROGRAM LISTING

```
3 RANDOM
5 CLEAR1500
10 CLS
15 PRINT"STOMPER IS HUNTING HIS BOOTS, WAIT A FEW
   SECONDS PLEASE."
17 GOTO 30
20 PRINT"THIS IS A VOICE INPUT PROGRAM WHICH INCLUDES
   GRAPHICS"
22 PRINT"AND SOUND EFFECTS. DISCONNECT THE 'MIC' JACK.
   CONNECT"
24 PRINT"THE 'AUX' JACK TO AN AMPLIFIER. VOICE INPUT
   WILL BE"
26 PRINT"THROUGH THE RECORDER. DEPRESS THE 'RECORD' AND
   'PLAY'"
28 GOTO 30000
30 GOSUB1000:GOSUB1100:GOSUB1200:GOSUB1300:GOSUB1400:
   GOSUB1500
40 GOSUB1600
50 GOSUB1700:GOSUB1800:GOSUB1900:GOSUB2000:GOSUB2100:
   GOSUB2200:GOSUB2300
55 GOSUB2400:GOSUB2500
57 GOTO 20
60 DD=1
70 B=3
80 B1=(131+(64*B))
85 B2=B1
90 M=1
100 M1=45
105 CLS
110 GOTO 5000
1000 A$=""
1010 FOR I=1 TO 35
1020 READ X
1030 IF X>=0 THEN A$=A$+CHR$(128+X)ELSEA$=A$+CHR$(26)+
     STRING$(ABS(X),8)
1040 NEXT I
1050 DATA 0,0,0,0,0,0,0,0,-8
1060 DATA0,0,63,59,55,63,0,0,-8
1070 DATA 32,48,51,59,55,51,48,16,-8
1080 DATA 2,48,63,15,15,63,48,1
1090 RETURN
1100 B$=""
1110 FOR I=1 TO 30
1120 READ X
1130 IFX>=0THENB$=B$+CHR$(128+X)ELSEB$=B$+CHR$(26)+
     STRING$(ABS(X),8)
```

```
1140 NEXT I
1150 DATA 0,0,63,59,55,63,0,0,-8
1160 DATA 32,48,51,57,54,51,48,16,-8
1170 DATA 2,0,63,15,15,63,48,1,-8
1180 DATA 0,3,3
1190 RETURN
1200 C$=""
1210 FOR I =1 TO 30
1220 READ X
1230 IF X>=0 THENC$=C$+CHR$(128+X)ELSEC$=C$+CHR$(26)+
     STRING$(ABS(X),8)
1240 NEXT I
1250 DATA 0,0,63,59,55,63,0,0,-8
1260 DATA 32,48,51,57,54,51,48,16,-8
1270 DATA 2,0,63,15,15,63,48,1,-8
1280 DATA 0,12,15
1290 RETURN
1300 D$=""
1310 FOR I=1 TO 30
1320 READ X
1330 IF X>=0THEND$=D$+CHR$(128+X)ELSED$=D$+CHR$(26)+
     STRING$(ABS(X),8)
1340 NEXT I
1350 DATA 0,0,63,59,55,63,0,0,-8
1360 DATA 32,48,51,57,54,51,48,16,-8
1370 DATA 2,0,63,15,15,63,48,1,-8
1380 DATA 0,48,63
1390 RETURN
1400 E$=""
1410 FOR I=1 TO 36
1420 READ X
1430 IFX>=0THENE$=E$+CHR$(128+X)ELSEE$=E$+CHR$(26)+
     STRING$(ABS(X),8)
1440 NEXT  I
1450 DATA 0,0,63,59,55,63,0,0,-8
1460 DATA32,48,51,59,55,51,48,16,-8
1470 DATA 2,48,63,15,15,63,48,1,-8
1480 DATA  0,0,0,0,0,0,0,0,-0
1490 RETURN
1500 F$=""
1510 FORI=1 TO 13
1520 READ X
1530 IFX>=0THENF$=F$+CHR$(128+X)ELSEF$=F$+CHR$(26)+
     STRING$(ABS(X),8)
1540 NEXT I
1550 DATA 0,48,55,21,-7
1560 DATA 0,48,60,63,63,63,55,51
1570 RETURN
1600 G$=""
1610 FORI=1 TO 25
1620 READ X
1630 IFX>=0 THENG$=G$+CHR$(128+X)ELSEG$=G$+CHR$(26)+
     STRING$(ABS(X),8)
1640 NEXT I
1650 DATA 0,0,0,0,-7
1660 DATA0,0,0,48,55,21,0,0,-8
1670 DATA 48,60,63,63,63,55,3,0,-2
1680 DATA3,0
1690 RETURN
1700 H$=""
1710 FOR I=1 TO 14
```

```
1720 READ X
1730 IFX>=0THENH$=H$+CHR$(128+X)ELSEH$=H$+CHR$(26)
     +STRING$(ABS(X),8)
1740 NEXT I
1750 DATA 0,32,58,59,-7
1760 DATA0,32,56,62,63,63,63,51,17
1770 RETURN
1800 I$=""
1810 FOR I=1 TO 44
1820 READ X
1830 IFX>=0 THENI$=I$+CHR$(128+X)ELSEI$=I$+CHR$(26)+
     STRING$(ABS(X),8)
1840 NEXT I
1850 DATA 0,0,0,0,0,0,0,0,-8
1860 DATA 0,0,48,48,48,48,0,0,-8
1870 DATA 0,0,63,62,61,63,0,0,-8
1880 DATA 40,12,60,62,61,60,12,20,-8
1890 DATA 0,12,15,3,3,15,12,0
1895 RETURN
1900 J$=""
1910 FOR I=1 TO 44
1920 READ X
1930 IFX>=0THENJ$=J$+CHR$(128+X)ELSEJ$=J$+CHR$(26)+
     STRING$(ABS(X),8)
1940 NEXT I
1950 DATA 0,0,0,0,0,0,0,0,-8
1960 DATA 0,0,60,44,28,60,0,0,-8
1970 DATA 0,0,15,47,31,15,0,0,-8
1980 DATA 10,3,63,63,63,63,3,5,-8
1990 DATA 0,3,3,0,0,3,3,0
1995 RETURN
2000 K$=""
2010 FOR I=1 TO 44
2020 READ X
2030 IFX>=0THENK$=K$+CHR$(128+X)ELSEK$=K$+CHR$(26)+
     STRING$(ABS(X),8)
2040 NEXT I
2050 DATA 0,0,48,48,48,48,0,0,-8
2060 DATA0,0,63,62,61,63,0,0,-8
2070 DATA 40,12,60,62,61,60,12,20,-8
2080 DATA 0,12,15,3,3,15,12,0,-8
2090 DATA 0,0,0,0,0,0,0,0
2095 RETURN
2100 L$=""
2110 FOR I=1 TO 44
2120 READ X
2130 IFX>=0THENL$=L$+CHR$(128+X)ELSEL$=L$+CHR$(26)+
     STRING$(ABS(X),8)
2140 NEXT I
2150 DATA 0,0,60,44,28,60,0,0,-8
2160 DATA 0,0,15,47,31,15,0,0,-8
2170 DATA 10,3,63,63,63,63,3,5,-8
2180 DATA 0;3,3,0,0,3,3,0,-8
2190 DATA 0,0,0,0,0,0,0,0
2195 RETURN
2200 M$=""
2210 FOR I=1 TO 28
2220 READ X
2230 IFX>=0THENM$=M$+CHR$(128+X)ELSEM$=M$+CHR$(26)+
     STRING$(ABS(X),8)
2240 NEXT I
```

```
2250 DATA 0,0,0,0,-7
2260 DATA 0,0,0,0,28,20,0,-7
2270 DATA 0,48,60,63,63,29,12,-7
2280 DATA 3,3,3,3,3,3,12
2290 RETURN
2300 N$=""
2310 FOR I=1 TO 28
2320 READ X
2330 IFX>=0THENN$=N$+CHR$(128+X)ELSEN$=N$+CHR$(26)+
     STRING$(ABS(X),8)
2340 NEXT I
2350 DATA 0,0,0,0,-7
2360 DATA 0,0,0,0,48,16,0,-7
2370 DATA 0,0,48,60,61,53,48,-7
2380 DATA 12,15,15,15,15,13,48
2390 RETURN
2400 O$=""
2410 FOR I=1 TO 71
2420 READX
2430 IFX>=0THENO$=O$+CHR$(128+X)ELSEO$=O$+CHR$(26)+
     STRING$(ABS(X),8)
2440 NEXT I
2450 DATA 23,3,3,3,3,3,3,3,3,3,21,-11
2460 DATA 21,0,0,0,0,0,0,0,0,0,21,-11
2470 DATA 23,3,7,3,3,3,3,3,3,3,21,-11
2480 DATA 21,0,0,0,0,0,0,0,0,0,21,-11
2485 DATA 21,0,0,0,0,0,0,0,0,0,21,-11
2490 DATA 21,63,42,21,63,42,21,63,42,21,21
2495 RETURN
2500 P$=""
2510 FORI=1TO71
2520 READX
2530 IFX>=0THENP$=P$+CHR$(128+X)ELSEP$=P$+CHR$(26)+
     STRING$(ABS(X),8)
2540 NEXT I
2550 DATA 23,3,3,3,3,3,3,3,3,3,21,-11
2560 DATA 21,0,0,0,0,0,0,0,0,0,21,-11
2570 DATA 23,3,3,3,3,3,3,3,3,3,21,-11
2580 DATA 21,0,0,0,0,0,0,0,0,0,21,-11
2590 DATA 21,0,0,0,0,0,0,0,0,0,21,-11
2600 DATA 21,0,42,21,0,42,21,63,42,21,21
2610 RETURN
5000 PRINT@45,E$
5005 PRINT@1005,A$;:PRINT@B2,F$;
5010 OUT255,00:PRINT@B2,H$;
5020 B2=B2+1
5025 IFB2-B1>54THEN7000
5030 IFINP(255)>200 THEN 9000
5050 GOTO 5005
5100 PRINT@M1,E$;:PRINT@B2,F$;:OUT255,00:PRINT@M1,B$;:
     PRINT@B2,H$;:OUT25
5,02
5110 B2=B2+1
5120 IFINP(255).255 THEN 9000
5130 IFB2-B1>40 THEN 15000
5140 PRINT@M1,C$;:PRINT@M1,D$;:PRINT@B2,F$;:PRINT@M1,
     C$;:PRINT@M1,B $;:GOTO 5100
5300 PRINT@M1,E$;:PRINT@B2,F$;:OUT255,00:PRINT@M1,B$;:
     PRINT@B2,H$;: OUT255,02
5310 B2=B2+1
```

```
5315 IFB2-B1>54THEN7000
5320 IFINP(255)>200  THEN 9000
5340 PRINT@M1,C$;:PRINT@M1,D$;:PRINT@B2,F$;:PRINT@M1,
     C$;:PRINT@M1,B $;:GOTO 5300
5500 PRINT@M1,L$;:PRINT@B2,F$;
5510 PRINT@M1,K$;:PRINT@B2,H$;:OUT255,00
5520 B2=B2+1:PRINT@M1,A$;
5525 IFB2-B1>54THEN7000
5530 PRINT@B2,F$;:IFINP(255)>200  THEN 9000
5540 M1=M1+64:IFM1=749THEN9500
5550 PRINT@M1,L$;:PRINT@B2,H$;
5560 PRINT@M1,K$;:B2=B2+1:PRINT@B2,F$;
5570 PRINT@M1,A$;:PRINT@B2,H$;
5575 IFB2-B1>54THEN7000
5580 IF INP(255)>200 THEN 9000
5590 M1=M1+64:IFM1=749THEN9500
5610 GOTO5500
5800 PRINT@M1,L$;:PRINT@B2,F$;
5810 PRINT@M1,K$;:PRINT@B2,H$;:OUT255,00
5820 B2=B2+1:PRINT@M1,A$;
5830 PRINT@B2,F$;:IFINP(255)>200 THEN9000
5840 IFB2-B1>37 THEN20000
5842 M1=M1+64
5845 IFM1>=749 THEN 9500
5850 PRINT@M1,L$;:PRINT@B2,H$;
5860 PRINT@M1,K$;:B2=B2+1:PRINT@B2,F$;
5870 PRINT@M1,A$;:PRINT@B2,H$;
5880 IFINP(255)>200 THEN9000
5890 IFB2-B1>37THEN20000
5900 M1=M1+64:GOTO5800
6000 PRINT@M1,K$;:PRINT@B2,F$;
6010 PRINT@M1,L$;:PRINT@B2,H$;:OUT255,00
6020 B2=B2+1:PRINT@M1,E$;:M1=M1-64
6025 IFB2-B1>54THEN7000
6030 PRINT@B2,F$;:IFINP(255)>200  THEN 9000
6040 IFM1=45 THEN 6100
6045 B2=B2+1
6050 PRINT@M1,K$;:PRINT@B2,H$;
6060 PRINT@M1,L$;:B2=B2+1:PRINT@B2,F$;
6070 PRINT@M1,E$;:PRINT@B2,H$;:M1=M1-64
6075 IFB2-B1>54THEN7000
6080 IFINP(255)>200 THEN 9000
6090 IFM1=45 THEN 6100ELSE6000
6100 PRINT@45,E$;:PRINT@1005,A$;
6110 GOTO9500
6300 PRINT@M1,K$;:PRINT@B2,F$;
6310 PRINT@M1,L$;:PRINT@B2,H$;:OUT255,00
6320 B2=B2+1:M1=M1-64:PRINT@M1,A$;
6330 PRINT@B2,F$;:IFINP(255)>200  THEN 9000
6340 IFB2-B1>37 THEN 20000
6350 PRINT@M1,K$;:PRINT@B2,H$;
6360 PRINT@M1,L$;:B2=B2+1:PRINT@B2,F$;
6370 M1=M1-64:PRINT@M1,A$;:PRINT@B2,H$;
6380 IFINP(255)>200 THEN 9000
6390 IFB2-B1>37 THEN 20000ELSE6300
6500 PRINT@M1,E$;:PRINT@B2,F$;
6510 OUT255,00:PRINT@B2,H$;
6520 B2=B2+1
6525 IF B2-B1>54THEN7000
6530 IF INP(255)>200 THEN 9000 ELSE6500
6700 PRINT@M1,E$;:PRINT@B2,F$;
```

```
6710 OUT255,00:PRINT@B2,H$;
6720 B2=B2+1:IFINP(255)>200 THEN 9000
6730 IF(B2-B1)>37 THEN20000ELSE6700
6900 PRINT@M1,E$;:PRINT@B2,F$;:OUT255,00:PRINT@M1,B$;:
     PRINT@B2,H$;:OUT255,02
6910 B2=B2+1
6920 IFINP(255)>200THEN9000
6930 IFB2-B1>37 THEN 20000ELSE6900
7000 SC=SC-1
7010 IFSC=-10 THEN 20000ELSE15120
9000 Q=0
9005 FOR D=1 TO 30
9010 OUT255,00
9020 X1= INP(255)
9030 IF X1>200 THEN9100
9040 NEXT D
9050 IF Q,4 THEN 9200
9060 IF Q,6 THEN 9300
9070 DD=3
9080 GOTO 9500
9100 Q=Q+1
9110 GOTO 9040
9200 DD=1:GOTO 9400
9300 DD=2:GOTO 9400
9400 IF M=1 THEN 9450
9410 IF M=12 THEN 9480
9420 GOTO 9500
9450 DD=2:GOTO9500
9480 DD=1:GOTO 9500
9500 M=(M1+19)/64
9508 IFM1=45 THEN 10000
9510 IF M1=1005 THEN 10000
9520 IF M1>=749 THEN 12000
9530 GOTO 11000
10000 M=(M1+19)/64
10002 B3=B2-B1
10005 IF DD=1 THEN 5000
10010 IF DD=2 THEN 10500
10020 M=(M1+19)/64
10030 IF M=B THEN 5100
10040 GOTO 5300
10500 B3=B2-B1
10510 MF=((41-B3)/1.5)+M
10520 IF(MF-B)>0 AND (MF-B)<5 THEN 5800
10530 GOTO 5500
11000 B3=B2-B1
11005 IFDD=1THEN11600
11010 IF DD=2 THEN 11300
11020 IF B=M THEN 5100
11030 IF (M-B)>0 AND (M-B)<5  THEN 6900
11040 GOTO 5300
11300 B3=B2-B1
11310 MF=((41-B3)/1.5)+M
11320 IF (MF-B)>0 AND (MF=B)<5 THEN 5800
11330 GOTO 5500
11600 B3=B2-B1
11610 MF=M-((41-B3)/1.5)
11620 IF (MF-B)>0AND(MF-B)<5 THEN 6300
11630 GOTO 6000
12000 B3=B2-B1
12005 IFDD=1 THEN 12600
```

```
12010  IF DD=2 THEN 12300
12020  IF (M-B3)>0 AND (M-B3)<5 THEN 6900
12030  GOTO 5300
12300  IF(M-B)>0 AND (M-B)<5 THEN 6700
12310  GOTO 6500
12600  MF=M-((41-B3)/1.5)
12610  IF(MF-B)>0AND(MF-B)<5 THEN 6300
12620  GOTO 6000
15000  PRINT@B2,G$;:OUT255,00:OUT255,02:PRINT@B2,M$;:OUT
       255,00:OUT 255,02:PRINT@B2,N$;:OUT255,00:OUT255,02
15010  B2=B2+64
15020  IF B2>832THEN15100
15030  GOTO 15000
15100  CLS
15110  PRINT@M1,E$;:SC=SC+1
15120  PRINT@1015,SC;
15130  B=10*(RND(0)):B=INT(B)
15135  IF B=0 THEN B=1
15140  B1=(131+(64*B))
15150  B2=B1
15160  GOTO 9500
20000  CLS
20005  P=0
20007  PRINT@415,"MONSTER WINS";
20010  PRINT@400,F$;:OUT255,00:OUT255,02:PRINT@337,
       G$;:P=P+1
20015  OUT255,00:OUT255,02:OUT255,00:OUT255,02
20020  IF P=50 THEN 20040
20030  GOTO 20010
20040  INPUT"TO PLAY AGAIN, HIT THE ENTER KEY";B9
20042  SC=0
20045  CLS
20050  GOTO 60
30000  PRINT"BUTTONS WHILE PUSHING THE LATCH AT
       THE REAR OF THE"
30010  PRINT"TAPE COMPARTMENT--SEE PICTURE BELOW."
30015  PRINT@960,"DEPRESS ANY KEY TO CONTINUE";
30020  PRINT@540,O$;:PRINT@540,P$;:Z$=INKEY$
30030  IFZ$=""THEN30020 ELSE 30040
30040  CLS
30050  PRINT"MONSTERS COME FROM THE LEFT,'STOMPER' IS AT
       THE"
30060  PRINT"RIGHT. STOMPER UNDERSTANDS'UP','DOWN',AND "
30070  PRINT"'STOMPEM'.STOMPER JUMPS UP BEFORE
       HE STOMPS."
30080  PRINT"IF THE MONSTER HITS STOMPER
       (OR VISA VERSA)--"
30090  PRINT"TOO BAD!  THE SCORE IS DISPLAYED
       AT THE LOWER"
30100  PRINT"RIGHT PORTION OF THE SCREEN.
       YOU HAVE A CREDIT"
30110  PRINT"LIMIT OF NINE POINTS.
       GET CLOSE TO THE MICROPHONE"
30120  PRINT"TO HELP STOMPER UNDERSTAND.
       REMEMBER THAT HE HEARS"
30130  PRINT"EVERYTHING THAT IS GOING ON IN YOUR ROOM."
30132  PRINT"  HINT: MONSTERS HAVE FIENDISH
       ODORS WHICH EXTEND"
30133  PRINT" SOME DISTANCE BENEATH THEIR BODIES"
30135  INPUT"DEPRESS ENTER TO CONTINUE";Z$
30150  GOTO 60
```

Chapter 11

Voxbox Typewriter

Worth mentioning is the Voxbox, a peripheral unit designed for the TRS-80 Model I computer and sold by Radio Shack. This unit is being discontinued, but many people own them and a few probably exist on store shelves. The unit first retailed for $179, but was reduced to $49 in 1980; thus it represents a bargain for those who can find and use it. Using the Voxbox requires a TRS-80 Model I, Level II, with at least 16K of RAM, and a cassette recorder. It works with or without the expansion interface.

This device includes a push-to-talk microphone, power supply, connecting cables, software, and the decoder unit itself. Although it connects to the card edge connector at the rear of the keyboard unit (unless the expansion interface unit is involved) an additional connector is supplied on the Voxbox so that you can use a printer or a peripheral device. The Voxbox includes a machine-language driver program which must be loaded when you turn on the computer. BASIC programs may then access this program by means of the USR command. Included with the unit is a Plot program which displays the characteristics detected when a word is spoken. Also included is an Inventory Demo program which illustrates how a voice-controlled inventory system might be operated. This program operates from an imaginary inventory and could not be used without rewriting for "real world" purposes. Finally, there is a Lunar program which simulates landing a spacecraft on the moon. No graphics are included, and I lost interest in it quickly.

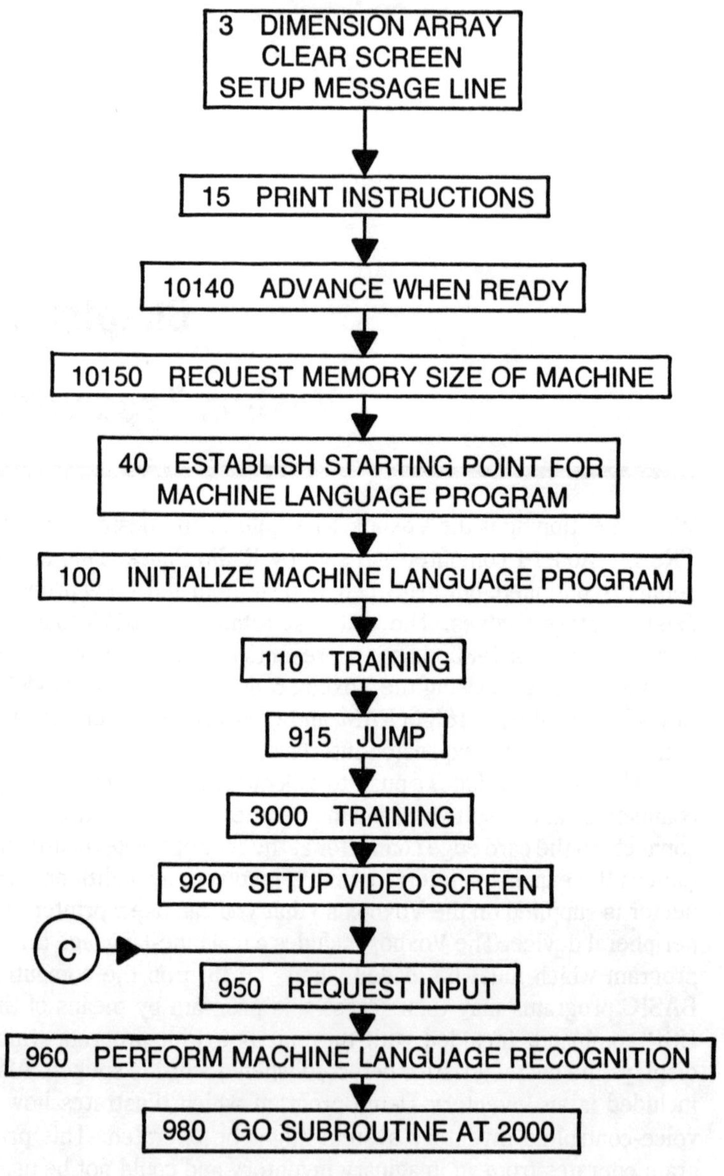

Fig. 11-1. Flowchart of Voxbox program.

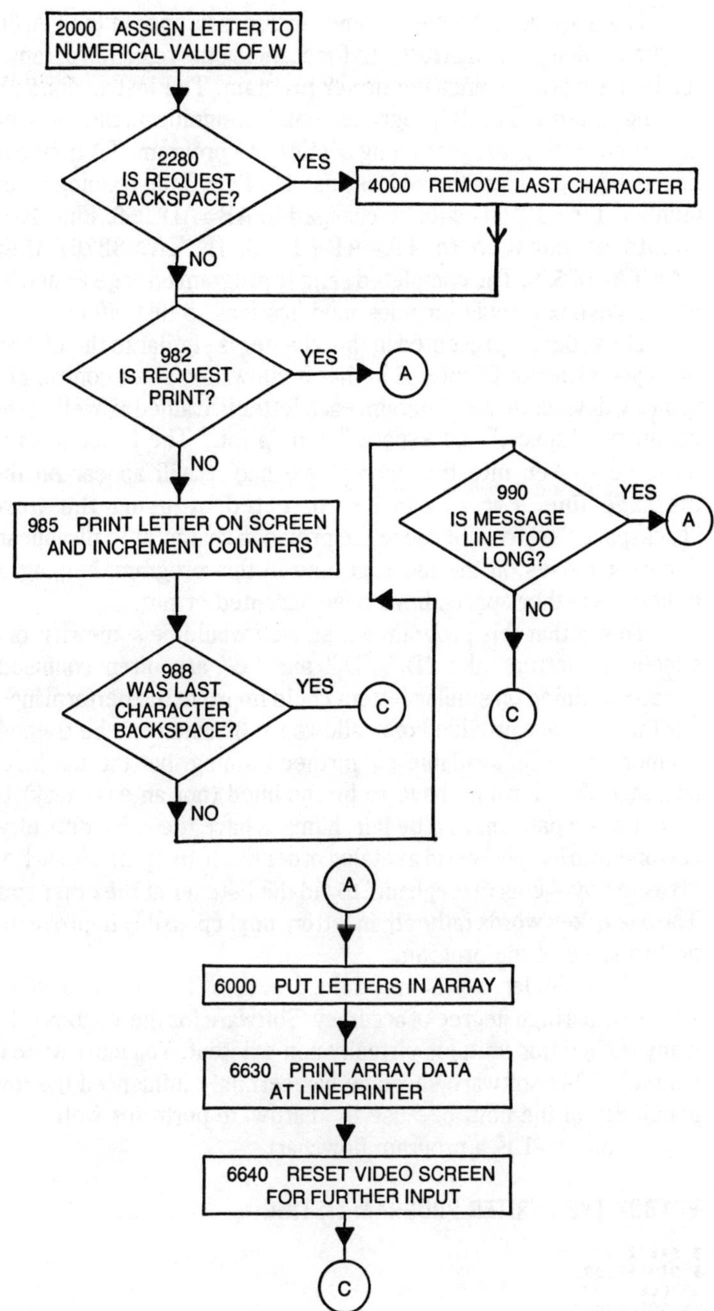

Fig. 11-1. Continued from page 88.

The 32-page instruction manual includes listings of the BASIC programs along with instructions for changing the rejection parameter in the machine language driver program. The instructions for writing your own BASIC programs contain a significant flaw on page 23. When setting up the training section of a program, TA (found in line 1010) represents the address used to POKE the training index number. Line 1010 should be changed to AB=AD*256. Line 1020 should be changed to TA=AB+1018: IF TA>32767 then TA=TA−65536. The completed sample program on page 25 and 26 of the Voxbox manual includes modifications to this effect.

The program presented in this chapter is similar to the Listening Typewriter of Chapter 6 in that it allows for voice control of a printing device. In this program, each letter is trained as well as the commands "space," "backspace," and "print." The letter desired must be spoken into the microphone and it will appear on the message line. Errors can be corrected by using the word "backspace," which will cause the previous character to disappear. A cursor moves on the message line in this program, helping to indicate whether spaces have been accepted or not.

To say that this program works well would be somewhat of a deception; letters like "B," "D," and "E" are often confused. Further training on similar letters could improve the performance, but the software provided only allows for 32 sounds to be trained. Memory space is available for further training, but the machine-language driver would have to be modified (not an easy task) to accept more patterns. To be fair, humans have the same difficulty. Anyone who has phoned in a catalog order has to use phrases such as "B as in boy—E as in elephant" to aid the listener at the other end. The use of key words rather than letters might possibly improve the performance of the program.

When similar words are trained several times, the Voxbox works with a high degree of accuracy. Software for the Voxbox (like many recognition units) is virtually non-existent. You must write it yourself. This software shortage has certainly influenced the low popularity of the unit, because the hardware performs well.

Figure 11-1 is a program flowchart.

VOXBOX TYPEWRITER PROGRAM LISTING

```
3 S=832
5 DIMS$(100)
10 CLS
15 GOTO10000
20 PRINT@0,"IS THIS A 16K, 32K OR 48K SYSTEM"
30 INPUT"   (TYPE 16, 32 OR 48)";MS
```

```
40 IF MS=16 THEN AD =112:GOTO80
50 IF MS=32 THEN AD =176:GOTO80
60 IF MS=48 THEN AD =240:GOTO80
70 GOTO 30
80 POKE16526,6
90 POKE16527,AD
100 X=USR(0)
110 TR=0
120 PRINT "SAY 'A'"
130 GOSUB 5000
140 TR=1
150 PRINT"SAY 'B'"
160 GOSUB 5000
170 TR=2
180 PRINT"SAY 'C'"
190 GOSUB 5000
200 TR=3
210 PRINT "SAY 'D'"
220 GOSUB 5000
230 TR=4
240 PRINT "SAY 'E'"
250 GOSUB 5000
260 TR=5
270 PRINT "SAY 'F'"
280 GOSUB 5000
290 TR=6
300 PRINT "SAY 'G'"
310 GOSUB 5000
320 TR=7
330 PRINT "SAY 'H'"
340 GOSUB 5000
350 TR=8
360 PRINT "SAY 'I'"
370 GOSUB 5000
380 TR=9
390 PRINT "SAY 'J'"
400 GOSUB 5000
410 TR=10
420 PRINT "SAY 'K'"
430 GOSUB 5000
440 TR=11
450 PRINT "SAY 'L'"
460 GOSUB 5000
470 TR=12
480 PRINT "SAY 'M'"
490 GOSUB 5000
500 TR=13
510 PRINT "SAY 'N'"
520 GOSUB 5000
530 TR=14
540 PRINT "SAY 'O'"
550 GOSUB 5000
560 TR=15
570 PRINT "SAY 'P'"
580 GOSUB 5000
590 TR=16
600 PRINT "SAY 'Q'"
610 GOSUB 5000
620 TR=17
630 PRINT "SAY 'R'"
640 GOSUB 5000
650 TR=18
660 PRINT "SAY 'S'"
670 GOSUB 5000
680 TR=19
690 PRINT "SAY 'T'"
700 GOSUB 5000
710 TR=20
720 PRINT "SAY 'U'"
730 GOSUB 5000
740 TR=21
750 PRINT "SAY 'V'"
```

```
760 GOSUB 5000
770 TR=22
780 PRINT "SAY 'W'"
790 GOSUB 5000
800 TR=23
810 PRINT "SAY 'X'"
820 GOSUB 5000
830 TR=24
840 PRINT "SAY 'Y'"
850 GOSUB 5000
860 TR=25
870 PRINT "SAY 'Z'"
880 GOSUB 5000
890 TR=26
900 PRINT "SAY 'SPACE'"
910 GOSUB 5000
915 GOSUB3000
920 CLS
930 POKE 16526,3
940 POKE 16547,AD
945 PRINT@893,"X"
946 POKE16192,140
950 PRINT@20,"NEXT LETTER"
960 X=USR(0)
970 W=PEEK(TA)
975 SK=0
980 GOSUB 2000
982 IF W=28 THEN 6000
985 PRINT@S,W$
986 POKE(15361+S),140
987 S$(S-832)=W$
988 IFSK=1GOTO950
990 S=S+1
995 IFS=894 THEN 6000
1000 GOTO 950
2000 IFW=0 W$="A"
2005 PRINT@100,"        "
2010 IFW=1 W$="B"
2020 IFW=2 W$="C"
2030 IFW=3 W$="D"
2040 IFW=4 W$="E"
2050 IFW=5 W$="F"
2060 IFW=6 W$="G"
2070 IFW=7 W$="H"
2080 IFW=8 W$="I"
2090 IFW=9 W$="J"
2100 IFW=10 W$="K"
2110 IFW=11 W$="L"
2120 IFW=12 W$="M"
2130 IFW=13 W$="N"
2140 IF W=14 W$="O"
2150 IFW=15 W$="P"
2160 IFW=16 W$="Q"
2170 IFW=17 W$="R"
2180 IFW=18 W$="S"
2190 IFW=19 W$="T"
2200 IFW=20 W$="U"
2210 IFW=21 W$="V"
2220 IFW=22 W$="W"
2230 IFW=23 W$="X"
2240 IFW=24 W$="Y"
2250 IFW=25 W$="Z"
2270 IF W=26 THEN W$=" "
2280 IF W=27 GOSUB 4000
2300 RETURN
3000 TR=27
3010 PRINT"SAY 'BACKSPACE'"
3020 GOSUB 5000
3030 TR=28
3040 PRINT"SAY 'PRINT'"
3050 GOSUB 5000
3060 RETURN
```

```
4000 W$=""
4005 PRINT@(S+1)," "
4010 S=S-1
4015 SK=1
4020 POKE(15360+S),140
4030 RETURN
5000 IF AD=112 THEN DD=28672
5002 IF AD=176 THEN DD=45056
5004 IF AD=240 THEN DD=61440
5006 TA =DD+1018
5008 IF DD.32767 THEN TA=TA-65536
5020 POKE 16526,0
5030 POKE 16527,AD
5040 POKETA,TR
5050 X=USR(0)
5060 IF PEEK(TA),.0 THEN GOTO 5090
5070 RETURN
5090 PRINT"ERROR"
5100 GOTO 5020
6000 A$=S$(0)
6010 B$=S$(1)
6020 C$=S$(2)
6030 D$=S$(3)
6040 E$=S$(4)
6050 F$=S$(5)
6060 G$=S$(6)
6070 H$=S$(7)
6080 I$=S$(8)
6090 J$=S$(9)
6100 K$=S$(10)
6110 L$=S$(11)
6120 M$=S$(12)
6130 N$=S$(13)
6140 O$=S$(14)
6150 P$=S$(15)
6160 Q$=S$(16)
6170 R$=S$(17)
6180 T$=S$(18)
6190 U$=S$(19)
6200 V$=S$(20)
6210 X$=S$(21)
6220 Y$=S$(22)
6230 Z$=S$(23)
6240 A1$=S$(24)
6250 B1$=S$(25)
6260 C1$=S$(26)
6270 D1$=S$(27)
6280 E1$=S$(28)
6290 F1$=S$(29)
6300 G1$=S$(30)
6310 H1$=S$(31)
6320 I1$=S$(32)
6330 J1$=S$(33)
6340 K1$=S$(34)
6350 L1$=S$(35)
6360 M1$=S$(36)
6370 N1$=S$(37)
6380 O1$=S$(38)
6390 P1$=S$(39)
6400 Q1$=S$(40)
6410 R1$=S$(41)
6420 S1$=S$(42)
6430 T1$=S$(43)
6440 U1$=S$(44)
6450 V1$=S$(45)
6460 W1$=S$(46)
6470 X1$=S$(47)
6480 Y1$=S$(48)
6490 Z1$=S$(49)
6500 A2$=S$(50)
6510 B2$=S$(51)
6520 C2$=S$(52)
```

```
6530 D2$=S$(53)
6540 E2$=S$(54)
6550 F2$=S$(55)
6560 G2$=S$(56)
6570 H2$=S$(57)
6580 I2$=S$(58)
6590 J2$=S$(59)
6600 K2$=S$(60)
6610 L2$=S$(61)
6620 M2$=S$(62)
6630 LPRINTA$;B$;C$;D$;E$;F$;G$;H$;I$;J$;K$;L$;M$;N$;O$;P$;Q$;R$;
T$;U$;V$;X$;Y$;Z$;A1$;B1$;C1$;D1$;E1$;F1$;G1$;H1$;J1$;K1$;L1$;M1$;
N1$;O1$;P1$;Q1$;R1$;S1$;T1$;U1$;V1$;W1$;X1$;Y1$;Z1$;A2$;B2$;C2$;D2
$;F2$;F2$;G2$;H2$;I2$;J2$;K2$;L2$;M2$
6640 CLS
6650 S=832
6660 PRINT@893,"X"
6670 GOTO950
10000 PRINT"THIS PROGRAM CONSISTS OF A LEARNING AND AN"
10010 PRINT"OPERATING PHASE. FIRST YOU MUST SPEAK ALL THE"
10020 PRINT"LETTERS AND A FEW WORDS AS THEY ARE REQUESTED."
10030 PRINT
10040 PRINT"       AFTER THIS TRAINING, YOU WILL BE ASKED"
10050 PRINT"FOR THE NEXT LETTER.  SAY THAT LETTER AND IT"
10060 PRINT"SHOULD APPEAR AT THE BOTTOM OF THE SCREEN."
10070 PRINT"IF IT DOES NOT APPEAR, SAY 'BACKSPACE' AND THE"
10080 PRINT"INCORRECT LETTER OR SPACE WILL BE REMOVED."
10090 PRINT"       SAY 'PRINT' TO CAUSE A LINE TO BE PRINTED."
10100 PRINT
10110 PRINT"       IF YOU RUN INTO THE STAR AT THE END OF THE"
10120 PRINT"LINE, THE PROGRAM WILL CAUSE THE LINE TO PRINT"
10130 PRINT"AUTOMATICALLY."
10140 INPUT"HIT THE ENTER KEY TO CONTINUE";RZ
10150 CLS
10160 GOTO 20
```

Chapter 12
Basic Electronics

To the uninitiated, the diagrams and strange little "bugs" found in electronic circuits are bewildering, but they need not be mysterious (see Fig. 12-1 for circuit elements). It is not difficult to build or understand circuits, but some preliminary concepts and information need to be presented to give you the knowledge you need to construct the projects in this book. *Integrated circuits*—ICs—are basic building blocks of complex devices. ICs can be thought of as "black box" devices—it is only necessary to know what comes out for certain inputs. It is no more necessary for you to understand the internal workings of a silicon chip than it is for a bus driver to understand the workings of a diesel engine. Digital integrated circuits take information, which is either high or low (positive supply voltage or negative supply voltage), and perform logical or mathematical operations. The pins on the IC may be classified in one of three ways. Either they are for power supply, for inputs, or for outputs. Integrated circuits need not be digital; some types are called *linear*. Linear ICs perform nondigital functions. An audio amplifier and a timer are examples of linear integrated circuits. Linear circuits may be connected to capacitors, resistors, potentiometers, crystals, and other such devices to control the operation of the circuit. Linear circuits have up to four types of pins: power supply, input, output, and control. Digital circuits, it should be pointed out, can directly control other digital circuits without the need for resistors, capacitors, and other components.

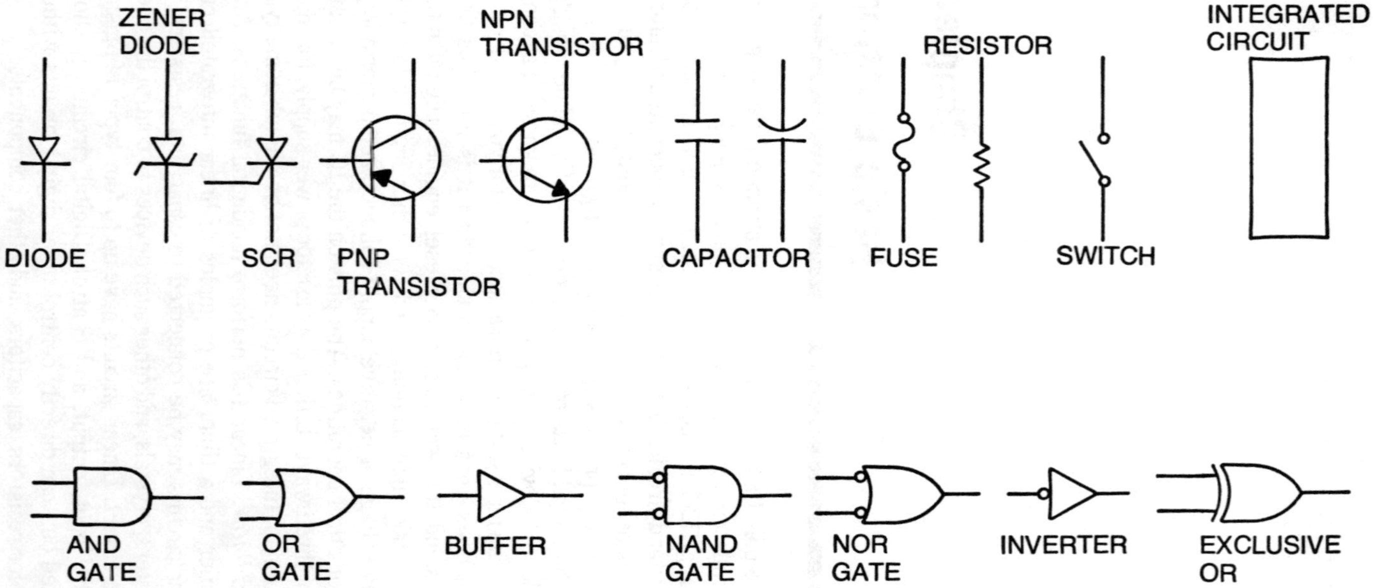

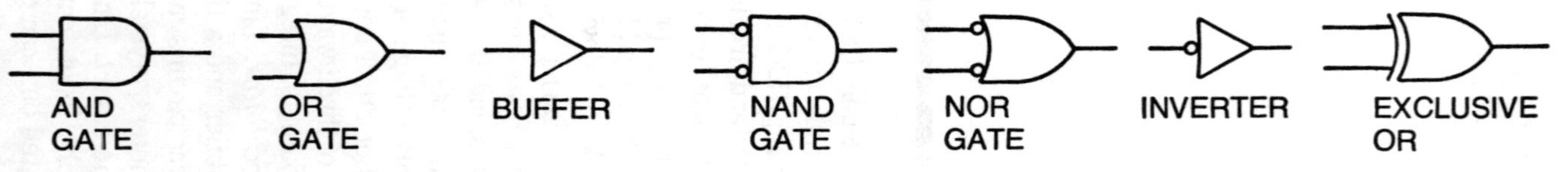

Fig. 12-1. Circuit symbols.

All electronic circuits require energy and for that reason some form of power supply must be provided. Some integrated circuits will tolerate little variance in the voltage supplied. Therefore, they must have a regulated direct current supply. Batteries provide smooth, ripple-free direct current (ripple is the bumps found in rectified alternating current, see Fig 12-2), but the voltage they supply changes with the energy being drawn by various devices and the voltage decreases as the battery is drained. Regulator integrated circuits (linear ICs) will take any reasonable voltage, such as 9 volts from a battery, and regulate it to some lower voltage, such as 5 volts. These are much simpler to design and use than the complex regulated supplies built a few years ago. A complete supply from an alternating source requires a transformer to reduce the voltage from the outlet to a lower level such as 12 volts. This alternating voltage can be converted to a rippled nonalternating voltage by the use of diodes. The ripple can be smoothed out with a capacitor and the raw dc (direct current) voltage can be applied to the input of an IC regulator. The regulator has an output pin and a ground; the

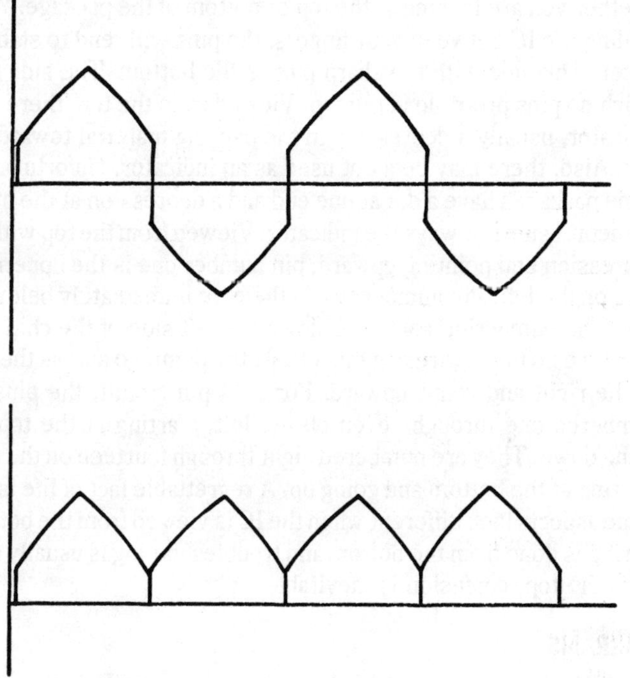

Fig. 12-2. Alternating voltage before and after rectification.

ground is tied to negative for reference, and output is the regulated voltage supply. A small capacitor is often placed across the input and the output to ground to enable the IC to respond more rapidly to changes in the input or output.

Regulator ICs, like many other linears, have a power rating (usually one amp or more) which indicates how much power they can handle. This rating assumes proper heat dissipation, a situation that occurs if the circuit is securely fastened to a piece of metal where the heat it generates can be carried away. Without this heat sink, the unit is good for only a fraction of its rating—perhaps one-tenth or less of what the specifications claim.

IC PACKAGE

Digital integrated circuits are primarily housed in *dual inline packages* (Fig. 12-3). This means that the devices are packaged in a rectangular piece of plastic or ceramic with wires protruding from the two longer sides. There is a standard numbering system that can be used to quickly find a desired pin (the wires coming from the IC are called pins). To use the numbering system, you must know whether you are looking at the top or bottom of the package. When holding the IC between your fingers, the pins will tend to stab one finger. The side with the sharp pins is the bottom. The side from which no pins protrude is the top. Viewed from the top, there is an indicator, usually a depression in the packing material toward one end. Also, there may be a dot used as an indicator. Unfortunately, some packages have a dot at one end and a depression at the other; the depression is always the indicator. Viewed from the top with the depression end pointing upward, pin number one is the uppermost wire on the left. Pin number two is the wire immediately below pin one. The numbering continues down the left side of the chip until there are no more wires on the left. At the point, go across the chip to the right and count upward. For a 14-pin circuit, the pins are numbered one through seven on the left, starting at the top and going down. They are numbered eight through fourteen on the right starting at the bottom and going up. A regrettable fact of life is that some aspects look different when the IC is viewed from the bottom. Wiring is done from the bottom and troubleshooting is usually done from the top; confusion is inevitable.

DIAGRAMS

Circuit diagrams may be drawn in many ways. The ones in this book include block diagrams showing the general concepts ac-

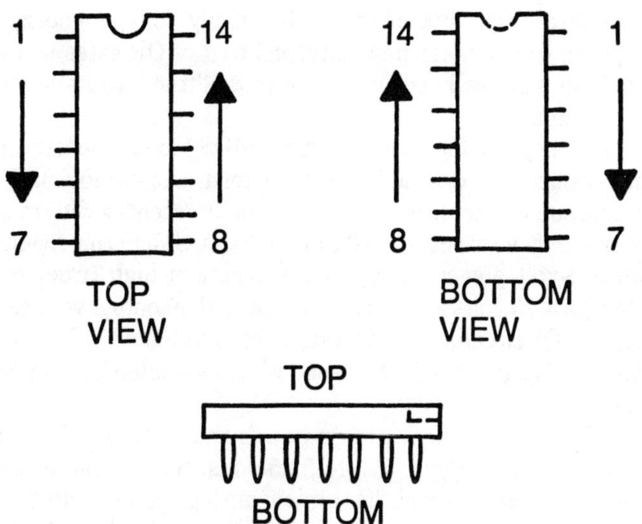

Fig. 12-3. Integrated circuit numbering.

complished, and wiring diagrams showing the interconnections of all components. Logic diagrams indicating all logic functions performed are not practical due to the large number of functions performed by some of the microprocessor related circuits. The wiring diagrams are actually hybrid drawings showing some of the logic symbols and some logic blocks. Each logic unit on the diagram has a number inside the figure. That number represents the integrated circuit used and the commercial circuit type (number used to purchase the circuit or look it up in a technical reference manual). Some integrated circuits contain six or more logic gates, and these gates may be drawn separately, but they will all have the same number inside the figure—indicating that they are physically contained in the same package. The numbers outside the figure represent pin numbers. Components such as resistors, capacitors, and transistors will also be shown. On these devices it will be necessary to examine the package they come in to determine which pin is which. Resistors are not polarity-sensitive and one lead is as good as another for wiring. The primary flow of diagrams is from left to right, though it is sometimes necessary to bring a signal back to the left after it has been created.

LOGIC FAMILIES

Digital logic integrated circuits are not all the same. There are several families of logic circuits that perform the same function in nonidentical ways. For example, the supply voltage, energy consumption, speed, noise immunity, and cost of OR gates will vary, though all units will require one or more "true" inputs to yield a "ture" output.

Two popular logic families are CMOS (complimentary metal oxide semiconductor) ant TTL (transistor-transistor logic). CMOS logic consumes very little power and usually accepts a wide range of power supply voltages, from 3 to 18 volts. A CMOS chip, operating from a 5-volt power supply has a minimum high (true) output voltage of 4.75 volts and a.maximum low (false) output voltage of .3 volts. CMOS circuits tend to be static-sensitive and can be damaged if the pins are touched by someone who has scuffed his feet on the carpet.

TTL logic consumes more power and tolerates the limited voltage supply range of 4.75 to 5.25 volts. Such a chip operating from a 5-volt power supply has a minimum high output voltage of 2.5 volts and a maximum low output voltage of 1.5 volts. CMOS and TTL circuits can be used in the same circuits operating from a 5-volt power supply, but they may or may not communicate successfully with one another. TTL circuits have a greater output power capability and thus can drive larger loads than CMOS circuits, though neither can handle much. There are exceptions to the rules, some CMOS circuits are designed to interface with and accept TTL levels. External pull-up resistors can be used to pull TTL high levels up to an acceptable level for CMOS.

Most processors are TTL compatible. The Z-80 and 8080 as well as the 1802 microprocessor interface directly to TTL memory circuits, because TTL memories are the most common and economical.

CONSTRUCTION AIDS

When you build individual circuits, you must install sockets. Because wire wrapping is a fast method of building unique devices, sockets are mandatory for such construction. Although it is possible to wrap wire directly to the legs of integrated circuits, it is not wise to do so. If the circuit fails, swapping it becomes a monumental task of unwrapping, restripping or lengthening wires. Likewise, the chance of damaging of CMOS circuit with static electricity is magnified if it must be handled 15 or 20 times as opposed to merely inserting it in a wired socket once. The pins of integrated circuits are not very long and the amount left after they are inserted through perforated board is minimal indeed, so it is rather difficult to make more than one connection on a pin.

The disadvantages of sockets include cost, along with the potential failure of an IC pin to contact a socket pin. Unless the total circuit is to be subjected to drastic environmental changes that could cause things to shrink and expand, it is doubtful whether printed circuits could actually prove more reliable than sockets. Printed circuits are cheaper to build on a mass basis. Sockets are highly desirable if a circuit is built up on a printed circuit board because soldered chips are most difficult to remove. It is also difficult to solder integrated circuits into place without subjecting the pins to excessive heat, which may cause failure.

Wire wrapping is a technique that greatly simplifies the construction of prototype circuits for the hobbyist. To build complex systems requires wiring connections from place to place. The old way of handling that situation was to cut a piece of wire, strip the ends, mechanically connect the two ends by bending or twisting the wire with pliers, and then apply solder—taking care not to create a cold solder joint or to overheat anything. In contrast, wire wrapping requires the use of small gauge wire (about #30) which is coated with a special insulation. This insulation can be easily stripped with a wire wrapping tool. There are two types of wire wrapping tools. The wire wrap pencil is manual and similar to the old mechanical system of wiring while the slit type tool involves a new technique and is much faster. The pencil requires taking the wire, cutting it and stripping the ends (easily accomplished by using a stripper built in the wiring pencil) then twisting four or five turns around whatever leads are to be connected. No soldering is required, the connection provides low resistance, and the process is much faster than the strip-and-solder method. Stripping dispensers along with precut and stripped wire are available to make the method even more convenient. The wire size is small and cannot be used for large power-handling jobs.

The slit type tool takes a pool of wire and feeds it down the center of a wrapping pencil. The tool must merely be rotated about the legs of a wire wrap socket four or five times (the tool slits the wire as it is rotated), then move on to the next point to be connected. When it is time to end the series of connections, a small lever is pushed on the slit pencil and the wire will be cut. This method is about six times as fast as the wiring pencil and the initial tool cost is modest. The disadvantage is that the tool must be used on wire wrap sockets (sockets with square posts) or it will not slit the wire. It cannot be used to wire to the leg of a transistor or a resistor because it will not slit the insulation from the wire. The wiring pencil can be used for connections to components, so long as the component lead is not too large in diameter (anything works up to the size of leads on ½-watt resistors). Wire wrap sockets along with the integrated circuits make a creation which is about three-quarters of an inch thick; if this is unacceptable (builting boards to fit in an Apple II computer, for example) there are other methods that use small wire and heat to remove the insulation, allowing for a thinner installation.

There are numerous types of board on which you can mount electronic projects. A pre-drilled phenolic board, dilled with integrated circuit spacing, is ideal. Plug-in boards can be purchased at greater expense, but they serve no purpose unless you already have something for them to plug into. To mount the phenolic board to its housing (metal case, wood, plastic, etc.) drill holes in the phenolic and add standoffs. If standoffs are not readily available a small diameter bolt of appropriate length can be used with several nuts placed on the bolt to achieve the desired standoff distance.

Another good tool for use in prototype construction is the modular integrated circuit breadboard socket (part #276-174 at Radio Shack) which will accept circuits directly into its holes. This socket has strips of commonly bussed holes (five common holes per IC pin spacing) which allow the placement of an integrated circuit and the addition of up to four wires leaving from that pin location. Solid wire from #22 to #30 can be used to interconnect pins. This hookup wire can be plugged into the holes and pulled out time after time, rapidly and without any special tools. Use of this breadboard unit allows for the building and testing of a design, then the rapid rearrangement of components to optimize the circuit (or make it work at all).

Static electricity is hazardous to many semiconductors, particularly CMOS and FET advices. Although modern integrated circuits are internally protected against static damage, they can be harmed, and care should be taken during handling and wiring. Static-sensitive components normally are packed in conductive foam; it is best to leave them in this foam until their final destination is prepared. Static electricity is most prevalent when the air is dry and physical objects are cool. Homes which are heated with forced-air are prime places for people (on a cold day) to scuff around and build up static charge. Possibly the best technique for static relief (short of ripping out carpet and installing a humidifier) is to touch a large metal object and discharge immediately before contacting static-sensitive devices.

ELECTRICAL RULES

For those not well versed in electricity, the next section explains Ohm's law and a few basic concepts that are important to an understanding of why odd little components are sprinkled about in electronic circuits (see Table 12-1).

$V=IR$, voltage is equal to current multiplied by resistance. That is Ohm's law and the essence of electrical engineering. Using algebra, there are two variations on that formula, $I=V/R$ and $R=V/I$. Before proceeding, an explanation is due concerning voltage, current, and resistance. *Voltage* is the potential force that will be used to cause action to occur. Imagine separating all men and all women; taking the men to one hill and the women to another hill miles away. For the men and women to get together requires desire; the greater the separation, the greater the desire required if they are to meet in the center. This is the concept of voltage. Voltage is the desire of electrons to get together with protons. The greater the separation, the greater the voltage. Consider the separated men and women again. Imagine a huge impenetrable ocean separating the sexes. That is the concept of resistance. *Resistance* is the blockage or bottlenecking of the flow of electrons. If the resistance is infinite, no electrons can flow and nothing happens; the voltage (potential) is preserved and nothing happens. Back to the example, allow one small ship to be released on the ocean; some men and women would leave their lands and join the others, but it would be a slow process. This is the analogy to *current*, the flow of electrons across the resistance. The less the resistance (more ships) the greater the flow (current). Given this analogy, you can see that a circuit must have resistance or there will be chaos—a large current flow and collapse of voltage.

Table 12-1. Formulas.

```
V=IR   V=Voltage
          I=Current
          R=Resistance
 I=V /R
R=V /I
P=I²R   P=Power
R(series)=R1 + R2 + R3
R(parallel)=((R1) (R2) (R3)) /(R1 + R2 + R3)
C=Capacitance:
  C(parallel)=C1 + C2 + C3
  C(series)= ((C1) (C2) (C3)) /(C1 + C2 + C3)
```

One other formula is important, $P=I^2R$ or power is equal to current times current times resistance. This formula is used to determine the power-handling requirements of various components. Power is measured in *watts*. Using the formula developed in the last paragraph, $R=V/I$ and substituting that in $P=I^2R$, you come up with the formula $P=(I^2)(V/I)$ which reduces to $P=VI$ or power equals voltage times current. When you install a resistor it is necessary to know what resistance to select (how many ohms) and what physical size (how many watts). Given the voltage supplied to a circuit and measuring the ohms, you can find the amps flowing in the area by using the formula $I=V/R$. With the current known it is possible to determine the power which will be dissipated by the resistor using $P=I^2R$ because I and R are known. Any wattage equal to higher than the calculated value will be sufficient. Note that the rating of the resistor is a value defined for free-air placement. Few resistors have that sort of air circulation, as they are normally confined on one side to a board. Thus a ½-watt resistor mounted against a board will not continuously tolerate one-half watt.

Resistors come in standard values and it is not always possible to purchase the value needed for a particular design. When this occurs, you have to combine available resistors to create the proper effective value. Resistors placed in series add mathematically; in other words a 100 ohm resistor in series with a 37 ohm resistor yields an effective resistance of 137 ohms. Resistors placed in parallel have an effective resistance equal to the product of the resistors divided by their sum. For example, 3 ohms paralleled with 5 ohms paralleled with 2 ohms is equal to: 3 times 5 times 2 divided by 3 plus 5 plus 2 or 30 divided by 10 for a total resistance of 3 ohms. The power capability required of each resistor is still calculated using $P=I^2R$ after using $I=V/R$ to determine the current flow. When dealing with a series combination of resistors, the voltage across each resistor is *not* equal to the total power supply voltage. The voltage across the resistors divides in proportion to the relative resistance of each unit. With a 5-volt power supply connected across a series combination of a 3.5 ohm resistor and a 1.5 ohm resistor; there would be 3.5 volts developed across the 3.5 volt resistor and 1.5 volts across the 1.5 ohm resistor.

Capacitors are often seen in circuits, and they can be used to accomplish numerous tasks. A *capacitor* is an energy storage device, it allows electrons to pile up or be released, depending upon whether the rest of the circuit is rising in voltage or falling. As a filter in power supplies, the capacitor charges when rectified alternating voltage rises and it discharges when the alternating voltage falls. The release of energy when the alternating wave is falling fills in the gap and creates a flatter waveshape. If the capacitor is large enough, the rectified wave will be almost as smooth as voltage from a battery. Stray voltage spikes can be induced into circuitry by the arching of brush type motors (sewing machines, for example) or other noise sources. These high stray voltages can damage integrated circuits or fool them into thinking a legitimate pulse has occurred. Voltage cannot rise rapidly across a capacitor unless that voltage is supported by a large amount of energy (high current); thus noise spikes, though large in voltage, will collapse to negligible values when placed against capacitors. For this reason, capacitors are frequently employed at various points to "eat" noise.

Capacitors may be manufactured from various materials and the different types vary in cost, reliability, temperature stability, storage capacity, and polarization. Some capacitors will accept positive or negative voltage on either terminal and they are known as nonpolarized capacitors. This type is frequently found on refrigerator motors and other alternating current devices. Polarized capacitors accept positive voltage on one end and negative on the other; they are not to be reversed or they will quickly fail. These are typically found in direct current applications where polarity is controlled, such as electronic circuits, power supplies in particular. The polarity marking is usually a band near the end where positive voltage is to be applied. Some manufacturers ring the unit with minus signs and arrows pointing to one end; that is the end which should have negative voltage applied to it.

Capacitors add directly in parallel; a 30 microfarad capacitor and a 15 microfarad capacitor in parallel have a combined capacitance of 45 microfarads. In series they combine by using the project of the units divided by the sum. With the 30 and 15 units, the series combination would equal 30 times 15 (450) divided by 30 plus 15 (45) for a total of ten microfarads.

Soldering, if it is deemed necessary, should be done with the lowest wattage iron possible. The joint (not the solder) should be heated with the iron and the solder should be placed against the joint until it melts and is drawn into the connection. Solder should not be used to make connections; the connections should be physically good before the iron is brought near. Solder merely secures the joint. Cold solder joints are dull-appearing spots where the hot solder was dropped onto the connection; this type of joint may not work or function electrically.

A permanent black marking pen can be used to denote integrated circuit numbers upon the back of perforated boards during wiring. Placing a dot in the position of the number one pin will help eliminate the confusion that occurs when trying to convert from the top to bottom views of data sheets or schematics.

A list of parts suppliers is given at the back of this book. They offer the types of parts and tools needed to begin electronic construction. Also listed are several magazines which carry excellent advertisements and articles.

SOFTWARE

Software is a necessary concern when dealing with computer systems. *Software* is a set of instructions which tell the hardware (physical circuitry) what to do. There are numerous "languages" which may be used to program computers, BASIC, FORTRAN, COBOL, and many others. Thse are high-level languages, because they accept English language instructions such as JUMP and GOTO. *Assembly language* is a lower-level language. Assembly-language programming uses codes like LDA which represent a processor operation. Assembly language does not directly support complicated operations, such as multiplying numbers or calling subroutines. Numerous codes must be combined to achieve the same goal which a single high-level instruction could accomplish. The bottom level of software is *machine-language* programming. Machine language is the actual code used by the integrated circuit to perform its tasks. Although it is the lowest level language, it is also the most difficult to use; but it is the only one that does not require other programs to make it work. BASIC for example, is a program contained (usually) in read only memory (ROM) within a computer such as the TRS-80. Upon receipt of a command such as GOTO, the program determines that actions are necessary to accomplish that goal and does all the necessary machine-language manipulations to accomplish the task. Machine-language programming is dependent entirely upon the type of microprocessor integrated circuit used; the instruction sets (that tell the microprocessor exactly what to do) vary from unit to unit.

A reasonable question to ask would be, "Why does anyone want to program in machine language?" There are many reasons for doing so. First, machine language is fast. All other languages ultimately must arrive at machine code to run; the "middleman" is eliminated if high-level languages are not used. Machine language is up to 300 times faster than BASIC, an important factor when dealing with graphics or rapidly occurring events. Machine language can be used to write programs that occupy a minimal amount of memory space—an important consideration when trying to save money on hardware (extra memory costs more). Machine language is an excellent learning tool; anyone who can program in machine code can easily master the more simple higher languages.

Speech recognition, particularly continuous recognition and speaker-independent recognition, will require rapid processing of significant quantities of data. The fastest handling of this data will be through machine language programming. An understanding of these principles will enable the designer to take in and put out information in whatever form is most convenient. Knowing how to write this type of program will enable the experimentalist to built inexpensive dedicated computer systems for burglar alarms, toys, test equipment, speech recognizers, or anything that you can imagine.

Before delving into the specifics of the 1802 microprocessor instructions, there are several fundamental concepts that must be covered. The hexadecimal numbering system is used for instructions and memory location identification rather than base ten numbers. Base ten numbers are the ones used in everyday life, seven plus seven equals 14 and the like. Base ten numbers are set up on a multiples-of-ten basis. Perhaps you have heard statements such as "His salary is in the six-figures range." That would mean that the person being referred to earns more than $100,000. Each digit in the base ten system represents ten times as much as the digit immediately to the right. Consider the number 439; it is composed of four times 100 plus three times ten plus nine times one. Hexadecimal, or base 16, is not so easy to handle mentally, but it is a logical system for handling digital data. Because a digital bit (the smallest amount of information a computer can record) can be only high or low in voltage (one or zero) it has but two states. Everything must be based upon a system which in its natural state utilizes multiples of two. A system based upon multiples of two is called the binary system. The binary system is inconvenient to use because of the length of the numbers. To establish the number 55,000 (base ten) in binary (base two) would require 16 digits. To avoid long numbers, yet remain consistent with the multiples of two, the hexadecimal system was devised. Four binary bits have a maximum number of possible distinct combinations equal to 16 (base ten). These numbers are represented in the hex system as shown in Table 12-2. Note that hex numbers are identical to base ten numbers until ten (base ten) is reached, then we have A. B represents 11, C repre-

Table 12-2. Numbering Systems

Base Ten	Base Sixteen
0	0
1	1
2	2
3	3
4	4
5	5
6	6
7	7
8	8
9	9
10	A
11	B
12	C
13	D
14	E
15	F
16	10

Decimal numbers are constructed as in the example below:

14328 =

1 × 10,000 plus	4B37=
4 × 1,000 plus	4 × 4,096 plus
3 × 100 plus	B × 256 plus
2 × 10 plus	3 × 16 plus
8 × 1.	7 × 1.

sents 12, D represents 13, E represents 14, and F represents 15. Zero is the sixteenth number in the system just as zero is the tenth number in the base ten system. A factor which is certain to cause confusion when dealing with computers is the place where numbering starts. To find the fifth memory location physically within a system, look for address location four—remember that the first memory location is address location zero.

Most common microprocessors are eight-bit machines. This means that they manipulate eight bits at one time. Eight bits can be represented by two binary groups of four or by two hexadecimal numbers. The hex system will be used. Computers are not very smart; they can only do a few very simple tasks. They can move bits around from one place to another, they can add in binary, and they can compare two numbers and tell which is greater or if the two are equal. That is about it. Everything else from space war games, to complex math, to industrial control, depends upon the ability of someone to reduce complex problems to these very simple manipulations.

Chapter 13

1802 Microprocessor Instructions

The 1802 microprocessor integrated circuit was chosen for this recognizer because it is well suited for control applications. Other types are better suited for math just as some are best for operating color graphics on televisions. Most microprocessor circuits can be adapted to most projects; the speed of operation and difficulty of programming will be influenced by the microprocessor chosen. Please note that the instruction set given here and the program listed will not work for any type of microprocessor other than the 1802.

The internal register arrangement of the 1802 is shown in Fig. 13-1. The number of bits handled by each register is also shown. There are 16 general-purpose 16-bit registers, R(O).1 through R(F).1. Because this is an eight-bit microprocessor, it can handle only eight bits at a time, not 16. These 16 registers are therefore broken down into 32 eight-bit registers. The registers are nonetheless often used in groups of two with the ending designation (R(?).1 referring to the high-order eight bits and the designation (R?).0 referring to the low-oreder eight bits. The "?" in the parentheses could be any hexadecimal number from O to F. These registers can be used to store information or to point to memory locations. The 1802 (as most microprocessors) will readily address up to 64,000 eight-bit groups or *bytes* of memory. Recall that 16 bits are necessary to define a unique location from a group of over 64,000. Any of these 16-bit register pairs can be sequentially placed (eight bits at a

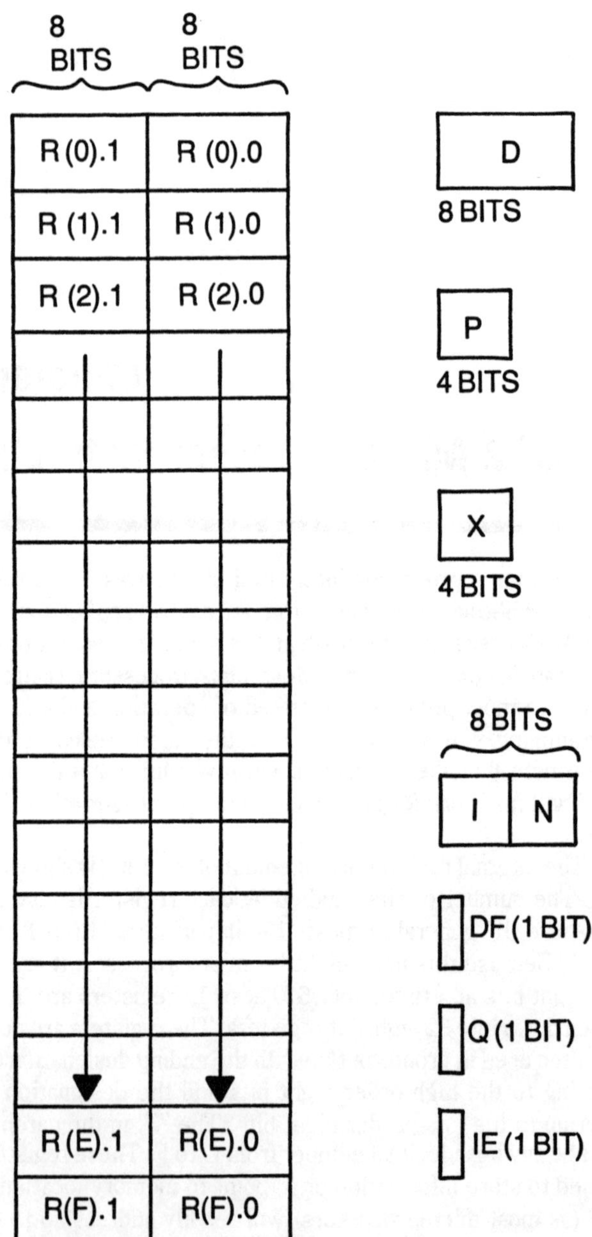

Fig. 13-1. 1802 register arrangement.

time) on the memory address lines to define a specific spot in memory. These 16 bits can also be placed in the 16-bit A register where they may be increased or decreased one number at a time. Form the A register they can be returned to the register from which they came or placed in another register. Registers N, P, and X are four-bit registers which hold a binary code equivalent to one digit of a hexadecimal number. This binary code is usd to refer to one of the 16-bit register paris. Register T is a temporary eight-bit register. I is a four-bit register used along with the N register to hold the code being executed. Note that the N register may act as a special code, depending upon the instruction being input. The D register is the primary place where comparisons occur and through which information is usually passed. The ALU (arithmetic-logic-unit) is an eight-bit unit which performs arithmetic and logic operations. It takes the byte in the D register and a byte on the data bus (obtained from memory), performs its function and places the result in the D register. A single-bit register DF is set to 1 or 0 depending upon whether a carry, no carry, no borrow, or borrow has occurred. Q is a flip-flop which can be set high or low and can be tested (asked whether it is high or low) by proper instruction command. IE is the interrupt enable flip-flop which may be used to allow or disallow interrupts. There are 93 primary instructions listed in Table 13-1. These are broken into nine groups: memory reference, register operations, logic operations, arithmetic operations, short branch, long branch, skip, control, and input-output. Each group and instruction will be described in the following pages.

MEMORY REFERENCE

The memory reference group is used to get information into and out of memory locations. A typical computer has an operating program to direct all activities. This is normally placed in some form of permanent memory, which cannot be accidentally written upon. Unless the system is dedicated to perform a very specific task without processing input information, there will be volatile memory which may be written into, erased, and changed at will. Where these two types of memory are located is dependent upon the physical construction of the system. Frequently, the operating program fills the lower numbered spaces in memory while the RAM is located in the upper parts. Part of the operating program (a few bytes) must be placed in the lowest part of memory. When the computer system is turned on, it will begin to sequence through memory, starting at the lowest possible address. Whatever it finds in the lowest spot will be

Table 13-1. 1802 Primary Instruction Set.

INSTRUCTION	CODE	OPERATION
Memory Reference		
LOAD VIA N	0N	$M(R(N)) \to D$; FOR N NOT 0
LOAD ADVANCE	4N	$M(R(N)) \to D$; $R(N)+1$
LOAD VIA X	F0	$M(R(X)) \to D$
LOAD VIA X AND ADVANCE	72	$M(R(X)) \to D$; $R(X)+1$
LOAD IMMEDIATE	F8	$M(R(P)) \to D$; $R(P)+1$
STORE VIA N	5N	$D \to M(R(N))$
STORE VIA X AND DECREMENT	73	$D \to M(R(X))$; $R(X)-1$
Register Operations		
INCREMENT REGISTER N	1N	$R(N)+1$
DECREMENT REGISTER N	2N	$R(N)-1$
INCREMENT REGISTER X	60	$R(X)+1$
GET LOW REG N	8N	$R(N).0 \to D$
PUT LOW REG N	AN	$D \to R(N).0$
GET HIGH REG N	9N	$R(N).1 \to D$
PUT HIGH REG N	BN	$D \to R(N).1$
Logic Operations		
OR	F1	$M(R(X))$ OR $D \to D$
OR IMMEDIATE	F9	$M(R(P))$ OR $D \to D$; $R(P)+1$
EXCLUSIVE OR	F3	$M(R(X))$ XOR $D \to D$
EXCLUSIVE OR IMMEDIATE	FB	$M(R(P))$ XOR $D \to D$; $R(P)+1$
AND	F2	$M(R(X))$ AND $D \to D$
AND IMMEDIATE	FA	$M(R(P))$ AND $D \to D$; $R(P)+1$
SHIFT RIGHT	F6	SHIFT D RIGHT, LSB(D) $\to$ DF, $0 \to$ MSB(D)
SHIFT RIGHT WITH CARRY RING SHIFT RIGHT	76	SHIFT D RIGHT, LSB(D) $\to$ DF, DF $\to$ MSB(D)
SHIFT LEFT	FE	SHIFT D LEFT, MSB(D) $\to$ DF, $0 \to$ LSB(D)
SHIFT LEFT WITH CARRY RING SHIFT LEFT	7E	SHIFT D LEFT, MSB(D) $\to$ DF, DF $\to$ LSB(D)
Arithmetic Operations		
ADD	F4	$M(R(X))$ + $D \to$ DF,D
ADD IMMEDIATE	FC	$M(R(P))$ + $D \to$ DF, D; $R(P)+1$
ADD WITH CARRY	74	$M(R(X))$ + D + DF $\to$ DF,D
ADD WITH CARRY IMMEDIATE	7C	$M(R(P))$ + D + DF $\to$ DF,D $R(P)$ + 1
SUBTRACT D	F5	$M(R(X))-D \to$ DF,D
SUBTRACT D IMMEDIATE	FD	$M(R(P))-D \to$ DF, D; $R(P)+1$
SUBTRACT D WITH BORROW	75	$M(R(X))-D-$(NOTDF) $\to$ DF, D
SUBTRACT D WITH BORROW, IMMEDIATE	7D	$M(R(P))-D-$(NOT DF) $\to$ DF, D; $R(P)$ + 1
SUBTRACT MEMORY	F7	$D-M(R(X)) \to$ DF, D
SUBTRACT MEMORY IMMEDIATE	FF	$D-M(R(P)) \to$ DF, D; $R(P)$ + 1
SUBTRACT MEMORY WITH BORROW	77	$D-M(R(X))-$(NOT DF) $\to$ DF, D
SUBTRACT MEMORY WITH BORROW, IMMEDIATE	7F	$D-M(R(P))-$(NOT DF) $\to$ DF, D $R(P)$ + 1

Branch Instructions--Short Branch

```
SHORT BRANCH                  30    M(R(P))→R(P).0
NO SHORT BRANCH               38    R(P) + 1
SHORT BRANCH IF D=0           32    IF D=0, M(R(P))→R(P).0
                                    ELSE R(P) + 1
SHORT BRANCH IF              3A    IF D NOT 0, M(R(P))→R(P).0
    D NOT 0                          ELSE R(P) + 1
SHORT BRANCH IF DF=1          33    IF DF=1, M(R(P))→R(P).0
SHORT BRANCH IF POS                 ELSE R(P) + 1
    OR ZERO
SHORT BRANCH IF EQUAL
    OR GREATER
SHORT BRANCH IF DF=0          3B    IF DF=0, M(R(P))→R(P).0
SHORT BRANCH IF MINUS               ELSE R(P) + 1
SHORT BRANCH IF LESS
SHORT BRANCH IF Q=1           31    IF Q=1, M(R(P))→R(P).0
                                    ELSE R(P) + 1
SHORT BRANCH IF Q=0           39    IF Q=0, M(R(P))→R(P).0
                                    ELSE R(P) + 1
SHORT BRANCH IF EF1=1         34    IF EF1=1, M(R(P))→R(P).0
    (1=Vss)                         ELSE R(P) +1
SHORT BRANCH IF EF1=0         3C    IF EF1=0, M(R(P))→R(P).0
    (0=Vcc)                         ELSE R(P) + 1
SHORT BRANCH IF EF2=1         35    IF EF2=1, M(R(P))→R(P).0
    (1=Vss)                         ELSE R(P) + 1
SHORT BRANCH IF EF2=0         3D    IF EF2=0, M(R(P))→R(P).0
    (0=Vcc)                         ELSE R(P) + 1
SHORT BRANCH IF EF3=1         36    IF EF3=1, M(R(P))→R(P).0
    (1=Vss)                         ELSE R(P) + 1
SHORT BRANCH IF EF3=0         3E    IF EF3=0, M(R(P))→R(P).0
    (0=Vcc)                         ELSE R(P) + 1
SHORT BRANCH IF EF4=1         37    IF EF4=1, M(R(P))→R(P).0
    (1=Vss)                         ELSE R(P) + 1
SHORT BRANCH IF EF4=0         3F    IF EF4=0, M(R(P))→R(P).0
    (0=Vcc)                         ELSE R(P) + 1
```

Branch Instructions--Long Branch

```
LONG BRANCH                   C0    M(R(P))→R(P).1
                                    M(R(P) + 1)→R(P).0
NO LONG BRANCH                C8    R(P) + 2
LONG BRANCH IF D=0            C2    IF D=0, M(R(P))→R(P).1
                                    M(R(P) + 1)→R(P).0
LONG BRANCH IF D NOT 0        CA    IF D NOT 0, M(R(P))→R(P).1
                                    M(R(P) + 1)→R(P).0
LONG BRANCH IF DF=1           C3    IF DF=1, M(R(P))→R(P).1
                                    M(R(P) + 1)→R(P).0
                                    ELSE R(P) + 2
LONG BRANCH IF DF=0           CB    IF DF=0, M(R(P))→R(P).1
                                    M(R(P) + 1)→R(P).0
                                    ELSE R(P) + 2
LONG BRANCH IF Q=1            C1    IF Q=1, M(R(P))→R(P).1
                                    M(R(P) + 1)→R(P).0
                                    ELSE R(P) + 2
LONG BRANCH IF Q=0            C9    IF Q=0, M(R(P))→R(P).1
                                    M(R(P) + 1)→R(P).0
                                    ELSE R(P) + 2
```

Skip Instructions

```
SHORT SKIP                    38    R(P) + 1
LONG SKIP                     C8    R(P) + 2
LONG SKIP IF D=0              CE    IF D=0, R(P) + 2
                                    ELSE CONTINUE
LONG SKIP IF D NOT 0          C6    IF D NOT 0, R(P) + 2
                                    ELSE CONTINUE
```

Table 13-1. Continued from page 113.

LONG SKIP IF DF=1	CF	IF DF=1, R(P) + 2 ELSE CONTINUE
LONG SKIP IF DF=0	C7	IF DF=0, R(P) + 2 ELSE CONTINUE
LONG SKIP IF Q=1	CD	IF Q=1, R(P) + 2 ELSE CONTINUE
LONG SKIP IF Q=0	C5	IF Q=0, R(P) + 2 ELSE CONTINUE
LONG SKIP IF IE=1	CC	IF IE=1, R(P) + 2 ELSE CONTINUE

Control Instructions

IDLE	00	WAIT FOR DMA OR INTERRUPT; M(R(0))→BUS
NO OPERATION	C4	CONTINUE
SET P	DN	N→P
SET X	EN	N→X
SET Q	7B	1→Q
RESET Q	7A	0→Q
SAVE	78	T→M(R(X))
PUSH X,P TO STACK	79	(X,P)→T; (X,P)→M(R(2)) THEN P→X; R(2)-1
RETURN	70	M(R(X))→(X,P); R(X) + 1 1→IE
DISABLE	71	M(R(X))→(X,P); R(X) + 1 0→IE

Input--Output Byte Transfer

OUTPUT 1	61	M(R(X))→BUS; R(X) + 1; N LINES = 1
OUTPUT 2	62	M(R(X))→BUS; R(X) + 1; N LINES = 2
OUTPUT 3	63	M(R(X))→BUS; R(X) + 1; N LINES = 3
OUTPUT 4	64	M(R(X))→BUS; R(X) + 1; N LINES = 4
OUTPUT 5	65	M(R(X))→BUS; R(X) + 1; N LINES = 5
OUTPUT 6	66	M(R(X))→BUS; R(X) + 1; N LINES = 6
OUTPUT 7	67	M(R(X))→BUS; R(X) + 1; N LINES = 7
INPUT 1	69	BUS→M(R(X)); BUS→D; N LINES = 1
INPUT 2	6A	BUS→M(R(X)); BUS→D; N LINES = 2
INPUT 3	6B	BUS→M(R(X)); BUS→D; N LINES = 3
INPUT 4	6C	BUS→M(R(X)); BUS→D; N LINES = 4
INPUT 5	6D	BUS→M(R(X)); BUS→D; N LINES = 5
INPUT 6	6E	BUS→M(R(X)); BUS→D; N LINES = 6
INPUT 7	6F	BUS→M(R(X)); BUS→D; N LINES = 7

assumed to be an instruction. It is therefore necessary that the first byte in the system be an instruction. That instruction could be merely a command to jump somewhere else and find the program, but such is infrequently the case.

The first instruction, LOAD VIA N takes a memory byte and loads it into the D register. Register N is a hexadecimal value from 1 to F (0 is not allowed; it conflicts with another instruction) and it determines which general purpose register pair is the data pointer. Suppose the value of N is 3; then the 16 bits in register pair R(3).1 and R(3).0 define the address of a memory location. Whatever is in that memory location will be moved to register D.

LOAD ADVANCE does the same thing as LOAD VIA N with one additional function. It takes the 16 bits in the general-purpose register pair and adds one to the total after it has placed the data in D.

LOAD VIA X takes a memory byte and loads it into the D register. The hexadecimal number is the X register that determines which register pair will contain the address of the memory byte to be moved. This differs from LOAD VIA N in that the instruction itself in LOAD VIA N determined which register pair would be the memory location pointer. The value in the X register has to be set with another instruction.

LOAD VIA X AND ADVANCE does the same as LOAD VIA X with one additional function. It takes the 16 bits in the general-purpose register pair and adds one to the contents of that register pair after moving the memory byte to the D register. It does not increase the value of the number stored in the X register.

LOAD IMMEDIATE takes the memory byte pointed to (the next byte in sequence in the operating program) and moves it into the D register. Register P is incremented by one so that the next byte it examines (in sequence in the operating program) will be an instruction.

STORE VIA N takes the contents of the D register and places those contents into memory. The value of N determines which general register pair is used to point out a memory address into which the value from D will be stored. The contents of the D register do not change.

STORE VIA X AND DECREMENT takes the contents of the D register and places those contents into memory. The memory location is determined by the contents of a general register pair; the hexadecimal number in register X defines the register pair (0 to F) that will point to the memory location. After placing the value from register D into memory, the contents of register D remain unchanged. The contents of the general register pair (the address of the memory location where the byte was stored) is decreased by one count.

REGISTERS

The next group of instructions allows for manipulations of the general-purpose registers. The manipulations include increasing or decreasing the numbers in the general purpose registers. These instructions also allow the programmer to put numbers into the registers or take them out. It needs to be noted here that all numbers going into or out from the registers must go through the D register.

INCREMENT REG N causes the value within a general-purpose register to be increased by one unit. The value of the N register determines which register pair is to be incremented. This instruction applies to the register pair, not to memory.

DECREMENT REG N causes the value within a general-purpose register to be decreased by one unit. The value of the N register determines which register pair is to be decremented.

INCREMENT REG X causes the value within a general-purpose register to be increased by one unit. The value within the X register determines which register pair is to be incremented. Another instruction is required to set a value in the X register which will be used to point to the general-purpose register that this instruction increments.

GET LOW REG N takes the value stored in a low-order member of a register pair and places that value into the D register. The value of the N register determines which register pair is being considered; the instruction itself defines the transfer to be the eight bits of the lower order into the D register.

PUT LOW REG N takes the number stored in register D and places the value in the low order member of a general register pair. The value of register N determines which register pair will have its low-order member replaced by the value that is in register D. Register D remains unchanged throughout this operation.

GET HIGH REG N take the value stored in a high-order member of a register pair and places that value into the D register. The value of the N register determines which register pair is being considered; the instruction itself defines the transfer to be the eight bits of the lower order into the D register.

PUT HIGH REG N takes the number stored in register D and places that value in the high-order member of a general register pair. The value of register N determines which register pair will have its low-order member replaced by the value that is in register D. Register D remains unchanged throughout this operation.

LOGIC

Logic operations are used to perform manipulations utilizing logic functions, or to test specific bits in a byte or to alter the structure of a byte.

OR performs the logical *or* function with two eight-bit operands. One operand is the byte stored in the D register, and the other operand is a memory byte. The memory byte's address is found in a general register pair, the pair defined by the hexadecimal digit stored in the X register. Each bit of one byte is compared to the corresponding bit of the other byte; if either bit is high, then the output bit for that location will be high. The result of this comparison is placed in the D register.

OR IMMEDIATE takes the data in register D and compares it with the next byte in the program sequence. The two bytes are given a corresponding bit by bit OR comparison and the result of the comparison is placed in the D register. The contents of the program counter are incremented by one. The program counter is a general-purpose register pair, the one designated by the four-bit register P. The number contained within this general-purpose register pair is the address of the memory location containing instruction byte of the program being run. This instruction is a two-byte instruction; the first byte tells the 1802 that the next byte in the program is not an instruction but rather information to be compared. The contents of the program counter always advance one count after executing an instruction; but the program counter must advance once (automatically) and once by force of the instruction to reach the next instruction in sequence.

EXCLUSIVE OR performs the *exclusive or* logic function upon two eight-bit operands. Onc operand is the byte stored in the D register and the other operand is a memory byte. The memory byte's address is found in a general register pair, the pair defined by the hexadecimal digit stored in the X register. Each bit of one byte is compared to the corresponding bit of the other byte; if one and only one bit is high then the output bit for that location will be high. The result of this comparison is placed into the D register.

EXCLUSIVE OR IMMEDIATE is very similar to EXCLU-SIVE OR, the difference being in the location of the two bytes to be compared. For this instruction, one byte is found in the D register while the other byte to be compared is found as the next byte in the program sequence. The contents of the program counter (general-purpose register pair) must be incremented by one because this is a two byte instruction.

AND takes two bytes and performs the logical *and* function, bit by bit on corresponding bits. The *and* function merely states that both bits must be high if the output is to be high. One of the two bytes being compared is found in the D register, the other is in a memory location whose address is in a general purpose register pair. The contents of register X point to the general purpose register pair which points to the memory location of the memory byte. The results of this AND operation are placed into the D register.

AND IMMEDIATE is the same as the AND function except that the bytes come from a different location and the program counter is incremented by one count. One of the two bytes comes from the D register while the other is the byte found next in the program sequence. The results are placed into the D register and the general-purpose register pair used as the program counter is incremented once because this is a two-byte instruction.

SHIFT RIGHT takes the contents of the D register and shifts the bits right one position. The rightmost bit (least significant bit) is moved into the DF register. The leftmost bit (most significant bit) has a zero shifted into its place.

SHIFT RIGHT WITH CARRY—RING SHIFT RIGHT takes the contents of the D register and shifts the bits right one position. The rightmost bit is moved into the DF register, and the bit formerly in the DF register is moved into the leftmost bit of the D register. In other words, nine bits are being handled and are moving in a ring, the ninth bit being whatever is in the DF register.

SHIFT LEFT takes the contents of the D register and shifts the bits left one position. The leftmost bit (most significant bit) is moved into the DF register. The rightmost bit (least significant bit) has a zero shifted into its place.

SHIFT LEFT WITH CARRY—RING SHIFT LEFT takes the contents of the D register and shifts the bits left one position. The leftmost bit is moved into the DF register and the bit formerly in the DF register is moved into the rightmost bit of the D register.

ARITHMETIC

The next group of instructions to be considered is the arithmetic group. All that can be done is to add or subtract bytes, but all other functions can be created by manipulating these and the logic functions.

ADD takes the contents of the D register and adds that to a byte from memory. The memory location is defined by the contents of a general register pair; that pair being specified by the contents of the X register. The result of the addition is placed in the D register. A *flag* is set in the DF register; a high bit means a carry has occurred, a low bit means no carry.

ADD IMMEDIATE adds the contents of the D register to the next byte in the program sequence. The DF register is set high if a carry occurs, low if not. The result of the addition is placed in the D register. The general register pair that serves as the program counter is incremented by one; this is necessary since this is a two-byte instruction.

ADD WITH CARRY takes the byte contained by register D and adds that to a byte from memory adding also the contents of the DF register. The memory location's address is the same as the contents of the general register pair pointed to by the contents of the X register. Results of this operation are placed in the D register with any carry causing the DF bit to be high; no carry and the DF bit is low.

ADD WITH CARRY IMMEDIATE takes the byte contained by register D and adds that to the byte next in the program sequence adding also the contents of the DF register. The results are placed in the D and DF registers. This is a two-byte instruction, thus the general-purpose register pointed to by the contents of register P is incremented by one.

Computers do not subtract well; they add. To subtract, this computer adds using the two's complement method. This takes each bit of the subtrahend and complements (makes high bit low and low bits high) it adding this to the minuend plus one.

SUBTRACT D takes a byte from memory and subtracts the byte in the D register, placing the result in the D register and setting a high or low in the DF register. If DF is high, then no borrow has occurred and D is a true positive number. If DF is low, then a borrow has occurred and the result in the D register is a two's complement.

SUBTRACT D IMMEDIATE takes a byte from memory and subtracts from it the byte in the D register, placing the result in the D register and setting a high or low flag in the DF register. The byte from memory is the next byte in the program sequence, thus making this a two byte instruction. The general register pair pointing to the memory location for the controlling program is advanced one count so that the next step in the program sequence will be an instruction.

SUBTRACT D WITH BORROW allows subtraction while keeping track of a possible previous borrow operation. It takes a byte from memory and from this subtracts the contents of the D register and the inverse of the DF register (high if DF is low, low if DF is high). The memory byte's address is found in the general-purpose register pair that is pointed out by the contents of the X register. The result of the subtraction is placed in the D register. If DF is high, then no borrow has occurred and the contents of D represent a true positive number. If DF is low, then a borrow has occurred and the contents of D represents a two's complement negative number.

SUBTRACT D WITH BORROW IMMEDIATE is the same as SUBTRACT D WITH BORROW except that the byte from which the D register is subtracted is found in the next position in the program memory. This instruction is a two-byte instruction, the second byte being data; of course, the program counter (general register pair) must be incremented by one count.

SUBTRACT MEMORY takes the information in the D register and subtracts a memory byte from the contents of D. The results of this subtraction go into the D and DF registers. The memory byte subtracted is found by taking the contents of register X which defines a general register pair and using the contents of that register pair as the address of the memory byte to be subtracted.

SUBTRACT MEMORY IMMEDIATE takes the information in the D register and subtracts from it a memory byte. The results of this subtraction go into the D and DF registers. The memory byte subtracted is the next byte in the program sequence, making this a two-byte instruction and calling for an advance of the program counter.

SUBTRACT MEMORY WITH BORROW takes the contents of the D register and subtracts from it a memory byte and the inverse of the DF register. This operation keeps up with any previous borrow operations which may have occurred. The memory byte is the one addressed by the general register pair which the contents of the X register points to. Results of this operation go into the D and DF registers, and the content of the DF register has the same meaning as it does in all other subtract operations.

SUBTRACT MEMORY WITH BORROW IMMEDIATE takes the contents of the D register and subtracts from it a memory byte and the inverse of the DF register. This operation is identical to SUBTRACT MEMORY WITH BORROW except that the byte subtracted is the next byte in the program sequence, making this a two-byte instruction. The program counter is advanced one count.

SHORT BRANCH

The next group is the short branch and limited test group set of instructions. They allow the program counter to jump anywhere within a group of 256 bytes when the appropriate conditions (if any) are met. The test instructions provide for a short branch jump if the test requirements are satisfied. An area of potential confusion exists in the instruction names. When the instruction says, *if EF1 = 1*, it means *if EF1 = low*. For these instructions only a one is taken to be low, and a zero is taken to be high.

SHORT BRANCH is an unconditional instruction which causes the program to jump to another spot a short distance away. The branching can only occur within 256-byte group. The contents of the low-order byte of a general register pair (the pair being used to address memory locations where the program is found) is changed to equal the next byte found in the program memory sequence. This is a two-byte instruction, the first byte being the actual instruction and the second byte being data. There is no forced additional count on the program count register because the program count register (general register pair) has a new value—the one assigned by this instruction. This is essentially a GOTO instruction which causes the program to jump somewhere away from the one-byte-at-a-time ascension which it normally follows.

NO SHORT BRANCH causes the program counter (general register pair containing the address of the memory byte which is the portion of the program being acted upon) to skip the next byte in sequence.

SHORT BRANCH IF D=0 is a conditional branch statement. If the contents of register D equal zero, then the low-order byte of the program counter (general register pair) will be changed to the value found in the next memory byte in the program sequence. If D equals zero, the program jumps to the prescribed location; otherwise, the program skips the next memory byte in sequence and operates upon the next instruction.

SHORT BRANCH IF D NOT ZERO is a conditional branch statement similar to SHORT BRANCH IF D=0. The only difference is that the program jumps to the prescribed location if the contents of D do not equal zero.

SHORT BRANCH IF DF=1, SHORT BRANCH IF POSITIVE OR ZERO, SHORT BRANCH IF EQUAL OR GREATER are descriptions of the same instruction. This instruction examines the value stored in the DF register. If that value is high then the low-order byte of the program counter (general register pair) will be changed to the value found in the next memory byte in the program sequence, otherwise, the next memory byte in the program sequence will be skipped.

SHORT BRANCH IF DF=0, SHORT BRANCH IF MINUS, SHORT BRANCH IF LESS are descriptions of the same instruction. This instruction examines the value stored in the DF register. If that value is low then the low-order byte of the program counter (general register pair) will be changed to the value found in the next memory byte in the program sequence; otherwise, the next memory byte in the program sequence will be skipped.

SHORT BRANCH IF Q=1 tests the output of the Q flip-flop; if it is high, the low-order byte of the program counter is replaced by the value found in the next memory byte. If this is not the case, the next memory byte in sequence is skipped over.

SHORT BRANCH IF Q=0 tests the output for the Q flip-flop; if it is low the low-order byte of the program counter is replaced by the value found in the next memory byte. If this is not so, the next memory byte in sequence is skipped.

SHORT BRANCH IF EF1=1 tests the input line EF1. If this line is low (remember that one means low and zero means high for the EF lines) then the low-order byte of the program counter is changed to the value of the next byte in the program sequence. If this is not the case, the next byte in the program sequence is skipped.

SHORT BRANCH IF EF1=0 tests the input line EF1. If this line is high (remember again that 1 means low and 0 means high for the EF lines) then the low-order byte of the program counter is changed to the value of the next byte in the program sequence. If this is not the case, the next byte in the program sequence is skipped.

Short branch for EF2, EF3, and EF4 are the same as for EF1, the only difference being which input line is being tested by the instruction.

LONG BRANCH

Long branch instructions are capable of moving the program counter anywhere within the 64,000 bytes of memory the processor is capable of addressing.

LONG BRANCH is an unconditional jump instruction that requires three bytes. The first byte is the instruction, the second byte replaces the high-order byte of the general register pair that is being used as the program counter (pointing to the memory location where the next instruction is to be found). The third byte replaces the low-order byte of the program counter. The next memory byte will be considered to be an instruction; its location is defined by the previous two bytes.

NO LONG BRANCH causes the program counter (general register pair which addresses the memory byte used in the program sequence) to skip the next two bytes in the program sequence. This is the same instruction as LONG SKIP.

LONG BRANCH IF D=0 causes the program to jump to a specified location if the contents of the D register are low. The program jumps by changing the contents of the program counter (general register pair) to the value specified in the second and third bytes of the LONG BRANCH instruction, the second byte replacing the high-order byte of the program counter and the third byte replacing the low order byte of the program counter. If the value in the D register is high, then the second and third bytes of this instruction are skipped.

LONG BRANCH IF D NOT ZERO is the same as the previous instruction except that the jump occurs if D is high and the continue occurs if D is low.

LONG BRANCH IF DF=1 is a three byte instruction that causes the program counter to jump to a new location if the contents of DF are high (the jump is accomplished as in the previous instructions). Of course the entire three bytes are skipped if the contents of DF are low.

LONG BRANCH IF DF=0 is similar to the previous instruction except that the jump occurs if the contents of the DF register are low. If the contents of DF are high, this three byte instruction is passed over with no further action.

LONG BRANCH IF Q=1 tests the value of the Q flip-flop. If it is high, then the program counter is changed as in all the other long branch instructions. If low, it is skipped as in the other instructions. This is also a three byte instruction.

LONG BRANCH IF Q=0 tests the value of the Q flip-flop and jumps if that value is low. Otherwise, the entire three-byte instruction is bypassed with no action.

SKIP

The SKIP instructions allow the processor to ignore the next one or two bytes in the instruction sequence. Most of these instructions require that some condition be met before the skip is allowed.

These instructions skip by advancing the program counter (general register pair) by one count or two counts. If the required conditions are not met, then the program counter advances normally with no special count, thus enabling the next byte in the program sequence to be executed.

SHORT SKIP is an arbitrary instruction that forces the program counter to advance one time (thus jumping over one byte). It is the only skip instruction that does not call for an advance of two counts. This is the same instruction as NO SHORT BRANCH.

LONG SKIP, the same instruction as NO LONG BRANCH, is arbitrary and forces the program counter to advance two counts (jumping two memory bytes).

LONG SKIP IF D=0 tests the value within the D register. If that value is low, then the program counter skips two counts; otherwise it continues in sequence.

LONG SKIP IF D NOT 0 examines the value within the D register and causes the program counter to skip two counts if the value found is high; otherwise the count continues in sequence.

LONG SKIP IF DF=1 examines the value within the DF register and causes the program counter to skip two counts if the value found is high; otherwise the count continues in sequence.

LONG SKIP IF DF=0 tests DF and causes the program counter to skip two counts if the value found is low; otherwise it continues in sequence.

LONG SKIP IF Q=1 examines the state of the Q flip-flop and skips two counts (program counter) if Q is high; otherwise it continues in sequence.

LONG SKIP IF Q=0 tests the Q flip-flop and skips two counts (program counter) if Q is low; otherwise it continues in sequence.

LONG SKIP IF IE=1 tests the IE register and causes the program counter to skip two counts if the value found is high; otherwise it continues in sequence.

CONTROL

The control group of instructions allow certain specialized functions to occur.

IDLE causes the program to stop where it is until an interrupt or direct memory access is received by the low indication of the DMA IN, DMA OUT, or INTERRUPT lines on the microprocessor circuit. The contents of the memory byte addressed by the general register pair zero are placed on the data bus.

NO OPERATION causes the program counter to proceed to the next step in the program sequence. This is a time waster and is frequently used when generating time delay.

SET P takes the last four bits of the instruction byte and places them into the P register. In other words, the contents of the N register are placed into the P register, then the program counter moves along to the next instruction.

SET X takes the last four bits of the instruction byte and places them into the X register. The contents of N, in other words, are moved into the X register; then on to the next instruction.

SET Q causes the Q flip-flop to assume the high state.

RESET Q causes the Q flip-flop to assume the low state.

Before moving into the next group of control instructions it is appropriate to consider the purpose of interrupts. *Interrupts* enable a computer to perform many tasks seemingly at the same time. Consider the task of using a computer to monitor a group of sensors used in a burglar alarm system for a home. The expense of a computer is great to devote entirely to such a purpose when one considers that the machine will operate day and night, perhaps never having to act upon a violation. A more reasonable approach would be to allow the computer to play games or perform other tasks and only handle the burglar alarm when a sensor has been violated. The interrupt line merely tells the computer that something that occurs rather infrequently has occurred. It is a problem for the program writer to establish priorities and determine when to "service" the interrupt. An analogous situation occurs when a telephone rings; the options include answering it immediately, answering it after some time, or ignoring it altogether.

The computer must remember where it was before "servicing" the interrupt if it is to resume normal operation after handling the special situation. When the interrupt line goes low, a certain sequence of events occurs if the interrupt enable flag, IE, is high. That sequence includes storing the existing values from the X and P registers in the eight-bit register T (temporary). The contents of P go into the lower four bits while X goes into the higher four bits. At the same time the value of one is forced into the P register and two into the X register. The IE register is set low, disabling any further interrupts until readied by program control.

SAVE causes the byte of information stored in the T register to be placed in the memory location addressed by a general register pair. The general register pair doing this addressing is the one defined by the value found in the register X.

MARK is a fairly complex instruction which does several things. First, it places the contents of the X and P registers in the temporary register T. Next, it moves the contents of register T into the memory location which is addressed by the contents of the general register pair number two. The value contained in register P is placed into register X. The value found in general register pair number two is decreased by a count of one.

RETURN places new values in the X and P registers. These values come from the memory byte that is addressed by a general register pair. Which general register pair addresses this memory location is determined by the contents of the register X. The contents of the general register pair located by X are increased one count. The interrupt enable flag IE is set to a high level.

DISABLE performs the same operation as "RETURN" except that the interrupt enable flag is set to a low level. This causes the processor to ignore the interrupt enable line in the event that it should be active.

INPUT-OUTPUT

The final group of instructions to be considered are the input and output group. These are used to get information into the processor from external sources and to pass information outside the processor.

OUTPUT causes the contents of a memory byte to be placed on the data bus while also pulling high one or more N lines from the processor. The memory byte to be placed on the bus is addressed by a general register pair. The general register pair used is the one pointed to by the contents of the X register. The three low-byte bits of the N register are placed onto the N lines during this step. This operation occurs very rapidly and must be latched by external circuitry if the data is to be observed.

INPUT takes a byte which is placed on the data bus (this byte must be placed on the data bus at the appropriate time—something that will be covered in the hardware description of the speech recognizer) and puts that byte into a memory location. The memory location is the one addressed by the general register pair which is located by the contents of the register X. The input byte from the data bus is also placed in the D register. The three N lines are pulled high in correspondence with the contents of the N register. If N is nine, then the N lines equal one; if N contains A, then the N lines equal two; etc.

Chapter 14

The Recognizer

Examining the recognizer, one can see that there are four major units which form the speech recognition device (Fig. 14-1). These four blocks are: input stage, processor stage, output stage, and power supply.

The input stage uses a microphone, an amplifier, frequency-selective filters, and squaring apparatus. Its purpose is to obtain sound from the air, break it into defined components, and prepare those components for processing.

The processing stage obtains its data from the input stage as well as the control switches. Given this information, it analyzes the data in a fashion determined by the program (software) by which it is operating. Included here are the processor (it makes decisions and shuffles information around) and the control switches (they tell the processor what functions are desired). Two groups of memory are utilized. One type of memory cannot be altered by program control or loss of power, that type (EPROM, or Erasable Programmable Read Only Memory) contains the resident program, the instructions which tell the processor what to do. The other type of memory (RAM) can be changed by program control and is subject to "forgetting" if power is removed. The EPROM controls all activity and the RAM is used to store input information and data which has been manipulated.

The output stage takes information from the processor and converts it to some usable form. In this case it causes lights to be on

127

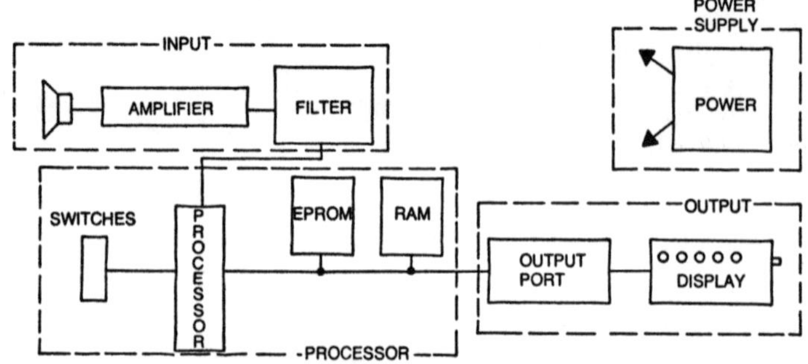

Fig. 14-1. Block diagram of The Recognizer.

or off and relays to be energized or not. The output stage by its electrical configuration takes information from the processor at a time when all electrical signals are right. Correct timing on the electrical signals is controlled by program commands to the processor. Which command to issue depends upon wiring of the output stage. Although it is possible to build a system by starting with either software or hardware and then making the other fit, it is usually easier to define the hardware first. This is because software, usually, is more easily changed than hardware.

The power supply is the final necessary component for a system. Criteria to be considered here include: regulation, source, and availability. Computer components work best when they perform within specified voltage ranges; therefore (considering how cheaply and easily regulation may be provided), it is best to regulate the supply. Most components do not simply fail if they are subjected to voltages which are out of tolerance; they become erratic and cause the system to occasionally do odd things.

Whether to use batteries or electricity from a wall plug is another consideration. Batteries will simplify cost of the supply itself, but they will be a bother as they must continually be recharged (more circuits and more expense) or replaced (more expense).

Availability is the final consideration. Can the system tolerate going down if the lights in the building blink? The speech recognition system shown here will have to be retrained upon power loss. This could be a real problem if the application were for a handicapped person who could not restart the system alone. A combination of battery and wall supply can provide better supply availability. Mobility of the unit would require the supply to have battery capability.

INPUT AND FILTERS

Construction of active filters is likely to be the most difficult task attempted in building a recognition unit. Design of such filters is a task which can best be described separately (see Sources). Difficulty arises with the actual value of components (as opposed to the value marked). Resistors and capacitors are always rated at a certain value plus or minus a few percent. Following the instructions given here should result in having three filters that will pass three different ranges of frequencies (see Fig. 14-2).

For a microphone I used the least expensive cassette microphone available. Rather than building an amplifier, I purchased Radio Shack's mini-amplifier (catalog number 277-1008), and it has proven to be adequate. The output of that amplifier comes into resistor R1 across which a voltage-varying wave is produced when sounds occur. The amplifier is powered by a battery (its own supply), and it must therefore be referenced to the Recognizer supply. This is the reason for connecting one side of the resistor to positive.

The operational amplifier (triangle in the middle of circuitry) is biased positive; therefore its output is positive except when a sound occurs and its pulse is negative. The 74LS367 is a Schmitt trigger gate. This tends to square the erratic pulse that comes from the operational amplifier. The various resistors and capacitors are used to bias and permit feedback in such a way as to cause the operational amplifier to pass a limited specific frequency range. The adjustable resistor (R13 from frequency one) is part of the biasing arrangement. Although values have been assigned for these potentiometers, they may well have to be set to something different. I would recommend that ten turn potentiometers be used because of the critical nature of tuning these filters.

As mentioned earlier, the output of the operational amplifiers is normally positive (high) and that is passed through the Schmitt trigger as a positive (high) signal. Only when sound is present does this signal go low. This point is emphasized to clear some confusion which may result. The output of the Schmitt trigger is tied directly to a EF line on the microprocessor circuit. In the software (instructions in a computer program) is a loop which effectively says that if the EF line is one, then jump to a recognize subroutine, otherwise, continue to loop (see 00,30; frequency program). That instruction would seem to be incorrect, based on the physical facts; since EF goes low when there is a sound and stays high when there

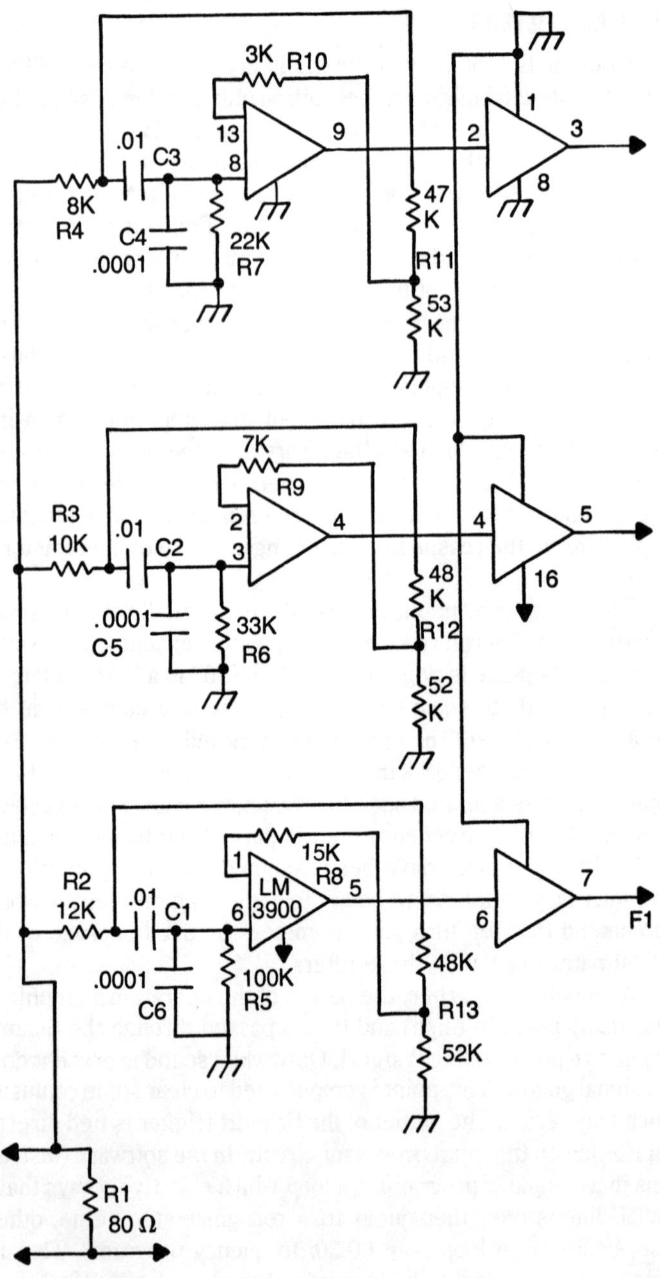

Fig. 14-2. Three-frequency bandpass filter for The Recognizer.

130

is not a sound. For the EF lines on the 1802 processor circuit, one is defined as a low and zero is defined as a high.

Each of the three frequency filters have the same setup but different component values. The concept here is simple; it is that low-frequency sounds will be passed by one filter, mid-frequency by another, and high-frequency by the third. Human utterances may contain any combination of these. The output of this input stage (F1, F2, and F3) could be tied through an input port to any computer and with appropriate software used for voice recognition. Obviously you could use more filters, each with a narrower passband, and gather more information to use in recognition determinations.

Without a signal generator and oscilloscope, these filters are difficult to tune, but not impossible. Attach a voltmeter between one of the output lines (F1) and ground. Hum a low note into the microphone and adjust R13 for maximum deflection on the meter. Perform a similar adjustment for F2 (midrange) and F3 (high-frequency).

PROCESSOR

One way to approach the processor stage is to consider the 1802 microprocessor circuit pin by pin (Fig. 14-3). Pins one and 39 (clock and crystal) are tied to Q1, R14, C7 and C8. These components (along with some things internal to the 1802) oscillate and provide timing for the processor. In the example built here, a 1 megahertz crystal was used as the timebase. Higher speed (larger numbers in megahertz) crystals may be used, but there are several things that should be understood before you attempt such actions. There are speed limitations within the 1802, about four megahertz for such a circuit operating from a 5-volt supply. Some versions of the 1802 will accept a 10-volt supply and the maximum frequency for running is about 6 megahertz then. The faster the speed of operation, the more radio frequency interference will be generated. This will show up on televisions and radios in the vicinity of the circuit. Putting the entire circuitry in a metal box will usually eliminate this problem. Lead length and circuit design become more important at higher speeds; wire wrap construction and wires running wildly about may not be acceptable due to inductance of these wires at the higher speeds. All components, including memory, must be capable of operating at the higher speeds. The faster the microprocessor is running, the lower must be the access time for memory circuits (the lower a memory's access time, the more it costs).

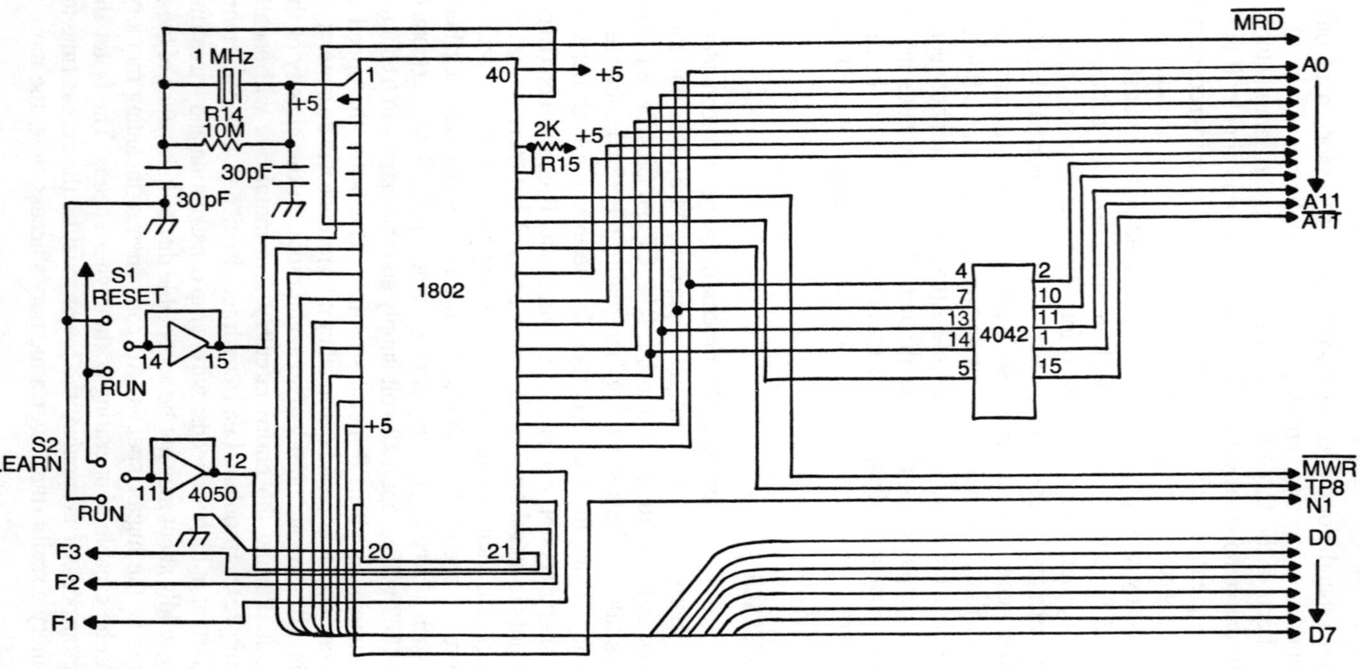

Fig. 14-3. Processor and memory stage of The Recognizer.

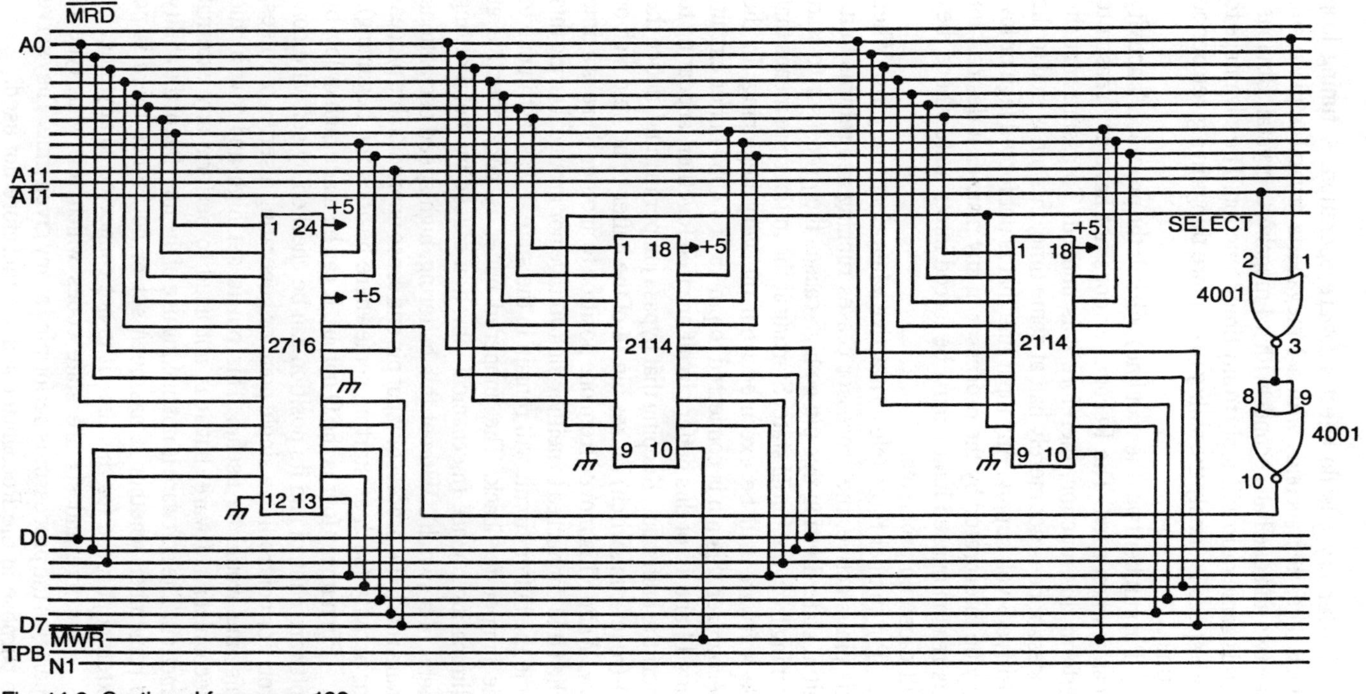

Fig. 14-3. Continued from page 132.

Faster crystals do affect software operation. A timing loop which takes ten seconds with a 1 megahertz crystal in place will take two and one half seconds with a 4 megahertz crystal. Obviously, this same ratio will apply to any timed function. The advantage to more speed is simply the ability to do more things in a given period of time.

Pin number two (the wait line) will halt the processor's activity cleanly when used. The Recognizer does not have any reason to perform this function; therefore it is unused. To assure that the processor does not merely halt at some time, this pin is tied to the positive 5-volt supply. Any input line that is not forced high or low may be interpreted by the processor in any manner it desires; for this reason unused inputs must be forced into a state where they will cause no problems.

Pin number three (clear) is active when electrically low. When this pin is active, the processor ceases running and returns to its initial state. Letting this pin go high causes the processor to start running from the initial state. Starting at the initial state means that the software will be executed from the very beginning. In the Recognizer this pin is connected to pin 15 of a 4050 buffer circuit. Pins 14 and 15 of this buffer circuit are tied together, appearing to short the buffer out. Keeping that bypass jumper in mind, notice the S1 (reset-run switch) causes pin 14 of the buffer to be held high or low. When S1 is moved from one position to another there is a time when it is connected to neither plus voltage nor ground. During this time the buffer circuit will remain in the state it was last in due to the jumper feedback. The jumpered buffer is very effective at eliminating bounce (mechanical vibration caused by metal hitting metal in a switch). Without this buffering, high-speed oscillations could reach the processor input pin and cause unpredictable processor activity (such as starting somewhere besides the beginning).

Pin number four is the Q output. It can be made high or low by software control and its position can be checked by software control. For controlling a single point or generating a series of pulses, this line would be useful. This pin is set high and low in the Recognizer software, but it is not used to perform any external function. The software is not making use of the line, but of the ability to remember whether it has been set or not. Since there is no external purpose for this line, it is not connected to anything.

Pins five and six are state codes which tell what type of operation the processor is performing at any given time. They serve no purpose in the Recognizer and are therefore not used.

Pin number seven (memory read) is used in conjunction with other outputs to determine when to read from memory. There are three memory circuits in the recognizer and they form two groups of memory which are to be handled. The 2716 circuit is an EPROM (Erasable Programmable Read Only Memory). The 1802 cannot put anything into this circuit, it can only take data out; therefore there is no reason to perform any activity upon the 2716 other than an occasional read. The 2716 contains 2048 address locations and each address location is composed of eight bits of memory.

There are two 2114 circuits which together form the second group of memory. The 2124 is a RAM (random access memory). The 1802 can put things into or take things out of these circuits; therefore it will be necessary to read from and write these chips. Each 2114 contains 1024 address locations and each location is composed of four bits of memory. Because the 1802 system is based upon the usage of eight bits it is necessary to use two four-bit memories for the storage and retrieval of eight-bit words.

A decision was made to have the 2716 placed in the memory system starting at location zero and ending at location 2047. The place in the memory system for the 2114 memory starts at address 2048 and ends at address 3071. The previously mentioned addresses were defined in the decimal system; to be consistent with the hexadecimal system used in the software listings the 2716 memory runs from 00,00 to 07,FF and the 2114 runs from 08,00 to 0B,FF. Although the placement of the memory is arbitrary, there is an overwhelming reason for putting the nonvolatile (EPROM) memory first. Nonvolatile memory will contain the program upon which the system operation is based; the processor will seek instructions starting at the lowest memory number and then work its way up.

Not forgetting the memory read line, it is necessary to consider several other lines to clear up the picture of memory addressing. Pins 25 through 32 are memory address lines, pin 25 being the least significant and pin 32 the most significant. Things get complicated at this point. To address 64,000 memory locations requires 16 address lines, yet only eight are provided. The 1802 sets the address lines twice for each address. The first time it sets the high-order eight bits; the second time it sets the low-order eight bits. While the high-order eight bits are set, pin number 34 (TPA) is made active. This causes the 4042 circuit in the Recognizer to take four bits on the input (pins four, seven, 13, and 14 of the 4042) and transfer that information to the output (pins two, 10, 11 and one of the 4042) and latch the output side such that that data will stay until the next pulsing of TPA, pin number 34 of the 1802. The 1802 then sets the low-order eight bits of the address. At this point there are twelve lines of address information available in the Recognizer, A0 through A7 direct from the 1802, and A8 through A11 latched via the 4042. The inverse of A11 is also brought out from the 4042. These lines are sufficient to address all the memory locations that will be used by the Recognizer. Upon completion of the address (while the address lines are still active), the memory read (pin seven) or memory write (pin 35) line is made active to indicate which operation is expected.

With this background it is possible to consider the 2716 (EPROM) and how it knows when it is supposed to output data onto the bus. Pin number 20 of the 2716 is the enable line for the memory. If pin number 20 goes low then it will place on the data bus whatever information is contained in the memory location which is defined by the bits on the address bus.

Examining pin 20 of the 2716 circuit, it can be seen that pin 10 of the 4001 is the source of this enabling signal. Pins eight and nine of the 4001 are tied together, thus the two-input NOR logic gate will function as an inverter. When the input to pins eight and nine is high, the output at pin 10 will be low and the 2716 will be enabled. Backing up from this point you arrive at pin number three of the 4001 circuit. For pin three to be high (translating through to activate the 2716) both input pins one and two must be low. If either pin number one or pin number two of the 4001 circuit are high, then the 2716 memory will be disabled. Address line A11 will be low until the memory address passes 07,FF. Address line A11 will then be high until the address passes 0F,FF; a point which will not occur with the Recognizer software. Because address line A11 is tied to pin number two of the 4001, the 2716 circuit can only be enabled if the address is less than 08,00 (or some points greater than 0F,FF—not possible in this system). To enable the 2716 requires that pin number one of the 4001 be low also. Pin number one is connected to the memory read line, a line which is normally high. Memory read goes low when the processor desires to read something from memory. Therefore you may conclude that the 2716 will only be enabled when the address is lower than 08,00, and a memory read operation is requested.

Mention has been made of the data bus that corresponds to pins eight through 15 on the 1802. The least significant bit on the bus is labeled D0 and that is associated with pin number 15. The most significant bit on the bus is labeled D7 and is associated with pin number eight. The data bus connects the 1802 processor with the 2716 (memory holding the program) with the 2114's (memory for temporary storage of data) and the 1852 (output port).

Selection of the 2114 circuits for read and write operations is probably the most complex portion of the processor circuitry. When the address lies between 08,00 and 0B,FF and a read or write operation is requested, these circuits must perform. Pin number eight on the 2114 is the chip enable line, when it is brought low then something is going to happen. When pin eight is low, the 2114 will either put data onto the data bus or take data off and store it in the location defined by the address lines. Whether it is putting or taking depends upon pin number ten of the 2114; a high causes the circuit to read (put data onto the bus) while a low causes it to take (write into storage). To restate this, when it is desired to store something in the RAM (2114), it is necessary for the memory address to be between 08,00 and 0B,FF, for the pin number eight of the 2114 to be low, and for pin number ten of the 2114 to be low. If it is desired to read something from the RAM (2114), the address must be between 08,00 and 0B,FF that pin number eight of the 2114 must be low, and pin number 10 of the 2114 must be high.

To accomplish the last task mentioned is easy for pin number ten on the 2114. Tying pin ten to the memory write line from the processor (pin 35 of the 1802) will cause this point to be high during any operation except a write (storage into memory). Pin number eight of the 2144 is more involved. It is connected to pin 11 of the 4011 circuit. Input pons 12 and 13 control output pin 11; they must both be high for pin 11 to be low (therefore enabling the 2114 to operate). Pin 12 of the 4011 is connected to the A11 address line which will be high during the address interval 08,00 to 0B,FF (it will also be low from 00,00 to 07,FF, disabling the 2114 circuits during those address intervals). Pin 13 of the 4011 must be high when a read or write operation is to occur—and no other time. Three of the NAND gates on the 4011 are wired to act as inverters; this was done to save the labor and expense of adding another circuit onto the board. Those three gates are the ones defined by pin combinations 1,2,3; 5,6,4; 8,9,10. The memory read signal (active when low, high most of the time) is inverted by the time it reaches pin three of the 4011 circuit. The memory write signal (active when low, high most of the time) is inverted by the time it reaches pin four of the 4011 circuit. Pins three and four of the 4011 are connected to pins 12 and 13 of the 4001 respectively. If either pin 12 or 13 of the 4001 is high, then pin 11 of 4001 will be low making eight and nine of 4011 low; which in turn makes 10 of 4011 high, making 13 of 4011 high. This occurs if memory read or memory write are active. The combination of the correct address and memory read or memory write active will enable the 2114 circuits.

Pins 16 and 40 on the 1802 are power supply pins requiring plus 5 volts.

Pins 17, 18, and 19 are input-output command pins defining which port is to be used for an input-output command. Pin 18 (N1) is wired in the Recognizer and it responds to an OUTPUT, PORT TWO command. The three bits NO (least significant), N1, and N2 (most significant) allow for the construction and definition of eight ports. The N1 line (pin 18 of the 1802) along with memory read (pin seven of the 1802) and TPB (pin 33 of the 1802) combine to tell the 1852 circuit that it is time to take the information on the data bus and put it (latched) onto the output lines, (4, 6, 8, 10, and 15) of the 1852.

Pin number 20 of the 1802 is where the negative power supply (ground) is placed on the processor.

Pins 21 through 24 represent EF4 to EF1 respectively. These lines may be examined by the processor under software control at any time desired, therefore forming a four-bit input port of sorts. Pins 36, 37, and 38 of the 1802 are various input output request lines not used in the Recognizer. They should be tied to positive 5 volts through a resistor to prevent them from causing some undersired operation.

OUTPUT

Output circuitry centers around the 1852 output port (see Fig. 14-4). The output port is tied to the data bus and some control lines. At the right moment (determined by a combination of memory read, N1, and TPB) the port moves into action. It takes the data on the bus and puts it on the output lines, latching it at the output. Latching the data simply means that the output will be set and remain in that state regardless of the data bus until the control lines from the correct combination again. It must be remembered that all the instructions from the memory and many other information transactions are conducted on the data bus. This port will handle up to eight outputs, though only five are wired. The one labeled "output 0" is the least significant bit of an output byte. This output port does not have the capability of handling much power; it cannot even turn a small light on or off. To amplify this signal, a small transistor (2N222) is used (Fig. 14-5). The output of the 1852 circuit is connected directly to

138

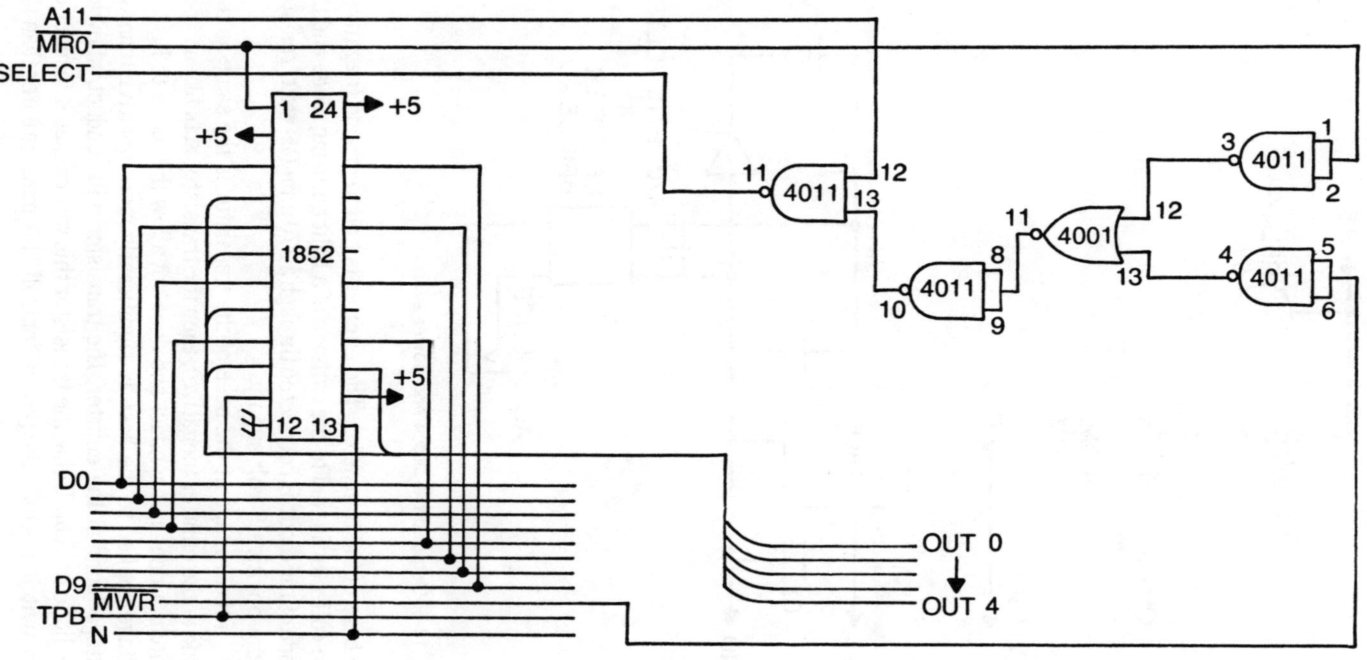

Fig. 14-4. Output stage of The Recognizer.

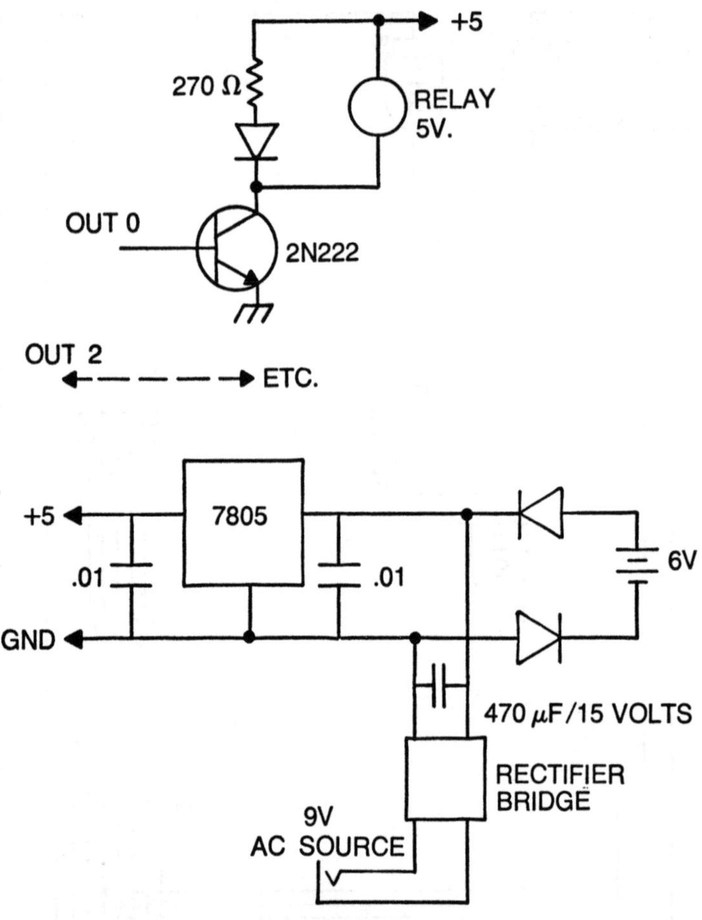

Fig. 14-5. Output drive circuit and power supply.

the base of the transistor. The emitter is tied to ground (negative). The collector is tied to the cathode of a light emitting diode and the anode of the diode is connected through a 270 ohm (½-watt) resistor to the positive 5-volt supply.

If the voltage at the base of the transistor is the same as that found at the emitter (negative), then the transistor acts like an open switch; it does not conduct and does not allow the diode to light. If voltage applied to the base is significantly more positive than the voltage found at the emitter, the transistor will conduct, allowing the diode to light. Using the transistor this way causes it to function as a switch in which the power controlled is much greater than the power required to control. The light emitting diode cannot tolerate more than about 2 volts across its leads, otherwise it will burn out. To limit this voltage (and the current which will overheat it) a 270 ohm resistor is placed in series with the supply. Each of the outputs is set up in the same fashion. The transistor can handle more load than the diode, therefore a relay coil can be placed in parallel with the diode-resistor combination, providing contacts for other activity.

The power supply shown is rather simple with 9 volts coming in through the jack supplied. This voltage is rectified (therefore it can be alternating or direct current, polarity does not matter) and is filtered with a capacitor; then it goes through diodes to the 7805 regulator circuit. The 7805 circuit takes the input and provides a constant 5 volt output. The battery shown is a backup supply utilizing a 6 volt battery. The diodes prevent the battery from taking current from the normal source (which is at 9 volts), yet they allow it to provide the energy if the other source fails. The 7805 circuit generates a significant amount of heat and it must be mounted on metal (preferably a commercial heat sink) to prevent damage from overheating. Note that the heat sink will get rather warm to the touch.

Chapter 15

Length for the Recognizer

Utilizing the Length program with the Recognizer provides a simple approach to sound recognition. As established here, the learn-run switch has no function and the run-reset switch has limited use. Moving this switch to the reset position then to run fully enables the system.

Upon operation of the run-reset switch, all lights will be off. After a sound is detected, there will always be a light on. Four words or phrases of varying length may be distinguished; for example, "go," "stop," "turn right," and "please turn to the left" work well. Natural speech must be used here, meaning that no significant gap is allowed between words. When a sound is detected, one of the lights will be selected for illumination, regardless of what the sound or word may be. Using a processor and software for this type of function is clearly a case of overkill; a much simpler system could be devised without the need for filters, processor, and memories.

This system can be effectively used for control at a distance from the microphone. Such a device can operate lights or a television without the necessity of having a sound pickup close to the lips of the operator. In order words ordinary room sounds could be eliminated with the volume control and only shouted commands used to exercise control. The sound pickup (microphone) would best be placed on the ceiling or away from point where it might be triggered by ordinary talking. Be forewarned that loud laughter, like you find at parties can operate this type of system.

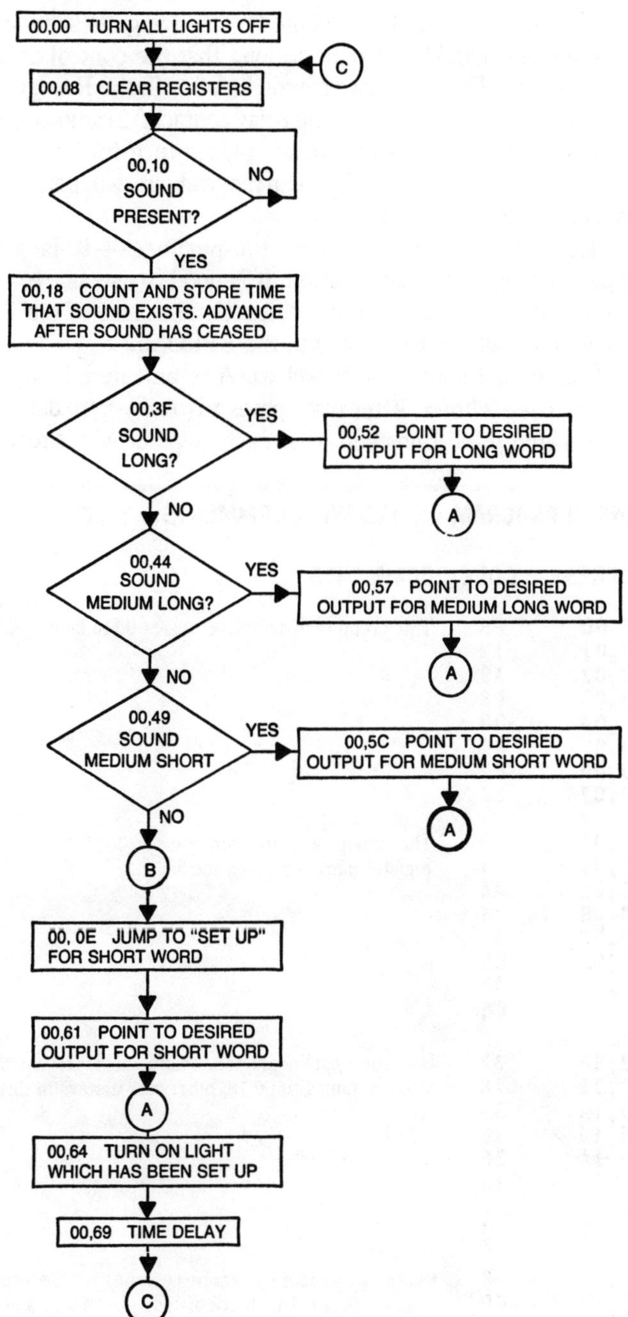

Fig. 15-1. Program flowchart of Length for The Recognizer.

More phrases could be accepted by changing the software, but the commands quickly become so long that the control delay becomes serious. Using the commands listed with the Recognizer, it is possible to control (by using the relay contacts) a radio-controlled toy. Remember that the command "please turn to the left" consumes so much time that the toy can move about two feet while the command is being issued.

This program was written for purposes—it is a fairly simple machine-language creation. It is good to use as a test upon the completion of Recognizer construction because of the limited likelihood of putting an error into the EPROM.

Figure 15-1 shows the flowchart. A commented listing of the machine code follows. After that comes a byte-by-byte description of the memory locations and what each step accomplishes.

LENGTH PROGRAM LISTING WITH COMMENTS

ADDRESS	CODE	COMMENTS
00,00	F8	This group of instructions causes 00 to be output.
00,01	79	
00,02	A9	
00,03	F8	
00,04	00	
00,05	B9	
00,06	E9	
00,07	62	
00,08	F8	This group of instructions causes 00,00 to be placed in
00,09	00	register pairs four, five and six.
00,0A	A4	
00,0B	B4	
00,0C	A5	
00,0D	B5	
00,0E	A6	
00,0F	B6	
00,10	34	Here the input lines are tested. If sound is present, then the
00,11	18	program jumps to 00,18; otherwise it stays in this loop.
00,12	35	
00,13	18	
00,14	36	
00,15	18	
00,16	30	
00,17	10	
00,18	F8	Reaching this address requires escape from the loop which
00,19	4F	began at 00,10. This block of code places the value 00,4F
00,1A	A7	into the general register pair number seven.
00,1B	F8	

ADDRESS	CODE	COMMENTS
00,1C	00	
00,1D	B7	
00,1E	34	These instructions test each input line for sound present or absent. If present, the program jumps to 00,32. If absent, it progresses without jumping.
00,1F	32	
00,20	35	
00,21	32	
00,22	36	
00,23	32	
00,24	27	These instructions decrement the value contained in register seven and cause the program to jump to 00,2A if that value is equal to zero. Otherwise, the program jumps to 00,1E.
00,25	87	
00,26	32	
00,27	2A	
00,28	30	
00,29	1E	
00,2A	15	Reached from 00,27, these instructions first increment the value in register five. If that value is equal to 10, then the program jumps to 00,3F. Otherwise, the program returns to 00,18.
00,2B	85	
00,2C	FD	
00,2D	10	
00,2E	32	
00,2F	3F	
00,30	30	
00,31	18	
00,32	14	Reached from 00,1F or 00,21 or 00,23, these instructions first increment the value contained by register four. Next, the value contained by register seven is decremented and then tested. If it equals zero, the program jumps to 00,18. If not equal to zero, this loop is run several times until it does. The C4 instructions are used to create about the same timing as occurs from 00,1E to 00,28.
00,33	27	
00,34	87	
00,35	32	
00,36	18	
00,37	C4	
00,38	C4	
00,39	C4	
00,3A	C4	
00,3B	C4	
00,3C	C4	
00,3D	30	
00,3E	33	
00,3F	84	This instruction takes the value held in the low order byte of general register pair number four and places it into the D register for testing. This instruction is reached from 00,2F.
00,40	FD	If the value held in register four is equal to or greater than 49 the program jumps to 00,52; otherwise it continues to 00,44.
00,41	49	
00,42	3B	
00,43	52	
00,44	84	If the value held in register four is equal to or greater than 32 the program jumps to 00,57; otherwise it continues to 00,49.
00,45	FD	
00,46	32	
00,47	3B	
00,48	57	

ADDRESS	CODE	COMMENTS
00,49	84	If the value held in register four is equal to or greater than 19 the program jumps to 00,5C; otherwise it continues to 00,4E.
00,4A	FD	
00,4B	19	
00,4C	3B	
00,4D	5C	
00,4E	C4	Since the value in register four is obviously less than 19, the program jumps to 00,61.
00,4F	C4	
00,50	30	
00,51	61	
00,52	F8	Reached from 00,43, this instruction places 75 into the low order byte of the nine register and then jumps to 00,64.
00,53	75	
00,54	A9	
00,55	30	
00,56	64	
00,57	F8	Reached from "00,48", this instruction places "76" into the low order byte of the nine register and then jumps to 00,64.
00,58	76	
00,59	A9	
00,5A	30	
00,5B	64	
00,5C	F8	Reached from 00,4D, this instruction places 77 into the low order byte of the nine register and then jumps to 00,64.
00,5D	77	
00,5E	A9	
00,5F	30	
00,60	64	
00,61	F8	Reached from 00,51, this instruction places 78 into the low order byte of the nine register.
00,62	78	
00,63	A9	
00,64	F8	These instructions cause the memory byte addressed by the contents of register pair number nine to be output.
00,65	00	
00,66	B9	
00,67	E9	
00,68	62	
00,69	F8	This is a time delay loop which will jump to 00,08 upon completion of the delay.
00,6A	FF	
00,6B	AA	
00,6C	F8	
00,6D	0F	
00,6E	BA	
00,6F	2A	
00,70	9A	
00,71	32	
00,72	08	
00,73	30	
00,74	6F	
00,75	08	Indicates the longest word

ADDRESS	CODE	COMMENTS
00,76	04	Indicates word next-to-longest
00,77	02	Indicates word next-to-shortest
00,78	01	Indicates the shortest word
00,79	00	Indicates nothing recognized

MEMORY LOCATION   (00,00)

Instruction   F8 79
Before Instruction   After Instruction
                              Register Pairs

Register	High	Low		Register	High	Low
0	00	00		0	00	02
1	?	?		1	?	?
2	?	?		2	?	?
3	?	?		3	?	?
4	?	?		4	?	?
5	?	?		5	?	?
6	?	?		6	?	?
7	?	?		7	?	?
8	?	?		8	?	?
9	?	?		9	?	?
A	?	?		A	?	?
B	?	?		B	?	?
C	?	?		C	?	?
D	?	?		D	?	?
E	?	?		E	?	?
F	?	?		F	?	?

Eight Bit Register

Register	Contents		Register	Contents
D	?		D	79

Four and One Bit Registers

Register	Contents		Register	Contents
I	F		I	7
N	8		N	9
X	?		X	?
P	0		P	0
DF	?		DF	?

This instruction places 79 into the D register. This step is one
of a series designed to force an output of 00 as soon as the program
runs. The 00 will cause all output lines to be low, thus all light
emitting diodes will be off and all relays will be in non-energized
state.

Instruction A9

Before Instruction				After Instruction		
				Register Pairs		
Register	High	Low		Register	High	Low
0	00	02		0	00	03
1	?	?		1	?	?
2	?	?		2	?	?
3	?	?		3	?	?
4	?	?		4	?	?
5	?	?		5	?	?
6	?	?		6	?	?
7	?	?		7	?	?
8	?	?		8	?	?
9	?	?		9	?	79
A	?	?		A	?	?
B	?	?		B	?	?
C	?	?		C	?	?
D	?	?		D	?	?
E	?	?		E	?	?
F	?	?		F	?	?

Eight Bit Register			
Register	Contents	Register	Contents
D	79	D	79

Four and One Bit Registers			
Register	Contents	Register	Contents
I	A	I	A
N	9	N	9
X	?	X	?
P	0	P	0
DF	?	DF	?

Contents of the D register 79 are placed in the low order byte of the general register pair number nine. The 1802 microprocessor circuit will only output a byte from a memory location; therefore it is necessary to define which location (memory address 00 79) will contain the desired data.

Instruction   F8 00

Before Instruction			After Instruction		
			Register Pairs		
Register	High	Low	Register	High	Low
0	00	03	0	00	05
1	?	?	1	?	?
2	?	?	2	?	?
3	?	?	3	?	?
4	?	?	4	?	?
5	?	?	5	?	?
6	?	?	6	?	?
7	?	?	7	?	?
8	?	?	8	?	?
9	?	79	9	?	79
A	?	?	A	?	?
B	?	?	B	?	?
C	?	?	C	?	?
D	?	?	D	?	?
E	?	?	E	?	?
F	?	?	F	?	?
			Eight Bit Register		
Register	Contents		Register	Contents	
D	79		D	00	
			Four and One Bit Registers		
Register	Contents		Register	Contents	
I	F		I	0	
N	8		N	0	
X	?		X	?	
P	0		P	0	
DF	?		DF	?	

The high-order byte of general register pair number nine is set to 00. Although that may be the contents of that location on power-up of the microprocessor, it is a good programming habit to assume that data is correct only if placed there under program control.

Instruction B9
Before Instruction

After Instruction

Register Pairs

Register	High	Low		Register	High	Low
0	00	05		0	00	06
1	?	?		1	?	?
2	?	?		2	?	?
3	?	?		3	?	?
4	?	?		4	?	?
5	?	?		5	?	?
6	?	?		6	?	?
7	?	?		7	?	?
8	?	?		8	?	?
9	?	79		9	00	79
A	?	?		A	?	?
B	?	?		B	?	?
C	?	?		C	?	?
D	?	?		D	?	?
E	?	?		E	?	?
F	?	?		F	?	?

Eight Bit Register

Register	Contents		Register	Contents
D	00		D	00

Four and One Bit Registers

Register	Contents		Register	Contents
I	B		I	B
N	9		N	9
X	?		X	?
P	0		P	0
DF	?		DF	?

Again the contents of the D register (now 00) are being moved; this time to the high order byte of general register pair number nine. The D register is the common place through which most data is moved. This completes the loading of a general register pair with an address.

Instruction   E9
Before Instruction | | | | After Instruction

Register Pairs

Register	High	Low		Register	High	Low
0	00	06		0	00	07
1	?	?		1	?	?
2	?	?		2	?	?
3	?	?		3	?	?
4	?	?		4	?	?
5	?	?		5	?	?
6	?	?		6	?	?
7	?	?		7	?	?
8	?	?		8	?	?
9	00	79		9	00	79
A	?	?		A	?	?
B	?	?		B	?	?
C	?	?		C	?	?
D	?	?		D	?	?
E	?	?		E	?	?
F	?	?		F	?	?

Eight Bit Register

Register	Contents		Register	Contents
D	00		D	00

Four and One Bit Registers

Register	Contents		Register	Contents
I	E		I	E
N	9		N	9
X	?		X	9
P	0		P	0
DF	?		DF	?

In the instruction E9 the E is the instruction itself while the
second number (9 in this case) is the data being moved. The
contents of the X register are changed to the same thing as the
number following the E.

Instruction 62

Before Instruction			After Instruction		
			Register Pairs		
Register	High	Low	Register	High	Low
0	00	07	0	00	08
1	?	?	1	?	?
2	?	?	2	?	?
3	?	?	3	?	?
4	?	?	4	?	?
5	?	?	5	?	?
6	?	?	6	?	?
7	?	?	7	?	?
8	?	?	8	?	?
9	00	79	9	00	79
A	?	?	A	?	?
B	?	?	B	?	?
C	?	?	C	?	?
D	?	?	D	?	?
E	?	?	E	?	?
F	?	?	F	?	?
		Eight Bit Register			
Register	Contents		Register	Contents	
D	00		D	00	
	Four and One Bit Registers				
Register	Contents		Register	Contents	
I	6		I	6	
N	2		N	2	
X	9		X	9	
P	0		P	0	
DF	?		DF	?	

The 62 causes the memory byte addressed by the general register pair pointed to by X to be placed on the bus for output on port number two. What this means is that the contents of X (9) point to general register pair number nine. General register pair number nine contains the number 00,79 which is the address of the memory byte to be output. Examine memory location 00,79 to see that 00 is the data being output.

Instruction   F8 00

Before Instruction				After Instruction Register Pairs		
Register	High	Low		Register	High	Low
0	00	08		0	00	0A
1	?	?		1	?	?
2	?	?		2	?	?
3	?	?		3	?	?
4	?	?		4	?	?
5	?	?		5	?	?
6	?	?		6	?	?
7	?	?		7	?	?
8	?	?		8	?	?
9	00	79		9	00	79
A	?	?		A	?	?
B	?	?		B	?	?
C	?	?		C	?	?
D	?	?		D	?	?
E	?	?		E	?	?
F	?	?		F	?	?

Eight Bit Register

Register	Contents		Register	Contents
D	00		D	00

Four and One Bit Registers

Register	Contents		Register	Contents
I	F		I	0
N	8		N	0
X	9		X	9
P	0		P	0
DF	?		DF	?

This instruction places 00 in the D register. Why was this done, considering the fact that 00 is the number already contained in D? The answer is programming inefficiency; I did not know what the contents of D might be when I was writing this step.

Instruction   A4

Before Instruction			After Instruction Register Pairs		
Register	High	Low	Register	High	Low
0	00	0A	0	00	0B
1	?	?	1	?	?
2	?	?	2	?	?
3	?	?	3	?	?
4	?	?	4	?	00
5	?	?	5	?	?
6	?	?	6	?	?
7	?	?	7	?	?
8	?	?	8	?	?
9	00	79	9	00	79
A	?	?	A	?	?
B	?	?	B	?	?
C	?	?	C	?	?
D	?	?	D	?	?
E	?	?	E	?	?
F	?	?	F	?	?

Eight Bit Register

Register	Contents	Register	Contents
D	00	D	00

Four and One Bit Registers

Register	Contents	Register	Contents
I	A	I	A
N	4	N	4
X	9	X	9
P	0	P	0
DF	?	DF	?

The purpose of this and the next five instructions is to insure that register pairs, four, five, and six start with a value of 00,00. This is a preliminary part of the program, establishing empty registers for possible future use. The low order byte of general purpose register pair number four is set to 00 with this step.

Instruction B4

Before Instruction				After Instruction		
			Register Pairs			
Register	High	Low		Register	High	Low
0	00	0B		0	00	0C
1	?	?		1	?	?
2	?	?		2	?	?
3	?	?		3	?	?
4	?	00		4	00	00
5	?	?		5	?	?
6	?	?		6	?	?
7	?	?		7	?	?
8	?	?		8	?	?
9	00	79		9	00	79
A	?	?		A	?	?
B	?	?		B	?	?
C	?	?		C	?	?
D	?	?		D	?	?
E	?	?		E	?	?
F	?	?		F	?	?

Eight Bit Register

Register	Contents		Register	Contents
D	00		D	00

Four and One Bit Registers

Register	Contents		Register	Contents
I	B		I	B
N	4		N	4
X	9		X	9
P	0		P	0
DF	?		DF	?

Here the high order byte of general register pair number four is
given the value 00.

Instruction A5

Before Instruction			After Instruction		
			Register Pairs		
Register	High	Low	Register	High	Low
0	00	0C	0	00	0D
1	?	?	1	?	?
2	?	?	2	?	?
3	?	?	3	?	?
4	00	00	4	00	00
5	?	?	5	?	00
6	?	?	6	?	?
7	?	?	7	?	?
8	?	?	8	?	?
9	00	79	9	00	79
A	?	?	A	?	?
B	?	?	B	?	?
C	?	?	C	?	?
D	?	?	D	?	?
E	?	?	E	?	?
F	?	?	F	?	?

Eight Bit Register

Register	Contents	Register	Contents
D	00	D	00

Four and One Bit Registers

Register	Contents	Register	Contents
I	A	I	A
N	5	N	5
X	9	X	9
P	0	P	0
DF	?	DF	?

Here the low order byte of general register pair number five is given the value 00.

Instruction   B5

Before Instruction				After Instruction		
			Register Pairs			
Register	High	Low		Register	High	Low
0	00	0D		0	00	0E
1	?	?		1	?	?
2	?	?		2	?	?
3	?	?		3	?	?
4	00	00		4	00	00
5	?	00		5	00	00
6	?	?		6	?	?
7	?	?		7	?	?
8	?	?		8	?	?
9	00	79		9	00	79
A	?	?		A	?	?
B	?	?		B	?	?
C	?	?		C	?	?
D	?	?		D	?	?
E	?	?		E	?	?
F	?	?		F	?	?

Eight Bit Register

Register	Contents		Register	Contents
D	00		D	00

Four and One Bit Registers

Register	Contents		Register	Contents
I	B		I	B
N	5		N	5
X	9		X	9
P	0		P	0
DF	?		DF	?

The high order byte of general register pair number five is given the value 00.

Instruction A6

	Before Instruction				After Instruction	
				Register Pairs		
Register	High	Low		Register	High	Low
0	00	0E		0	00	0F
1	?	?		1	?	?
2	?	?		2	?	?
3	?	?		3	?	?
4	00	00		4	00	00
5	00	00		5	00	00
6	?	?		6	?	00
7	?	?		7	?	?
8	?	?		8	?	?
9	00	79		9	00	79
A	?	?		A	?	?
B	?	?		B	?	?
C	?	?		C	?	?
D	?	?		D	?	?
E	?	?		E	?	?
F	?	?		F	?	?

Eight Bit Register

Register	Contents		Register	Contents
D	00		D	00

Four and One Bit Registers

Register	Contents		Register	Contents
I	A		I	A
N	6		N	6
X	9		X	9
P	0		P	0
DF	?		DF	?

The low order byte of general register pair number six is given the value 00.

Instruction B6
Before Instruction   After Instruction
                                          Register Pairs

Register	High	Low		Register	High	Low
0	00	0F		0	00	10
1	?	?		1	?	?
2	?	?		2	?	?
3	?	?		3	?	?
4	00	00		4	00	00
5	00	00		5	00	00
6	?	00		6	00	00
7	?	?		7	?	?
8	?	?		8	?	?
9	00	79		9	00	79
A	?	?		A	?	?
B	?	?		B	?	?
C	?	?		C	?	?
D	?	?		D	?	?
E	?	?		E	?	?
F	?	?		F	?	?

Eight Bit Register

Register	Contents		Register	Contents
D	00		D	00

Four and One Bit Registers

Register	Contents		Register	Contents
I	B		I	B
N	6		N	6
X	9		X	9
P	0		P	0
DF	?		DF	?

The high order byte of general register pair number six is
given the value 00.

Instruction   34 18

| Before Instruction | | | | After Instruction | | |
| Register Pairs | | | | | | | |
Register	High	Low		Register	High	Low
0	00	10		0	00	12
1	?	?		1	?	?
2	?	?		2	?	?
3	?	?		3	?	?
4	00	00		4	00	00
5	00	00		5	00	00
6	00	00		6	00	00
7	?	?		7	?	?
8	?	?		8	?	?
9	00	79		9	00	79
A	?	?		A	?	?
B	?	?		B	?	?
C	?	?		C	?	?
D	?	?		D	?	?
E	?	?		E	?	?
F	?	?		F	?	?

Eight Bit Register

Register	Contents		Register	Contents
D	00		D	00

Four and One Bit Registers

Register	Contents		Register	Contents
I	3		I	1
N	4		N	8
X	9		X	9
P	0		P	0
DF	?		DF	?

This instruction tests the input line, EF1. If EF1 is low (remember that an electrical low is a 1 for the EF lines) then the program counter is changed to 18. This segment of the program is testing the input lines to determine if sound is present or not. No sound results in a high input to the EF line which results in the program testing the next EF line as indicated above. If sound were present and affecting the above line, then general register pair number zero (low byte) would be changed to the value 18 and that would be the next instruction used.

Instruction   35 18

Before Instruction			After Instruction		
			Register Pairs		
Register	High	Low	Register	High	Low
0	00	12	0	00	14
1	?	?	1	?	?
2	?	?	2	?	?
3	?	?	3	?	?
4	00	00	4	00	00
5	00	00	5	00	00
6	00	00	6	00	00
7	?	?	7	?	?
8	?	?	8	?	?
9	00	79	9	00	79
A	?	?	A	?	?
B	?	?	B	?	?
C	?	?	C	?	?
D	?	?	D	?	?
E	?	?	E	?	?
F	?	?	F	?	?

Eight Bit Register			
Register	Contents	Register	Contents
D	00	D	00

Four and One Bit Registers			
Register	Contents	Register	Contents
I	3	I	1
N	5	N	8
X	9	X	9
P	0	P	0
DF	?	DF	?

Similar to the previous instruction, this one tests the EF2 line. If sound is present (electrical low on EF2) then the program counter is relocated to memory byte location 00,18. The register contents above assume that no sound was found, thus the program continues to the next step.

Instruction 36 18

Before Instruction			After Instruction		
			Register Pairs		
Register	High	Low	Register	High	Low
0	00	14	0	00	16
1	?	?	1	?	?
2	?	?	2	?	?
3	?	?	3	?	?
4	00	00	4	00	00
5	00	00	5	00	00
6	00	00	6	00	00
7	?	?	7	?	?
8	?	?	8	?	?
9	00	79	9	00	79
A	?	?	A	?	?
B	?	?	B	?	?
C	?	?	C	?	?
D	?	?	D	?	?
E	?	?	E	?	?
F	?	?	F	?	?

Eight Bit Register			
Register	Contents	Register	Contents
D	00	D	00

Four and One Bit Registers			
Register	Contents	Register	Contents
I	3	I	1
N	6	N	8
X	9	X	9
P	0	P	0
DF	?	DF	?

Again the instruction is a test of an external line, EF3. If sound
is present (remember that sound being present causes an electrical
low in this hardware system; sound present could cause an electrical high—calling for a different instruction—if the hardware were
put together differently) then the program moves to byte 00,18. The
register contents listed assume no sound, thus the program advances to byte 00,16.

Instruction   30 10

Before Instruction			After Instruction		
			Register Pairs		
Register	High	Low	Register	High	Low
0	00	16	0	00	10
1	?	?	1	?	?
2	?	?	2	?	?
3	?	?	3	?	?
4	00	00	4	00	00
5	00	00	5	00	00
6	00	00	6	00	00
7	?	?	7	?	?
8	?	?	8	?	?
9	00	79	9	00	79
A	?	?	A	?	?
B	?	?	B	?	?
C	?	?	C	?	?
D	?	?	D	?	?
E	?	?	E	?	?
F	?	?	F	?	?

			Eight Bit Register		
Register	Contents		Register	Contents	
D	00		D	00	

			Four and One Bit Registers		
Register	Contents		Register	Contents	
I	3		I	1	
N	0		N	0	
X	9		X	9	
P	0		P	0	
DF	?		DF	?	

Reaching this point in the program means that the outputs of
the three filters have been tested and found to indicate no sound
present. Logically, what must be done is to continue testing these
filter outputs until sound occurs. This instruction causes the program counter (register pair number zero) to hold a value 00,10. The
next instruction to be executed will be the one at memory location
00,10. The program will remain in this loop until a sound occurs.

Instruction F8 4F

Before Instruction			After Instruction		
			Register Pairs		
Register	High	Low	Register	High	Low
0	00	18	0	00	1A
1	?	?	1	?	?
2	?	?	2	?	?
3	?	?	3	?	?
4	00	00	4	00	00
5	00	00	5	00	00
6	00	00	6	00	00
7	?	?	7	?	?
8	?	?	8	?	?
9	00	79	9	00	79
A	?	?	A	?	?
B	?	?	B	?	?
C	?	?	C	?	?
D	?	?	D	?	?
E	?	?	E	?	?
F	?	?	F	?	?

Eight Bit Register			
Register	Contents	Register	Contents
D	00	D	4F

Four and One Bit Registers			
Register	Contents	Register	Contents
I	F	I	4
N	8	N	F
X	9	X	9
P	0	P	0
DF	?	DF	?

The only way to reach this point is to find a sound at instruction 00,10; 00,12; or 00,14. The program has determined that a sound exists, it now must figure out how long it exists and based upon that cause the appropriate output line to become active. Because the microprocessor executes instructions so rapidly and words occur so slowly, time delays must be introduced into the program. This step places 4F into the D register. 4F is a number that will be placed in a register and decreased one count at a time to achieve a timing goal.

Instruction   A7

Before Instruction				After Instruction		
			Register Pairs			
Register	High	Low		Register	High	Low
0	00	1A		0	00	1B
1	?	?		1	?	?
2	?	?		2	?	?
3	?	?		3	?	?
4	00	00		4	00	00
5	00	00		5	00	00
6	00	00		6	00	00
7	?	?		7	?	4F
8	?	?		8	?	?
9	00	79		9	00	79
A	?	?		A	?	?
B	?	?		B	?	?
C	?	?		C	?	?
D	?	?		D	?	?
E	?	?		E	?	?
F	?	?		F	?	?

Eight Bit Register			
Register	Contents	Register	Contents
D	4F	D	4F

Four and One Bit Registers			
Register	Contents	Register	Contents
I	A	I	A
N	7	N	7
X	9	X	9
P	0	P	0
DF	?	DF	?

The value in the D register (4F) is placed into register 7, low byte, where it may be accessed later in the program.

Instruction   F8 00

Before Instruction			After Instruction		
			Register Pairs		
Register	High	Low	Register	High	Low
0	00	1B	0	00	1D
1	?	?	1	?	?
2	?	?	2	?	?
3	?	?	3	?	?
4	00	00	4	00	00
5	00	00	5	00	00
6	00	00	6	00	00
7	?	4F	7	?	4F
8	?	?	8	?	?
9	00	79	9	00	79
A	?	?	A	?	?
B	?	?	B	?	?
C	?	?	C	?	?
D	?	?	D	?	?
E	?	?	E	?	?
F	?	?	F	?	?

Eight Bit Register

Register	Contents	Register	Contents
D	4F	D	00

Four and One Bit Registers

Register	Contents	Register	Contents
I	F	I	0
N	8	N	0
X	9	X	9
P	0	P	0
DF	?	DF	?

This instruction is used to insure that the value 00 is present in the high order byte of register pair number seven. As the program turns out, it is not necessary that this step and the following one be performed. Although I reworked this program several times, it seems to be possible to continue finding better and shorter ways the program could have been written. To remove these bytes would require changing addresses throughout the program, an effort not worth the time involved.

Instruction B7
Before Instruction   After Instruction
                            Register Pairs

Register	High	Low		Register	High	Low
0	00	1D		0	00	1E
1	?	?		1	?	?
2	?	?		2	?	?
3	?	?		3	?	?
4	00	00		4	00	00
5	00	00		5	00	00
6	00	00		6	00	00
7	?	4F		7	00	4F
8	?	?		8	?	?
9	00	79		9	00	79
A	?	?		A	?	?
B	?	?		B	?	?
C	?	?		C	?	?
D	?	?		D	?	?
E	?	?		E	?	?
F	?	?		F	?	?

Eight Bit Register

Register	Contents		Register	Contents
D	00		D	00

Four and One Bit Registers

Register	Contents		Register	Contents
I	B		I	B
N	7		N	7
X	9		X	9
P	0		P	0
DF	?		DF	?

This step takes the value in the D register (00) and places it in
the high order byte of general register pair number seven.

Instruction   34 32

Before Instruction				After Instruction		
				Register Pairs		
Register	High	Low		Register	High	Low
0	00	1E		0	00	20
1	?	?		1	?	?
2	?	?		2	?	?
3	?	?		3	?	?
4	00	00		4	00	00
5	00	00		5	00	00
6	00	00		6	00	00
7	00	4F		7	00	4F
8	?	?		8	?	?
9	00	79		9	00	79
A	?	?		A	?	?
B	?	?		B	?	?
C	?	?		C	?	?
D	?	?		D	?	?
E	?	?		E	?	?
F	?	?		F	?	?

Eight Bit Register

| Register | Contents | | Register | Contents |
| D | 00 | | D | 00 |

Four and One Bit Registers

Register	Contents		Register	Contents
I	3		I	3
N	4		N	2
X	9		X	9
P	0		P	0
DF	?		DF	?

Again the EF lines (EF1 in this case) are being tested to see if sound is present. If sound is present, the program will proceed to the instruction at location 00,32; otherwise it will continue.

Instruction   35 32
Before Instruction

After Instruction

Register Pairs

Register	High	Low		Register	High	Low
0	00	20		0	00	22
1	?	?		1	?	?
2	?	?		2	?	?
3	?	?		3	?	?
4	00	00		4	00	00
5	00	00		5	00	00
6	00	00		6	00	00
7	00	4F		7	00	4F
8	?	?		8	?	?
9	00	79		9	00	79
A	?	?		A	?	?
B	?	?		B	?	?
C	?	?		C	?	?
D	?	?		D	?	?
E	?	?		E	?	?
F	?	?		F	?	?

Eight Bit Register

Register	Contents		Register	Contents
D	00		D	00

Four and One Bit Registers

Register	Contents		Register	Contents
I	3		I	3
N	5		N	2
X	9		X	9
P	0		P	0
DF	?		DF	?

The input line, EF2 is tested by this instruction. If the line is electrically low the program counter is set to 00,32; otherwise it continues to 00,22. The register contents shown above indicate a high input on EF2, no sound present.

Instruction   36 32

Before Instruction			After Instruction Register Pairs		
Register	High	Low	Register	High	Low
0	00	22	0	00	24
1	?	?	1	?	?
2	?	?	2	?	?
3	?	?	3	?	?
4	00	00	4	00	00
5	00	00	5	00	00
6	00	00	6	00	00
7	00	4F	7	00	4F
8	?	?	8	?	?
9	00	79	9	00	79
A	?	?	A	?	?
B	?	?	B	?	?
C	?	?	C	?	?
D	?	?	D	?	?
E	?	?	E	?	?
F	?	?	F	?	?

Eight Bit Register

Register	Contents	Register	Contents
D	00	D	00

Four and One Bit Registers

Register	Contents	Register	Contents
I	3	I	3
N	6	N	2
X	9	X	9
P	0	P	0
DF	?	DF	?

If the input line EF3 is electrically low, then program control is transferred to the instruction byte at location 00,32; otherwise, the program continues at byte 00,24. The assumption used above is that EF3 remains electrically high.

Instruction   27

Before Instruction			After Instruction		
			Register Pairs		
Register	High	Low	Register	High	Low
0	00	24	0	00	25
1	?	?	1	?	?
2	?	?	2	?	?
3	?	?	3	?	?
4	00	00	4	00	00
5	00	00	5	00	00
6	00	00	6	00	00
7	00	4F	7	00	4E
8	?	?	8	?	?
9	00	79	9	00	79
A	?	?	A	?	?
B	?	?	B	?	?
C	?	?	C	?	?
D	?	?	D	?	?
E	?	?	E	?	?
F	?	?	F	?	?
		Eight Bit Register			
Register	Contents		Register	Contents	
D	00		D	00	
		Four and One Bit Registers			
Register	Contents		Register	Contents	
I	2		I	2	
N	7		N	7	
X	9		X	9	
P	0		P	0	
DF	?		DF	?	

The only way to reach this point in the program is to have
detected a sound and then fail to detect sound on a following test
(00,1E; 00,20; 00,22). This instruction decreases the value held in
register number seven by one count (note the value 4E instead of
4F). Remember that the next time the program comes through this
point it will subtract one from the value held in register seven, but
the value held in register seven can be 4F or any smaller quantity
(depending on how many times the program has been through this
loop).

Instruction 87

Before Instruction				After Instruction		
				Register Pairs		
Register	High	Low		Register	High	Low
0	00	25		0	00	26
1	?	?		1	?	?
2	?	?		2	?	?
3	?	?		3	?	?
4	00	00		4	00	00
5	00	00		5	00	00
6	00	00		6	00	00
7	00	4E		7	00	4E
8	?	?		8	?	?
9	00	79		9	00	79
A	?	?		A	?	?
B	?	?		B	?	?
C	?	?		C	?	?
D	?	?		D	?	?
E	?	?		E	?	?
F	?	?		F	?	?

Eight Bit Register

Register	Contents		Register	Contents
D	00		D	4E

Four and One Bit Registers

Register	Contents		Register	Contents
I	8		I	8
N	7		N	7
X	9		X	9
P	0		P	0
DF	?		DF	?

This instruction moves the low order byte of general register pair number seven into the D register. In other words, the number found in the low order byte of register pair seven can now be found in the D register.

Instruction   32 2A

Before Instruction			After Instruction		
			Register Pairs		
Register	High	Low	Register	High	Low
0	00	26	0	00	28
1	?	?	1	?	?
2	?	?	2	?	?
3	?	?	3	?	?
4	00	00	4	00	00
5	00	00	5	00	00
6	00	00	6	00	00
7	00	4E	7	00	4E
8	?	?	8	?	?
9	00	79	9	00	79
A	?	?	A	?	?
B	?	?	B	?	?
C	?	?	C	?	?
D	?	?	D	?	?
E	?	?	E	?	?
F	?	?	F	?	?

Eight Bit Register

Register	Contents	Register	Contents
D	4E	D	4E

Four and One Bit Registers

Register	Contents	Register	Contents
I	3	I	2
N	2	N	A
X	9	X	9
P	0	P	0
DF	?	DF	?

This instruction tests the contents of the D register. If the contents of D equal zero, then the program counter would change to 00,2A and that is where the next instruction would be found. Because the contents of register D equal 4E, the program advances to the next instruction in sequence, 00,28.

Instruction 30 1E
Before Instruction

Register	High	Low
0	00	28
1	?	?
2	?	?
3	?	?
4	00	00
5	00	00
6	00	00
7	00	4E
8	?	?
9	00	79
A	?	?
B	?	?
C	?	?
D	?	?
E	?	?
F	?	?

After Instruction
Register Pairs

Register	High	Low
0	00	1E
1	?	?
2	?	?
3	?	?
4	00	00
5	00	00
6	00	00
7	00	4E
8	?	?
9	00	79
A	?	?
B	?	?
C	?	?
D	?	?
E	?	?
F	?	?

Eight Bit Register

Register	Contents
D	4E

Register	Contents
D	4E

Four and One Bit Registers

Register	Contents
I	3
N	0
X	9
P	0
DF	?

Register	Contents
I	1
N	E
X	9
P	0
DF	?

This instruction defines the end of a loop. It causes the program to jump back to the instruction at 00,1E. This is accomplished by changing the low order byte of general register pair zero. There are two ways to escape this loop; if a sound is recognized, the program will advance to 00,32; if silence continues until register seven is decreased to the value zero then the program will move to 00,2A.

Instruction   15
Before Instruction

After Instruction

Register Pairs						
Register	High	Low		Register	High	Low
0	00	2A		0	00	2B
1	?	?		1	?	?
2	?	?		2	?	?
3	?	?		3	?	?
4	00	00		4	00	00
5	00	00		5	00	01
6	00	00		6	00	00
7	00	4E		7	00	4E
8	?	?		8	?	?
9	00	79		9	00	79
A	?	?		A	?	?
B	?	?		B	?	?
C	?	?		C	?	?
D	?	?		D	?	?
E	?	?		E	?	?
F	?	?		F	?	?

Eight Bit Register			
Register	Contents	Register	Contents
D	4E	D	4E

Four and One Bit Registers			
Register	Contents	Register	Contents
I	1	I	1
N	5	N	5
X	9	X	9
P	0	P	0
DF	?	DF	?

The only way to reach this point is to go through the loop (00,1E through 00,28) without recognizing a sound 79 times consecutively (79 equal 4F in bias 16 numbering system). This instruction increases the value found in register pair number five by one count. The count of 79 must occur 16 times before enough silence has elapsed to consider the word finished.

Instruction 85

Before Instruction				After Instruction		
			Register Pairs			
Register	High	Low		Register	High	Low
0	00	2B		0	00	2C
1	?	?		1	?	?
2	?	?		2	?	?
3	?	?		3	?	?
4	00	00		4	00	00
5	00	01		5	00	01
6	00	00		6	00	00
7	00	4E		7	00	4E
8	?	?		8	?	?
9	00	79		9	00	79
A	?	?		A	?	?
B	?	?		B	?	?
C	?	?		C	?	?
D	?	?		D	?	?
E	?	?		E	?	?
F	?	?		F	?	?

		Eight Bit Register		
Register	Contents		Register	Contents
D	4E		D	01

		Four and One Bit Registers		
Register	Contents		Register	Contents
I	8		I	8
N	5		N	5
X	9		X	9
P	0		P	0
DF	?		DF	?

This instruction moves the value found in the low order register of general pair number five into the D register.

Instruction   FD 10

Before Instruction			After Instruction		
			Register Pairs		
Register	High	Low	Register	High	Low
0	00	2C	0	00	2E
1	?	?	1	?	?
2	?	?	2	?	?
3	?	?	3	?	?
4	00	00	4	00	00
5	00	01	5	00	01
6	00	00	6	00	00
7	00	4E	7	00	4E
8	?	?	8	?	?
9	00	79	9	00	79
A	?	?	A	?	?
B	?	?	B	?	?
C	?	?	C	?	?
D	?	?	D	?	?
E	?	?	E	?	?
F	?	?	F	?	?

Eight Bit Register			
Register	Contents	Register	Contents
D	01	D	0F

Four and One Bit Registers			
Register	Contents	Register	Contents
I	F	I	1
N	D	N	0
X	9	X	9
P	0	P	0
DF	?	DF	1

This instruction subtracts the contents of register D form 10; the result of which is "0F." This result is placed in register D. The value "1" is placed in register DF to indicate that the result of this subtraction is a true positive number.

Instruction   32 3F

Before Instruction				After Instruction		
			Register Pairs			
Register	High	Low		Register	High	Low
0	00	2E		0	00	30
1	?	?		1	?	?
2	?	?		2	?	?
3	?	?		3	?	?
4	00	00		4	00	00
5	00	01		5	00	01
6	00	00		6	00	00
7	00	4E		7	00	4E
8	?	?		8	?	?
9	00	79		9	00	79
A	?	?		A	?	?
B	?	?		B	?	?
C	?	?		C	?	?
D	?	?		D	?	?
E	?	?		E	?	?
F	?	?		F	?	?
			Eight Bit Register			
Register	Contents			Register	Contents	
D	0F			D	0F	
			Four and One Bit Registers			
Register	Contents			Register	Contents	
I	3			I	3	
N	2			N	F	
X	9			X	9	
P	0			P	0	
DF	1			DF	1	

This instruction tests the contents of the D register and changes the program counter to 00,3F if those contents happen to be equal to zero. Since they are not, the program counter moves to 00,30. The location 00,3F is the address where a determination is made to the length of the spoken word.

Instruction   30 18

Before Instruction				After Instruction		
			Register Pairs			
Register	High	Low		Register	High	Low
0	00	30		0	00	18
1	?	?		1	?	?
2	?	?		2	?	?
3	?	?		3	?	?
4	00	00		4	00	00
5	00	01		5	00	01
6	00	00		6	00	00
7	00	4E		7	00	4E
8	?	?		8	?	?
9	00	79		9	00	79
A	?	?		A	?	?
B	?	?		B	?	?
C	?	?		C	?	?
D	?	?		D	?	?
E	?	?		E	?	?
F	?	?		F	?	?

Eight Bit Register

Register	Contents		Register	Contents
D	0F		D	0F

Four and One Bit Registers

Register	Contents		Register	Contents
I	3		I	1
N	0		N	8
X	9		X	9
P	0		P	0
DF	1		DF	1

This instruction is found at the end of a loop and it changes the program counter (register pair zero) to 00,18.

Instruction 14

Before Instruction			After Instruction		
			Register Pairs		
Register	High	Low	Register	High	Low
0	00	32	0	00	33
1	?	?	1	?	?
2	?	?	2	?	?
3	?	?	3	?	?
4	00	00	4	00	01
5	00	01	5	00	01
6	00	00	6	00	00
7	00	4E	7	00	4E
8	?	?	8	?	?
9	00	79	9	00	79
A	?	?	A	?	?
B	?	?	B	?	?
C	?	?	C	?	?
D	?	?	D	?	?
E	?	?	E	?	?
F	?	?	F	?	?

Eight Bit Register			
Register	Contents	Register	Contents
D	0F	D	0F

Four and One Bit Registers			
Register	Contents	Register	Contents
I	1	I	1
N	4	N	4
X	9	X	9
P	0	P	0
DF	1	DF	1

This step increases the value contained in register pair number
four by one count. The count in register number four will be used to
determine the length of the word.

Instruction 27

Before Instruction			After Instruction		
Register Pairs					
Register	High	Low	Register	High	Low
0	00	33	0	00	34
1	?	?	1	?	?
2	?	?	2	?	?
3	?	?	3	?	?
4	00	01	4	00	01
5	00	01	5	00	01
6	00	00	6	00	00
7	00	4E	7	00	4D
8	?	?	8	?	?
9	00	79	9	00	79
A	?	?	A	?	?
B	?	?	B	?	?
C	?	?	C	?	?
D	?	?	D	?	?
E	?	?	E	?	?
F	?	?	F	?	?

Eight Bit Register

| Register | Contents | Register | Contents |
| D | 0F | D | 0F |

Four and One Bit Registers

Register	Contents	Register	Contents
I	2	I	2
N	7	N	7
X	9	X	9
P	0	P	0
DF	1	DF	1

This instruction decreases the value contained in register pair number seven by one count. Consider the instructions at 00,1E; 00,20; and 00,22. One of those transferred the program to 00,32 therefore bypassing the timing loop instructions which commence at 00,24. This and the next group of instructions are used for timing.

Instruction 87

| Before Instruction | | | After Instruction
Register Pairs | | |
Register	High	Low	Register	High	Low
0	00	34	0	00	35
1	?	?	1	?	?
2	?	?	2	?	?
3	?	?	3	?	?
4	00	01	4	00	01
5	00	01	5	00	01
6	00	00	6	00	00
7	00	4D	7	00	4D
8	?	?	8	?	?
9	00	79	9	00	79
A	?	?	A	?	?
B	?	?	B	?	?
C	?	?	C	?	?
D	?	?	D	?	?
E	?	?	E	?	?
F	?	?	F	?	?

Eight Bit Register

Register	Contents	Register	Contents
D	0F	D	4D

Four and One Bit Registers

Register	Contents	Register	Contents
I	8	I	8
N	7	N	7
X	9	X	9
P	0	P	0
DF	1	DF	1

The contents of the low order byte of general register pair
number seven are placed into the D register.

Instruction   32 18
Before Instruction

After Instruction

Register Pairs

Register	High	Low	Register	High	Low
0	00	35	0	00	37
1	?	?	1	?	?
2	?	?	2	?	?
3	?	?	3	?	?
4	00	01	4	00	01
5	00	01	5	00	01
6	00	00	6	00	00
7	00	4D	7	00	4D
8	?	?	8	?	?
9	00	79	9	00	79
A	?	?	A	?	?
B	?	?	B	?	?
C	?	?	C	?	?
D	?	?	D	?	?
E	?	?	E	?	?
F	?	?	F	?	?

Eight Bit Register

Register	Contents	Register	Contents
D	4D	D	4D

Four and One Bit Registers

Register	Contents	Register	Contents
I	3	I	1
N	2	N	8
X	9	X	9
P	0	P	0
DF	1	DF	1

Should the contents of the D register equal zero, program execution would continue at location 00,18.

Instruction   C4

| Before Instruction | | | After Instruction
Register Pairs | | |
Register	High	Low	Register	High	Low
0	00	37	0	00	38
1	?	?	1	?	?
2	?	?	2	?	?
3	?	?	3	?	?
4	00	01	4	00	01
5	00	01	5	00	01
6	00	00	6	00	00
7	00	4D	7	00	4D
8	?	?	8	?	?
9	00	79	9	00	79
A	?	?	A	?	?
B	?	?	B	?	?
C	?	?	C	?	?
D	?	?	D	?	?
E	?	?	E	?	?
F	?	?	F	?	?

Eight Bit Register

Register	Contents	Register	Contents
D	4D	D	4D

Four and One Bit Registers

Register	Contents	Register	Contents
I	C	I	C
N	4	N	4
X	9	X	9
P	0	P	0
DF	1	DF	1

This and the five C4 instructions which follow do nothing but pass time. This portion of the program is a timing loop and those six "do nothing" commands correspond roughly to the time spent moving from 00,1E to 00,24. The idea is that the same timing loop time occur whether sound or silence initiates the timing.

Instruction   30 33

Before Instruction			After Instruction		
			Register Pairs		
Register	High	Low	Register	High	Low
0	00	3D	0	00	33
1	?	?	1	?	?
2	?	?	2	?	?
3	?	?	3	?	?
4	00	01	4	00	01
5	00	01	5	00	01
6	00	00	6	00	00
7	00	4D	7	00	4D
8	?	?	8	?	?
9	00	79	9	00	79
A	?	?	A	?	?
B	?	?	B	?	?
C	?	?	C	?	?
D	?	?	D	?	?
E	?	?	E	?	?
F	?	?	F	?	?
Eight Bit Register					
Register	Contents		Register	Contents	
D	4D		D	4D	
Four and One Bit Registers					
Register	Contents		Register	Contents	
I	3		I	3	
N	0		N	3	
X	9		X	9	
P	0		P	0	
DF	1		DF	1	

This instruction marks the end of a timing loop. It returns program control to location 00,33. The only way to escape the loop occurs at 00,35 when the contents of register number seven have been decreased to zero.

Instruction 84

Before Instruction			After Instruction		
			Register Pairs		
Register	High	Low	Register	High	Low
0	00	3F	0	00	40
1	?	?	1	?	?
2	?	?	2	?	?
3	?	?	3	?	?
4	00	01	4	00	01
5	00	01	5	00	01
6	00	00	6	00	00
7	00	4D	7	00	4D
8	?	?	8	?	?
9	00	79	9	00	79
A	?	?	A	?	?
B	?	?	B	?	?
C	?	?	C	?	?
D	?	?	D	?	?
E	?	?	E	?	?
F	?	?	F	?	?
		Eight Bit Register			
Register	Contents		Register	Contents	
D	00		D	01	
	Four and One Bit Registers				
Register	Contents		Register	Contents	
I	8		I	8	
N	4		N	4	
X	9		X	9	
P	0		P	0	
DF	1		DF	1	

The only way to get to this instruction is to jump from 00,2E and this only occurs when the contents of the D register equal zero. In physical terms, it means that a sound has occurred and has been followed by a sufficient period of silence. The contents of register four (low order byte) are not placed into the D register for examination.

Instruction FD 49

Before Instruction			After Instruction		
			Register Pairs		
Register	High	Low	Register	High	Low
0	00	40	0	00	42
1	?	?	1	?	?
2	?	?	2	?	?
3	?	?	3	?	?
4	00	01	4	00	01
5	00	01	5	00	01
6	00	00	6	00	00
7	00	4D	7	00	4D
8	?	?	8	?	?
9	00	79	9	00	79
A	?	?	A	?	?
B	?	?	B	?	?
C	?	?	C	?	?
D	?	?	D	?	?
E	?	?	E	?	?
F	?	?	F	?	?
			Eight Bit Register		
Register	Contents		Register	Contents	
D	01		D	48	
			Four and One Bit Registers		
Register	Contents		Register	Contents	
I	F		I	4	
N	D		N	9	
X	9		X	9	
P	0		P	0	
DF	1		DF	1	

Contents of register D are subtracted from 49. The results of
this subtraction are placed in the D register and the DF flag is also
set; the 1 indicating that no borrow occurred.

Instruction   3B 52

Before Instruction				After Instruction		
				Register Pairs		
Register	High	Low		Register	High	Low
0	00	42		0	00	44
1	?	?		1	?	?
2	?	?		2	?	?
3	?	?		3	?	?
4	00	01		4	00	01
5	00	01		5	00	01
6	00	00		6	00	00
7	00	4D		7	00	4D
8	?	?		8	?	?
9	00	79		9	00	79
A	?	?		A	?	?
B	?	?		B	?	?
C	?	?		C	?	?
D	?	?		D	?	?
E	?	?		E	?	?
F	?	?		F	?	?

Eight Bit Register

Register	Contents		Register	Contents
D	48		D	48

Four and One Bit Registers

Register	Contents		Register	Contents
I	3		I	5
N	B		N	2
X	9		X	9
P	0		P	0
DF	1		DF	1

This instruction tests the contents of the DF register. If DF equaled zero (meaning a borrow had occurred in the previous operation) then program control would jump to 00,52. Since no borrow occurred in the previous operation, the sound identifier (number in register pair number four) is less than 49.

Instruction 84
Before Instruction

| Register Pairs | | | | | | |
Register	High	Low		Register	High	Low
0	00	44		0	00	45
1	?	?		1	?	?
2	?	?		2	?	?
3	?	?		3	?	?
4	00	01		4	00	01
5	00	01		5	00	01
6	00	00		6	00	00
7	00	4D		7	00	4D
8	?	?		8	?	?
9	00	79		9	00	79
A	?	?		A	?	?
B	?	?		B	?	?
C	?	?		C	?	?
D	?	?		D	?	?
E	?	?		E	?	?
F	?	?		F	?	?

After Instruction

| Eight Bit Register | | |
Register	Contents		Register	Contents
D	48		D	01

| Four and One Bit Registers | | |
Register	Contents		Register	Contents
I	8		I	8
N	4		N	4
X	9		X	9
P	0		P	0
DF	1		DF	1

This step takes the contents of register four (low order byte) and places those contents into the D register.

Instruction FD 32

Before Instruction

Register	High	Low
0	00	45
1	?	?
2	?	?
3	?	?
4	00	01
5	00	01
6	00	00
7	00	4D
8	?	?
9	00	79
A	?	?
B	?	?
C	?	?
D	?	?
E	?	?
F	?	?

After Instruction

Register Pairs

Register	High	Low
0	00	47
1	?	?
2	?	?
3	?	?
4	00	01
5	00	01
6	00	00
7	00	4D
8	?	?
9	00	79
A	?	?
B	?	?
C	?	?
D	?	?
E	?	?
F	?	?

Eight Bit Register

Register	Contents		Register	Contents
D	01		D	31

Four and One Bit Registers

Register	Contents		Register	Contents
I	F		I	3
N	D		N	2
X	9		X	9
P	0		P	0
DF	1		DF	1

Contents of register D are subtracted from 32. The results of this subtraction are placed in the D register and the DF flag is also set, the 1 indicating that no borrow occurred.

Instruction   3B 57

Before Instruction			After Instruction		
Register Pairs					
Register	High	Low	Register	High	Low
0	00	47	0	00	49
1	?	?	1	?	?
2	?	?	2	?	?
3	?	?	3	?	?
4	00	01	4	00	01
5	00	01	5	00	01
6	00	00	6	00	00
7	00	4D	7	00	4D
8	?	?	8	?	?
9	00	79	9	00	79
A	?	?	A	?	?
B	?	?	B	?	?
C	?	?	C	?	?
D	?	?	D	?	?
E	?	?	E	?	?
F	?	?	F	?	?

Eight Bit Register

Register	Contents	Register	Contents
D	31	D	31

Four and One Bit Registers

Register	Contents	Register	Contents
I	3	I	5
N	B	N	7
X	9	X	9
P	0	P	0
DF	1	DF	1

This instruction tests the value contained by register DF. If the result had been zero, the program counter would have advanced to 00,57. The sound identifier (number contained in register four) is less than 32.

Instruction 84
Before Instruction

After Instruction

Register Pairs

Register	High	Low		Register	High	Low
0	00	49		0	00	4A
1	?	?		1	?	?
2	?	?		2	?	?
3	?	?		3	?	?
4	00	01		4	00	01
5	00	01		5	00	01
6	00	00		6	00	00
7	00	4D		7	00	4D
8	?	?		8	?	?
9	00	79		9	00	79
A	?	?		A	?	?
B	?	?		B	?	?
C	?	?		C	?	?
D	?	?		D	?	?
E	?	?		E	?	?
F	?	?		F	?	?

Eight Bit Register

Register	Contents		Register	Contents
D	31		D	01

Four and One Bit Registers

Register	Contents		Register	Contents
I	8		I	8
N	4		N	4
X	9		X	9
P	0		P	0
DF	1		DF	1

The sound identifier (number contained in register four) is moved into the D register again.

Instruction   FD 19
Before Instruction

Register	High	Low
0	00	4A
1	?	?
2	?	?
3	?	?
4	00	01
5	00	01
6	00	00
7	00	4D
8	?	?
9	00	79
A	?	?
B	?	?
C	?	?
D	?	?
E	?	?
F	?	?

After Instruction
Register Pairs

Register	High	Low
0	00	4C
1	?	?
2	?	?
3	?	?
4	00	01
5	00	01
6	00	00
7	00	4D
8	?	?
9	00	79
A	?	?
B	?	?
C	?	?
D	?	?
E	?	?
F	?	?

Eight Bit Register

Register	Contents	Register	Contents
D	01	D	18

Four and One Bit Registers

Register	Contents	Register	Contents
I	F	I	1
N	D	N	9
X	9	X	9
P	0	P	0
DF	1	DF	1

Contents of register D are subtracted from 19. The results of this subtraction are placed in the D register and the DF flag is also set, the 1 indicating that no borrow occurred.

Instruction 3B 5C

Before Instruction			After Instruction		
			Register Pairs		
Register	High	Low	Register	High	Low
0	00	4C	0	00	4E
1	?	?	1	?	?
2	?	?	2	?	?
3	?	?	3	?	?
4	00	01	4	00	01
5	00	01	5	00	01
6	00	00	6	00	00
7	00	4D	7	00	4D
8	?	?	8	?	?
9	00	79	9	00	79
A	?	?	A	?	?
B	?	?	B	?	?
C	?	?	C	?	?
D	?	?	D	?	?
E	?	?	E	?	?
F	?	?	F	?	?

Eight Bit Register			
Register	Contents	Register	Contents
D	18	D	18

Four and One Bit Registers			
Register	Contents	Register	Contents
I	3	I	5
N	B	N	C
X	9	X	9
P	0	P	0
DF	1	DF	1

This instruction tests the value contained by register DF. If the result had been zero, program counter would have advanced to 00,5C. The sound identifier (number contained in register four) is less than 19.

Instruction C4

| Before Instruction | | | After Instruction | | |
| | | | Register Pairs | | |
Register	High	Low	Register	High	Low
0	00	4E	0	00	4F
1	?	?	1	?	?
2	?	?	2	?	?
3	?	?	3	?	?
4	00	01	4	00	01
5	00	01	5	00	01
6	00	00	6	00	00
7	00	4D	7	00	4D
8	?	?	8	?	?
9	00	79	9	00	79
A	?	?	A	?	?
B	?	?	B	?	?
C	?	?	C	?	?
D	?	?	D	?	?
E	?	?	E	?	?
F	?	?	F	?	?

Eight Bit Register

Register	Contents	Register	Contents
D	18	D	18

Four and One Bit Registers

Register	Contents	Register	Contents
I	C	I	C
N	4	N	4
X	9	X	9
P	0	P	0
DF	1	DF	1

This instruction and the one following it (C4 at location 00,4F) do nothing but consume time. They exist because the previous version of the program contained an incorrect two-byte instruction; it was easier to delete the incorrect instruction and replace it with "do nothing" commands than to relocate addresses before and after this instruction.

196

Instruction 30 61
Before Instruction   After Instruction

Register Pairs

Register	High	Low		Register	High	Low
0	00	50		0	00	61
1	?	?		1	?	?
2	?	?		2	?	?
3	?	?		3	?	?
4	00	01		4	00	01
5	00	01		5	00	01
6	00	00		6	00	00
7	00	4D		7	00	4D
8	?	?		8	?	?
9	00	79		9	00	79
A	?	?		A	?	?
B	?	?		B	?	?
C	?	?		C	?	?
D	?	?		D	?	?
E	?	?		E	?	?
F	?	?		F	?	?

Eight Bit Register

Register	Contents		Register	Contents
D	18		D	18

Four and One Bit Registers

Register	Contents		Register	Contents
I	3		I	6
N	0		N	1
X	9		X	9
P	0		P	0
DF	1		DF	1

Because this sound had not proven to be one of the three possible longer sounds tested above, it must be the shortest sound of the four; therefore the program counter is set to 00,61 which is the address to commence an appropriate output. This instruction merely changes the low order byte of general register pair zero to 61.

Instruction   F8 75

Before Instruction			After Instruction		
			Register Pairs		
Register	High	Low	Register	High	Low
0	00	52	0	00	54
1	?	?	1	?	?
2	?	?	2	?	?
3	?	?	3	?	?
4	00	50	4	00	50
5	00	01	5	00	01
6	00	00	6	00	00
7	00	4D	7	00	4D
8	?	?	8	?	?
9	00	79	9	00	79
A	?	?	A	?	?
B	?	?	B	?	?
C	?	?	C	?	?
D	?	?	D	?	?
E	?	?	E	?	?
F	?	?	F	?	?

Eight Bit Register

Register	Contents	Register	Contents
D	F9	D	75

Four and One Bit Registers

Register	Contents	Register	Contents
I	F	I	7
N	8	N	5
X	9	X	9
P	0	P	0
DF	0	DF	0

The only way to reach this point would be to have a sound
identifier (number in register four) that is greater than 48. After the
subtraction the DF register would contain 0 and program control
would be transferred to this point. This instruction places 75 into
the D register; 75 is the low order byte of the memory address
which contains the output data for a long word.

Instruction A9

| Before Instruction | | | | After Instruction | | |
| Register Pairs | | | | | | |
Register	High	Low		Register	High	Low
0	00	54		0	00	55
1	?	?		1	?	?
2	?	?		2	?	?
3	?	?		3	?	?
4	00	50		4	00	50
5	00	01		5	00	01
6	00	00		6	00	00
7	00	4D		7	00	4D
8	?	?		8	?	?
9	00	79		9	00	75
A	?	?		A	?	?
B	?	?		B	?	?
C	?	?		C	?	?
D	?	?		D	?	?
E·	?	?		E	?	?
F	?	?		F	?	?

Eight Bit Register

Register	Contents		Register	Contents
D	75		D	75

Four and One Bit Registers

Register	Contents		Register	Contents
I	A		I	A
N	9		N	9
X	9		X	9
P	0		P	0
DF	0		DF	0

This instruction takes the value found in register D and transfers that value to the low order byte of general register pair number nine.

Instruction A9

Before Instruction				After Instruction		
			Register Pairs			
Register	High	Low		Register	High	Low
0	00	55		0	00	64
1	?	?		1	?	?
2	?	?		2	?	?
3	?	?		3	?	?
4	00	50		4	00	50
5	00	01		5	00	01
6	00	00		6	00	00
7	00	4D		7	00	4D
8	?	?		8	?	?
9	00	75		9	00	75
A	?	?		A	?	?
B	?	?		B	?	?
C	?	?		C	?	?
D	?	?		D	?	?
E	?	?		E	?	?
F	?	?		F	?	?

	Eight Bit Register		
Register	Contents	Register	Contents
D	75	D	75

	Four and One Bit Registers		
Register	Contents	Register	Contents
I	3	I	6
N	0	N	4
X	9	X	9
P	0	P	0
DF	0	DF	0

Control of the program is transferred to 00,64 by this instruction. This instruction completes the setup necessary for the output of a byte indicating that a long word has occurred.

Instruction F8 76

Before Instruction   After Instruction

Register Pairs

Register	High	Low		Register	High	Low
0	00	57		0	00	59
1	?	?		1	?	?
2	?	?		2	?	?
3	?	?		3	?	?
4	00	33		4	00	33
5	00	01		5	00	01
6	00	00		6	00	00
7	00	4D		7	00	4D
8	?	?		8	?	?
9	00	75		9	00	75
A	?	?		A	?	?
B	?	?		B	?	?
C	?	?		C	?	?
D	?	?		D	?	?
E	?	?		E	?	?
F	?	?		F	?	?

Eight Bit Register

Register	Contents		Register	Contents
D	FF		D	76

Four and One Bit Registers

Register	Contents		Register	Contents
I	F		I	7
N	8		N	6
X	9		X	9
P	0		P	0
DF	0		DF	0

To reach this point in the program requires that the sound identifier (number in register four) be greater than 31 and less than 4A (49 subtracted from 49 at location 00,40 would leave the DF register holding one). This step places 76 into the D register. 76 is the low order byte of the memory address for a data byte which will be the output of the word which is the third longest.

201

Instruction   A9

| Before Instruction | | | After Instruction
Register Pairs | | |
Register	High	Low	Register	High	Low
0	00	59	0	00	5A
1	?	?	1	?	?
2	?	?	2	?	?
3	?	?	3	?	?
4	00	33	4	00	33
5	00	01	5	00	01
6	00	00	6	00	00
7	00	4D	7	00	4D
8	?	?	8	?	?
9	00	75	9	00	76
A	?	?	A	?	?
B	?	?	B	?	?
C	?	?	C	?	?
D	?	?	D	?	?
E	?	?	E	?	?
F	?	?	F	?	?

Eight Bit Register

Register	Contents	Register	Contents
D	76	D	76

Four and One Bit Registers

Register	Contents	Register	Contents
I	A	I	A
N	9	N	9
X	9	X	9
P	0	P	0
DF	0	DF	0

This instruction places the value 76 into the D register.

Instruction   30 64

Before Instruction			After Instruction		
			Register Pairs		
Register	High	Low	Register	High	Low
0	00	5A	0	00	64
1	?	?	1	?	?
2	?	?	2	?	?
3	?	?	3	?	?
4	00	33	4	00	33
5	00	01	5	00	01
6	00	00	6	00	00
7	00	4D	7	00	4D
8	?	?	8	?	?
9	00	76	9	00	76
A	?	?	A	?	?
B	?	?	B	?	?
C	?	?	C	?	?
D	?	?	D	?	?
E	?	?	E	?	?
F	?	?	F	?	?

Eight Bit Register			
Register	Contents	Register	Contents
D	76	D	76

Four and One Bit Registers			
Register	Contents	Register	Contents
I	3	I	6
N	0	N	4
X	9	X	9
P	0	P	0
DF	0	DF	0

This instruction transfers control of the program to 00,64 where an output operation will occur. This is accomplished by moving the contents of the D register into the low order byte of general register pair zero.

Instruction   F8 77
Before Instruction

Register Pairs

Register	High	Low		Register	High	Low
0	00	5C		0	00	5E
1	?	?		1	?	?
2	?	?		2	?	?
3	?	?		3	?	?
4	00	1A		4	00	1A
5	00	01		5	00	01
6	00	00		6	00	00
7	00	4D		7	00	4D
8	?	?		8	?	?
9	00	76		9	00	76
A	?	?		A	?	?
B	?	?		B	?	?
C	?	?		C	?	?
D	?	?		D	?	?
E	?	?		E	?	?
F	?	?		F	?	?

After Instruction

Eight Bit Register

Register	Contents		Register	Contents
D	FF		D	77

Four and One Bit Registers

Register	Contents		Register	Contents
I	F		I	7
N	8		N	7
X	9		X	9
P	0		P	0
DF	0		DF	0

Reaching this place in the program requires that the sound identifier (number in register four) be greater than 18 and less than 32. The instruction here places 77 into the D register because 77 is the location of the data byte to be output as a representation of the word just longer than the shortest one.

Instruction   A9

Before Instruction				After Instruction		
			Register Pairs			
Register	High	Low		Register	High	Low
0	00	5E		0	00	5F
1	?	?		1	?	?
2	?	?		2	?	?
3	?	?		3	?	?
4	00	1A		4	00	1A
5	00	01		5	00	01
6	00	00		6	00	00
7	00	4D		7	00	4D
8	?	?		8	?	?
9	00	76		9	00	77
A	?	?		A	?	?
B	?	?		B	?	?
C	?	?		C	?	?
D	?	?		D	?	?
E	?	?		E	?	?
F	?	?		F	?	?

Eight Bit Register

Register	Contents		Register	Contents
D	77		D	77

Four and One Bit Registers

Register	Contents		Register	Contents
I	A		I	A
N	9		N	9
X	9		X	9
P	0		P	0
DF	0		DF	0

This instruction places the contents of the D register into the low order byte of general register pair number nine.

Instruction   30 64

Before Instruction			After Instruction		
Register Pairs					
Register	High	Low	Register	High	Low
0	00	5F	0	00	64
1	?	?	1	?	?
2	?	?	2	?	?
3	?	?	3	?	?
4	00	1A	4	00	1A
5	00	01	5	00	01
6	00	00	6	00	00
7	00	4D	7	00	4D
8	?	?	8	?	?
9	00	77	9	00	77
A	?	?	A	?	?
B	?	?	B	?	?
C	?	?	C	?	?
D	?	?	D	?	?
E	?	?	E	?	?
F	?	?	F	?	?

Eight Bit Register

| Register | Contents | Register | Contents |
| D | 77 | D | 77 |

Four and One Bit Registers

Register	Contents	Register	Contents
I	3	I	6
N	0	N	4
X	9	X	9
P	0	P	0
DF	0	DF	0

This instruction transfers control of the program to 00,64 where an output operation will occur. This is accomplished by moving the contents of the D register into the low order byte of general register pair zero.

Instruction   F8 78

Before Instruction			After Instruction		
			Register Pairs		
Register	High	Low	Register	High	Low
0	00	61	0	00	63
1	?	?	1	?	?
2	?	?	2	?	?
3	?	?	3	?	?
4	00	05	4	00	05
5	00	01	5	00	01
6	00	00	6	00	00
7	00	4D	7	00	4D
8	?	?	8	?	?
9	00	77	9	00	77
A	?	?	A	?	?
B	?	?	B	?	?
C	?	?	C	?	?
D	?	?	D	?	?
E	?	?	E	?	?
F	?	?	F	?	?

Eight Bit Register

Register	Contents	Register	Contents
D	77	D	78

Four and One Bit Registers

Register	Contents	Register	Contents
I	F	I	7
N	8	N	8
X	9	X	9
P	0	P	0
DF	0	DF	0

Reaching this place in the program requires that the sound identifier (number in register four) be less than 19. This instruction places 78 into the D register because the contents of the memory byte at location 00,78 represent the shortest word possible.

Instruction   A9

Before Instruction				After Instruction		
			Register Pairs			
Register	High	Low		Register	High	Low
0	00	63		0	00	64
1	?	?		1	?	?
2	?	?		2	?	?
3	?	?		3	?	?
4	00	05		4	00	05
5	00	01		5	00	01
6	00	00		6	00	00
7	00	4D		7	00	4D
8	?	?		8	?	?
9	00	77		9	00	78
A	?	?		A	?	?
B	?	?		B	?	?
C	?	?		C	?	?
D	?	?		D	?	?
E	?	?		E	?	?
F	?	?		F	?	?

Eight Bit Register			
Register	Contents	Register	Contents
D	78	D	78

Four and One Bit Registers			
Register	Contents	Register	Contents
I	A	I	A
N	9	N	9
X	9	X	9
P	0	P	0
DF	0	DF	0

This instruction places the contents of the D register into the low order byte of general register pair number nine.

Instruction   F8 00

Before Instruction			After Instruction Register Pairs		
Register	High	Low	Register	High	Low
0	00	64	0	00	66
1	?	?	1	?	?
2	?	?	2	?	?
3	?	?	3	?	?
4	00	05	4	00	05
5	00	01	5	00	01
6	00	00	6	00	00
7	00	4D	7	00	4D
8	?	?	8	?	?
9	00	78	9	00	78
A	?	?	A	?	?
B	?	?	B	?	?
C	?	?	C	?	?
D	?	?	D	?	?
E	?	?	E	?	?
F	?	?	F	?	?

Eight Bit Register

Register	Contents	Register	Contents
D	78	D	00

Four and One Bit Registers

Register	Contents	Register	Contents
I	F	I	0
N	8	N	0
X	9	X	9
P	0	P	0
DF	0	DF	0

This is the output section of the program, used to illuminate the appropriate light emitting diode after a sound has been decoded. Getting to this point requires either a jump from 00,55; 00,5A; 00,5F or falling through from 00,63. This instruction places 00 into the D register for transfer in the next step to another register.

Instruction B9

Before Instruction				After Instruction		
			Register Pairs			
Register	High	Low		Register	High	Low
0	00	66		0	00	67
1	?	?		1	?	?
2	?	?		2	?	?
3	?	?		3	?	?
4	00	05		4	00	05
5	00	01		5	00	01
6	00	00		6	00	00
7	00	4D		7	00	4D
8	?	?		8	?	?
9	00	78		9	00	78
A	?	?		A	?	?
B	?	?		B	?	?
C	?	?		C	?	?
D	?	?		D	?	?
E	?	?		E	?	?
F	?	?		F	?	?

Eight Bit Register

Register	Contents		Register	Contents
D	00		D	00

Four and One Bit Registers

Register	Contents		Register	Contents
I	B		I	B
N	9		N	9
X	9		X	9
P	0		P	0
DF	0		DF	0

The contents of D (00) are placed in the high order byte of general register pair number nine. As a programmer, it is not always obvious just what happens to be residing within a register; therefore, the safe thing to do is insert the desired value when needed rather than take a chance that things may work out. Even a chart like this one can be deceptive in a longer program; the contents of the registers may vary at any given point, depending upon the program path taken to arrive at that point.

Instruction   E9

Before Instruction			After Instruction		
			Register Pairs		
Register	High	Low	Register	High	Low
0	00	67	0	00	68
1	?	?	1	?	?
2	?	?	2	?	?
3	?	?	3	?	?
4	00	05	4	00	05
5	00	01	5	00	01
6	00	00	6	00	00
7	00	4D	7	00	4D
8	?	?	8	?	?
9	00	78	9	00	78
A	?	?	A	?	?
B	?	?	B	?	?
C	?	?	C	?	?
D	?	?	D	?	?
E	?	?	E	?	?
F	?	?	F	?	?

	Eight Bit Register		
Register	Contents	Register	Contents
D	00	D	00

	Four and One Bit Registers		
Register	Contents	Register	Contents
I	E	I	E
N	9	N	9
X	9	X	9
P	0	P	0
DF	0	DF	0

This instruction sets the value within the X register to 9. This instruction, like the last one, is not necessary in this program; but is part of a good practice; assuring that the pointer is pointing to the desired register pair. Remember that errors in software can be very difficult to find unless all code is written in understandable logical groupings.

Instruction 62

Before Instruction				After Instruction		
			Register Pairs			
Register	High	Low		Register	High	Low
0	00	68		0	00	69
1	?	?		1	?	?
2	?	?		2	?	?
3	?	?		3	?	?
4	00	05		4	00	05
5	00	01		5	00	01
6	00	00		6	00	00
7	00	4D		7	00	4D
8	?	?		8	?	?
9	00	78		9	00	78
A	?	?		A	?	?
B	?	?		B	?	?
C	?	?		C	?	?
D	?	?		D	?	?
E	?	?		E	?	?
F	?	?		F	?	?

	Eight Bit Register		
Register	Contents	Register	Contents
D	00	D	00

	Four and One Bit Registers		
Register	Contents	Register	Contents
I	6	I	6
N	2	N	2
X	9	X	9
P	0	P	0
DF	0	DF	0

The instruction causes the memory byte addressed by the
general register pair pointed to by the X register to be placed on the
output bus for output port number two. The X register points to
register pair number nine. Pair number nine addresses location
00,78. The contents of 00,78 (01) will be output. Port number two
refers to a hardware configuration which is wired to respond to an
"output port number two" instruction.

Instruction F8 FF

Before Instruction				After Instruction		
			Register Pairs			
Register	High	Low		Register	High	Low
0	00	69		0	00	6B
1	?	?		1	?	?
2	?	?		2	?	?
3	?	?		3	?	?
4	00	05		4	00	05
5	00	01		5	00	01
6	00	00		6	00	00
7	00	4D		7	00	4D
8	?	?		8	?	?
9	00	78		9	00	78
A	?	?		A	?	?
B	?	?		B	?	?
C	?	?		C	?	?
D	?	?		D	?	?
E	?	?		E	?	?
F	?	?		F	?	?

Eight Bit Register

Register	Contents		Register	Contents
D	00		D	FF

Four and One Bit Registers

Register	Contents		Register	Contents
I	F		I	F
N	8		N	F
X	9		X	9
P	0		P	0
DF	0		DF	0

This instruction is the first in a group designed to cause a time delay. After a word has been heard and decoded some time elapses before the system is allowed to listen for another word. The purpose of this is to prevent a long word (with a gap in the middle) from being interpreted two or three times. This particular instruction places FF into the D register.

Instruction AA

Before Instruction				After Instruction		
				Register Pairs		
Register	High	Low		Register	High	Low
0	00	6B		0	00	6C
1	?	?		1	?	?
2	?	?		2	?	?
3	?	?		3	?	?
4	00	05		4	00	05
5	00	01		5	00	01
6	00	00		6	00	00
7	00	4D		7	00	4D
8	?	?		8	?	?
9	00	78		9	00	78
A	?	?		A	?	FF
B	?	?		B	?	?
C	?	?		C	?	?
D	?	?		D	?	?
E	?	?		E	?	?
F	?	?		F	?	?
			Eight Bit Register			
Register	Contents			Register	Contents	
D	FF			D	FF	
		Four and One Bit Registers				
Register	Contents			Register	Contents	
I	A			I	A	
N	A			N	A	
X	9			X	9	
P	0			P	0	
DF	0			DF	0	

The low order byte of register pair A has been loaded with the value FF by this instruction.

Instruction   F8 0F
Before Instruction

After Instruction
Register Pairs

Register	High	Low		Register	High	Low
0	00	6C		0	00	6E
1	?	?		1	?	?
2	?	?		2	?	?
3	?	?		3	?	?
4	00	05		4	00	05
5	00	01		5	00	01
6	00	00		6	00	00
7	00	4D		7	00	4D
8	?	?		8	?	?
9	00	78		9	00	78
A	?	FF		A	?	FF
B	?	?		B	?	?
C	?	?		C	?	?
D	?	?		D	?	?
E	?	?		E	?	?
F	?	?		F	?	?

Eight Bit Register

Register	Contents		Register	Contents
D	FF		D	0F

Four and One Bit Registers

Register	Contents		Register	Contents
I	F		I	0
N	8		N	F
X	9		X	9
P	0		P	0
DF	0		DF	0

This instruction places 0F into the D register for transfer to another place later.

Instruction BA
Before Instruction   After Instruction

Register Pairs

Register	High	Low		Register	High	Low
0	00	6E		0	00	6F
1	?	?		1	?	?
2	?	?		2	?	?
3	?	?		3	?	?
4	00	05		4	00	05
5	00	01		5	00	01
6	00	00		6	00	00
7	00	4D		7	00	4D
8	?	?		8	?	?
9	00	78		9	00	78
A	?	FF		A	0F	FF
B	?	?		B	?	?
C	?	?		C	?	?
D	?	?		D	?	?
E	?	?		E	?	?
F	?	?		F	?	?

Eight Bit Register

Register	Contents		Register	Contents
D	0F		D	0F

Four and One Bit Registers

Register	Contents		Register	Contents
I	B		I	B
N	A		N	A
X	9		X	9
P	0		P	0
DF	0		DF	0

The contents of the D register 0F are transferred into the high order byte of register pair A with this instruction.

Instruction 2A

Before Instruction			After Instruction		
Register Pairs					
Register	High	Low	Register	High	Low
0	00	6F	0	00	70
1	?	?	1	?	?
2	?	?	2	?	?
3	?	?	3	?	?
4	00	05	4	00	05
5	00	01	5	00	01
6	00	00	6	00	00
7	00	4D	7	00	4D
8	?	?	8	?	?
9	00	78	9	00	78
A	0F	FF	A	0F	FE
B	?	?	B	?	?
C	?	?	C	?	?
D	?	?	D	?	?
E	?	?	E	?	?
F	?	?	F	?	?

Eight Bit Register

| Register | Contents | Register | Contents |
| D | 0F | D | 0F |

Four and One Bit Registers

Register	Contents	Register	Contents
I	2	I	2
N	A	N	A
X	9	X	9
P	0	P	0
DF	0	DF	0

This instruction decreases the contents of register pair A by one count form 0F,FF to 0F,FE. The operation of this timing loop is straightforward. A number (0F,FF) is placed into a register (A). The contents of that register are decreased by one count. The contents of the A register are tested; if zero then escape is provided from the loop. If the contents are not zero then another count is taken from the contents.

Instruction 9A

Before Instruction			After Instruction		
Register Pairs					
Register	High	Low	Register	High	Low
0	00	70	0	00	71
1	?	?	1	?	?
2	?	?	2	?	?
3	?	?	3	?	?
4	00	05	4	00	05
5	00	01	5	00	01
6	00	00	6	00	00
7	00	4D	7	00	4D
8	?	?	8	?	?
9	00	78	9	00	78
A	0F	FE	A	0F	FE
B	?	?	B	?	?
C	?	?	C	?	?
D	?	?	D	?	?
E	?	?	E	?	?
F	?	?	F	?	?
Eight Bit Register					
Register	Contents		Register	Contents	
D	0F		D	0F	
Four and One Bit Registers					
Register	Contents		Register	Contents	
I	9		I	9	
N	A		N	A	
X	9		X	9	
P	0		P	0	
DF	0		DF	0	

This instruction moves the high order byte of general register pair A into the D register. At this point, the contents of D equal the contents of high register A; but that will not be the case most of the time. As the rest of the loop is followed it will become obvious that register A is being decremented with each pass and the values therefore frequently changing.

Instruction   32 08
Before Instruction

Register	High	Low		Register	High	Low
0	00	71		0	00	73
1	?	?		1	?	?
2	?	?		2	?	?
3	?	?		3	?	?
4	00	05		4	00	05
5	00	01		5	00	01
6	00	00		6	00	00
7	00	4D		7	00	4D
8	?	?		8	?	?
9	00	78		9	00	78
A	0F	FE		A	0F	FE
B	?	?		B	?	?
C	?	?		C	?	?
D	?	?		D	?	?
E	?	?		E	?	?
F	?	?		F	?	?

After Instruction
Register Pairs

Eight Bit Register

Register	Contents		Register	Contents
D	0F		D	0F

Four and One Bit Registers

Register	Contents		Register	Contents
I	3		I	0
N	2		N	8
X	9		X	9
P	0		P	0
DF	0		DF	0

This instruction tests the contents of the D register. Were the results equal to zero (indicating that the loop had been run many times) the program would return to 00,08. Since that is not the case, the program counter advances to 00,73.

Instruction 30 6F

Before Instruction			After Instruction		
			Register Pairs		
Register	High	Low	Register	High	Low
0	00	73	0	00	6F
1	?	?	1	?	?
2	?	?	2	?	?
3	?	?	3	?	?
4	00	05	4	00	05
5	00	01	5	00	01
6	00	00	6	00	00
7	00	4D	7	00	4D
8	?	?	8	?	?
9	00	78	9	00	78
A	0F	FE	A	0F	FE
B	?	?	B	?	?
C	?	?	C	?	?
D	?	?	D	?	?
E	?	?	E	?	?
F	?	?	F	?	?

Eight Bit Register		
Register	Contents	Register	Contents
D	0F	D	0F

Four and One Bit Registers		
Register	Contents	Register	Contents
I	3	I	6
N	0	N	F
X	9	X	9
P	0	P	0
DF	0	DF	0

Reaching this place in the program indicates that the timing loop is in progress, but not finished. This instruction returns program control to 00.6F where the contents of register A are decremented and then tested again.

Instruction   08 (Data)
Before Instruction   After Instruction

Register Pairs

Register	High	Low		Register	High	Low
0	00	68		0	00	69
1	?	?		1	?	?
2	?	?		2	?	?
3	?	?		3	?	?
4	00	05		4	00	05
5	00	01		5	00	01
6	00	00		6	00	00
7	00	4D		7	00	4D
8	?	?		8	?	?
9	00	75		9	00	75
A	?	?		A	?	?
B	?	?		B	?	?
C	?	?		C	?	?
D	?	?		D	?	?
E	?	?		E	?	?
F	?	?		F	?	?

Eight Bit Register

Register	Contents		Register	Contents
D	00		D	00

Four and One Bit Registers

Register	Contents		Register	Contents
I	6		I	6
N	2		N	2
X	9		X	9
P	0		P	0
DF	0		DF	0

This is a data byte and it is only addressed as part of the
instruction 62 found at location 00,68. Note that the program area
starting at 00,52 sets up this data byte to be the one addressed by
the 62 instruction. This byte is "output" causing one line to be
electrically high (and one light-emitting diode lit), the one representing the longest word.

Instruction   04 (Data)

Before Instruction			After Instruction		
		Register Pairs			
Register	High	Low	Register	High	Low
0	00	68	0	00	69
1	?	?	1	?	?
2	?	?	2	?	?
3	?	?	3	?	?
4	00	05	4	00	05
5	00	01	5	00	01
6	00	00	6	00	00
7	00	4D	7	00	4D
8	?	?	8	?	?
9	00	76	9	00	76
A	?	?	A	?	?
B	?	?	B	?	?
C	?	?	C	?	?
D	?	?	D	?	?
E	?	?	E	?	?
F	?	?	F	?	?

	Eight Bit Register		
Register	Contents	Register	Contents
D	00	D	00

	Four and One Bit Registers		
Register	Contents	Register	Contents
I	6	I	6
N	2	N	2
X	9	X	9
P	0	P	0
DF	0	DF	0

This is a data byte and it is only addressed as part of the instruction 62 found at location 00,68. Note that the program area starting at 00,57 sets up this data byte to be the one addressed by the "62" instruction. This byte is "output" causing one line to be electrically high (and one light-emitting diode lit), the one representing the word next in length to the longest.

Instruction 02 (Data)

Before Instruction				After Instruction		
			Register Pairs			
Register	High	Low		Register	High	Low
0	00	68		0	00	69
1	?	?		1	?	?
2	?	?		2	?	?
3	?	?		3	?	?
4	00	05		4	00	05
5	00	01		5	00	01
6	00	00		6	00	00
7	00	4D		7	00	4D
8	?	?		8	?	?
9	00	77		9	00	77
A	?	?		A	?	?
B	?	?		B	?	?
C	?	?		C	?	?
D	?	?		D	?	?
E	?	?		E	?	?
F	?	?		F	?	?

	Eight Bit Register		
Register	Contents	Register	Contents
D	00	D	00

	Four and One Bit Registers		
Register	Contents	Register	Contents
I	6	I	6
N	2	N	2
X	9	X	9
P	0	P	0
DF	0	DF	0

This is a data byte and it is only addressed as part of the instruction 62 found at location 00,68. Note that the program area starting at 00,5C sets up this data byte to be the one addressed by the 62 instruction. This byte is "output" causing one line to be electrically high (and one light emitting diode lit), the one representing the word next in length to the shortest.

Instruction 01 (Data)

Before Instruction			After Instruction		
		Register Pairs			
Register	High	Low	Register	High	Low
0	00	68	0	00	69
1	?	?	1	?	?
2	?	?	2	?	?
3	?	?	3	?	?
4	00	05	4	00	05
5	00	01	5	00	01
6	00	00	6	00	00
7	00	4D	7	00	4D
8	?	?	8	?	?
9	00	78	9	00	78
A	?	?	A	?	?
B	?	?	B	?	?
C	?	?	C	?	?
D	?	?	D	?	?
E	?	?	E	?	?
F	?	?	F	?	?

	Eight Bit Register		
Register	Contents	Register	Contents
D	00	D	00

	Four and One Bit Registers		
Register	Contents	Register	Contents
I	6	I	6
N	2	N	2
X	9	X	9
P	0	P	0
DF	0	DF	0

This is a data byte and it is only addressed as part of the instruction 62 found at location 00,68. Note that the program area starting at 00,61 sets up this data byte to be the one addressed by the 62 instruction. This byte is "output" causing one line to be electrically high (and one light emitting diode lit), the one representing the shortest length word.

Instruction 00 (Data)
Before Instruction

Register	High	Low
0	00	07
1	?	?
2	?	?
3	?	?
4	?	?
5	?	?
6	?	?
7	?	?
8	?	?
9	00	79
A	?	?
B	?	?
C	?	?
D	?	?
E	?	?
F	?	?

Register	Contents
D	00

Register	Contents
I	6
N	2
X	9
P	0
DF	?

After Instruction
Register Pairs

Register	High	Low
0	00	08
1	?	?
2	?	?
3	?	?
4	?	?
5	?	?
6	?	?
7	?	?
8	?	?
9	00	79
A	?	?
B	?	?
C	?	?
D	?	?
E	?	?
F	?	?

Eight Bit Register

Register	Contents
D	00

Four and One Bit Registers

Register	Contents
I	6
N	2
X	9
P	0
DF	?

This is a data byte and it is only addressed as part of the instruction 62 found at location 00.07. Note that the program area starting at 00.00 sets up this data byte to be the one addressed by the 62 instruction. This byte is "output" causing all lines to be electrically low and all light-emitting diodes to be off.

Chapter 16

Frequency for the Recognizer

With the Frequency program the Recognizer becomes a powerful device for the deciphering of verbal sounds. With this program the system is speaker-dependent, meaning that the person using the device must also train it. To operate the system, you must first set the run-reset switch to the reset position, and then place the learn-run switch in the learn position. Set the amplifier to a loud (not distorted) position. Upon moving the run-reset switch to the run position, one light will be illuminated. This represents the first word, and it is wise to mark on a sheet of paper taped to the system which light represents which word. Upon detection of a sound, the Recognizer will illuminate an additional light (two lights on) indicating that sound is being input. If the input sound is too long (more than about 1.5 seconds) then it will be rejected and the light for the first word will be lit alone. If the learning process was successful, then the second light (alone) will be illuminated after the sound indicated (two lights on) situation has passed. Upon detection of the next sound, an additional light will come on (two lights lit) until the successful or unsuccessful completion of the learning for that word. Successful completion will be noted by illumination of the third light alone. Unsuccessful completion will be noted by the illumination again of the second position light alone. This process will be completed through the five words until the last word is learned, at which point all the lights will come on.

After the learning process has been completed, it is time to go into the run mode. First move the run-reset switch into the reset position. Next move the learn-run switch into the run position. Finally, move the reset-run switch back to the run position. All the lights should go out. When a sound is heard that the Recognizer determines to be one of the learned words, it will illuminate the

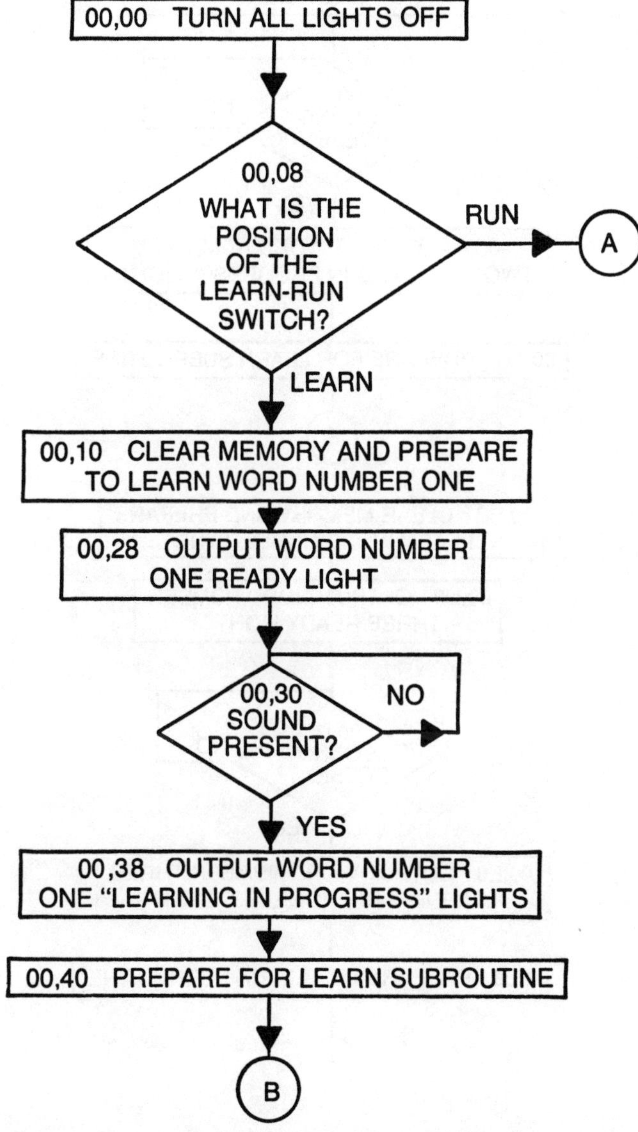

Fig. 16-1. Program flowchart of Frequency for The Recognizer.

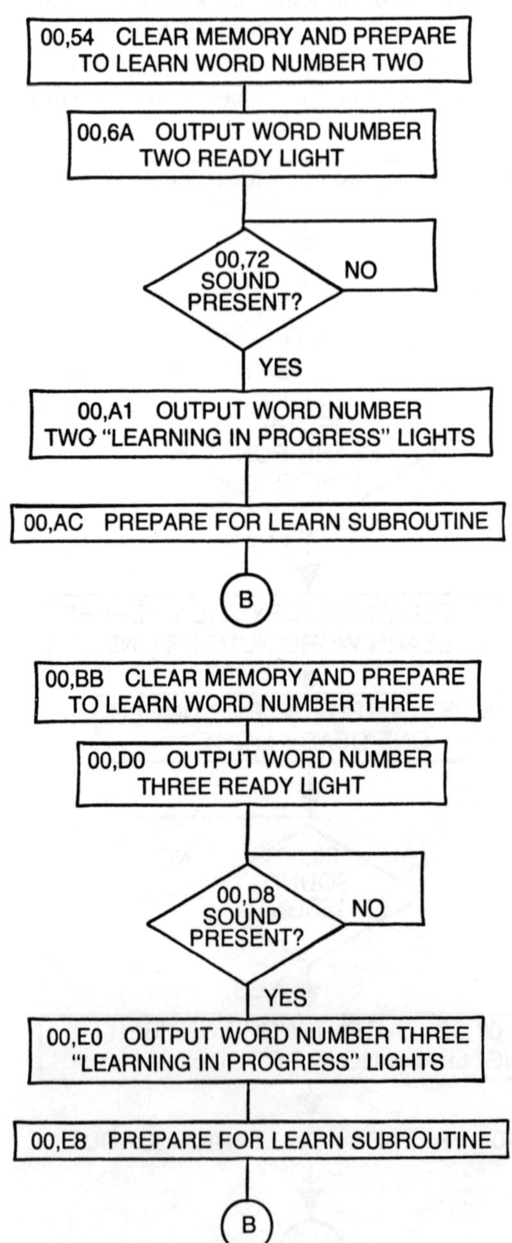

Fig. 16-1. Continued from page 227.

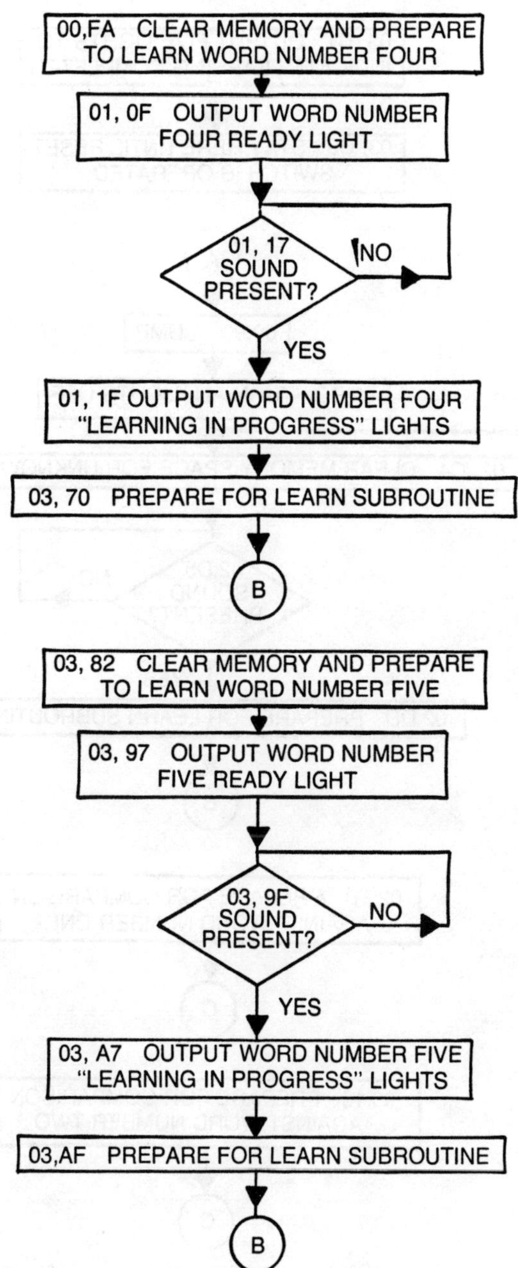

Fig. 16-1. Continued from page 228.

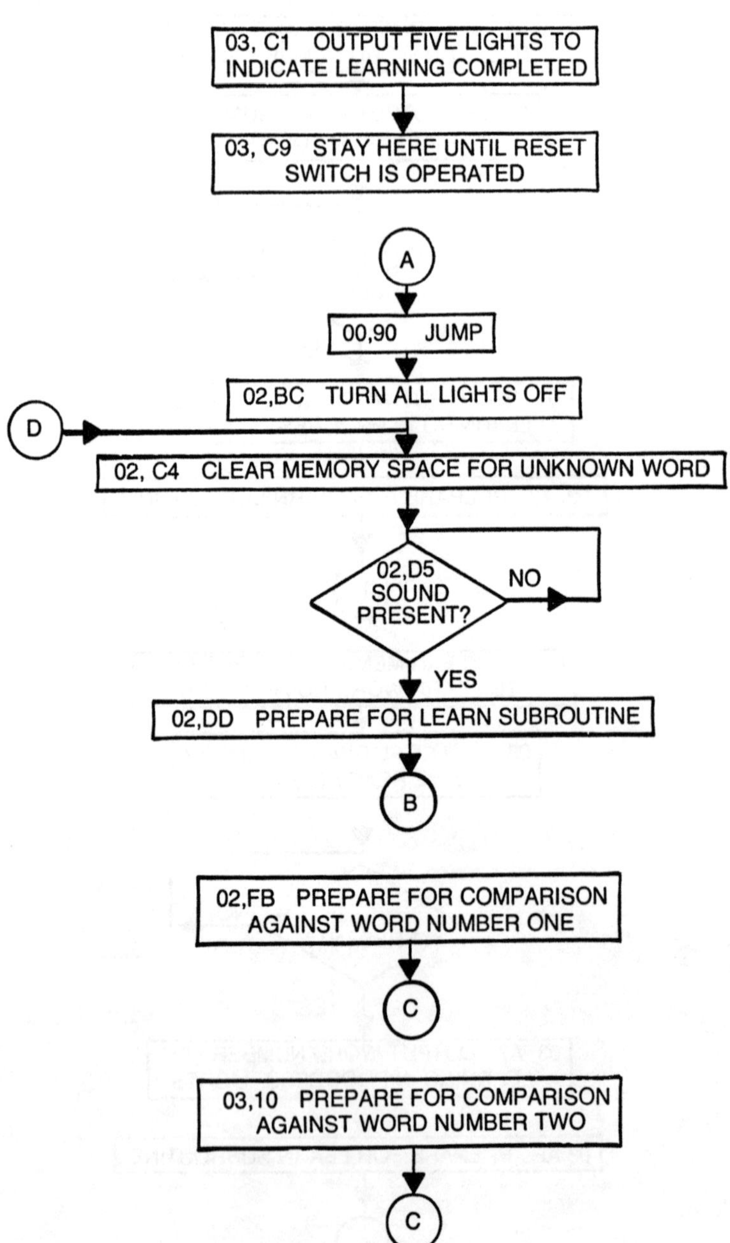

Fig. 16-1. Continued from page 229.

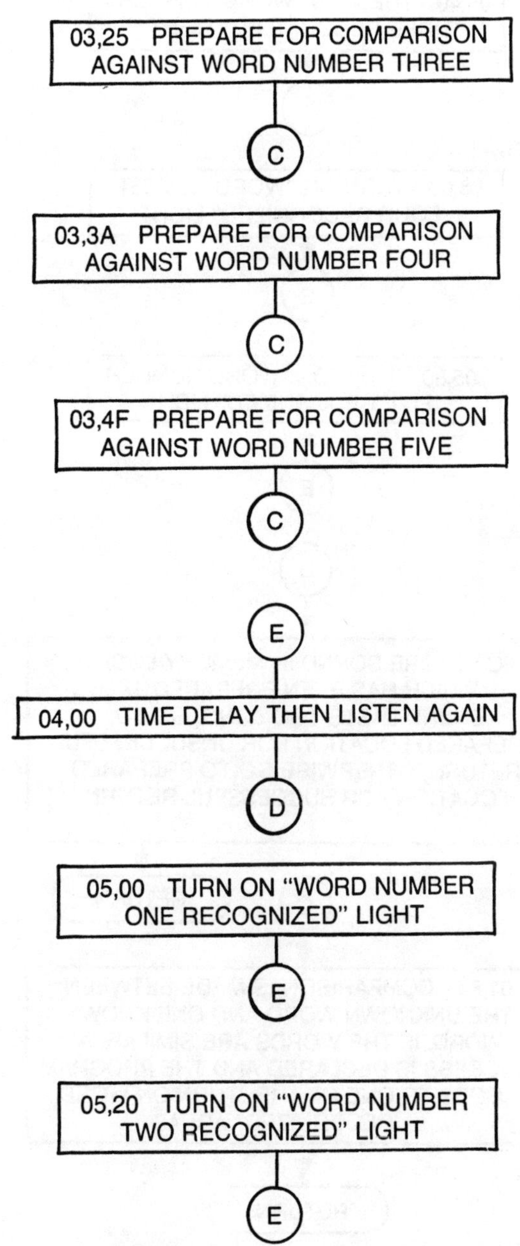

Fig. 16-1. Continued from page 230.

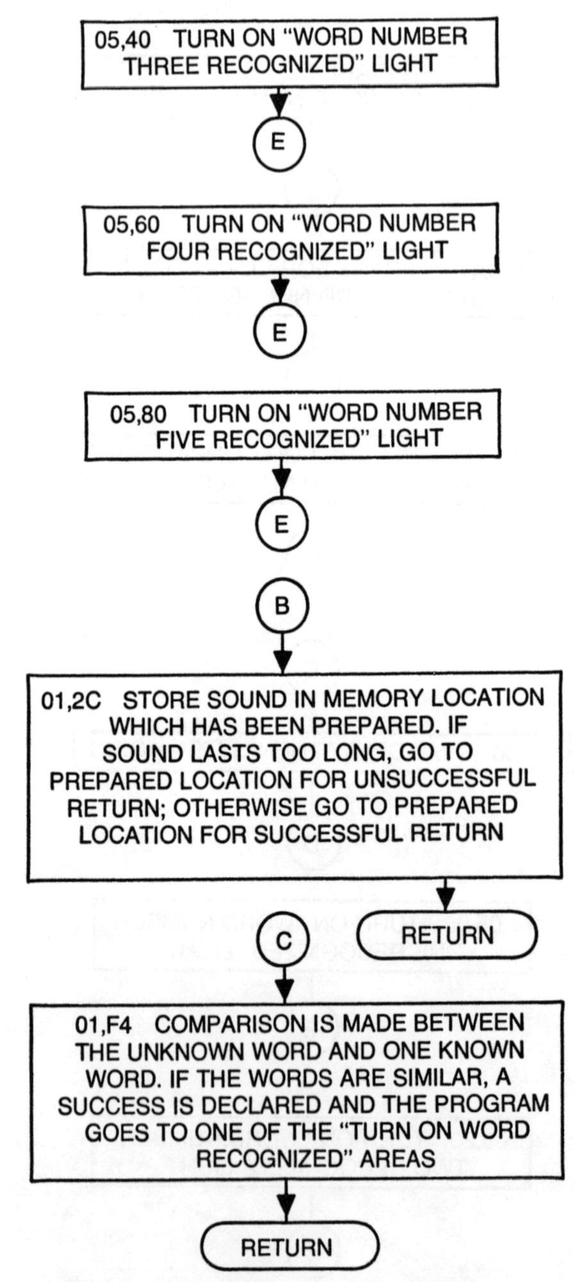

Fig. 16-1. Continued from page 231.

appropriate light (and operate the relay if one is wired). The light will stay illuminated until the Recognizer recognizes another word.

At memory location 02,16 is the validity parameter, 57. By trial and error this seems to be a number which works well. A higher number (up to 63) will result in greater accuracy but less likelihood of making a match at all. A lower number will result in more matches, but lower ability to distinguish between words.

The Recognizer works well when compared to devices available at this time. Room for improvement in software alone is tremendous. Each word is learned only one time; two or three patterns per word would better cover differences in an individual's speech. Also, 100 bytes of RAM are used for each pattern, and only three bits of each byte are filled. Nearly three times the resolution presently obtained could be gained by filling this unused space. Good use of memory space and increased memory supply could greatly enhance the information available for comparisons. The algorithm used here is very simple; store a pattern and compare it to the unknown pattern, and declare a match if the two are close enough. More sophisticated programs (which compensate for speed of speaking for example) could enhance the system potential.

Hardware improvements are possible, too. The new Electrically Alterable Programmable Read Only Memories could be trained and have the capability of remembering what was taught after the power has failed and returned. The cost is quite high now, but it is likely to fall rapidly on this new technology. More filters would provide more information. Multiple microprocessors can be placed under parallel control for rapid comparison to a large known vocabulary.

Figures 16-1 shows how the program progresses. Following is a commented listing that explains the operation of the software.

FREQUENCY PROGRAM LISTING WITH COMMENTS

00,00	F8	These instructions cause the contents of a memory byte to
00,01	80	be output. The address 00,80 is placed in register pair
00,02	A6	number six. The contents of register six 00,80 are used to
00,03	F8	address a memory byte, contents of which are 00. 00
00,04	00	causes all output lights to be off (00 means all off in this
00,05	B6	hardware system).
00,06	E6	
00,07	62	
00,08	C4	These instructions merely pass time and serve no useful
00,09	C4	purpose. Should one desire to do something else before
00,0A	C4	continuing this program, jump instructions could be substi-
00,0B	C4	tuted here.

| 00,0C | C4 |
| 00,0D | C4 |

| 00,0E | 3F | These instructions test the learn-run switch. If the switch |
| 00,0F | 90 | is in the learn mode, then the program goes to address |

These instructions test the learn-run switch. If the switch is in the learn mode, then the program goes to address 00,10. If the switch is in the run mode then the program goes to address 00,90. Position of the switch is determined by examining the state of the EF4 line (high or low), for the switch is physically tied to the EF4 line on the processor circuit.

00,10	F8
00,11	00
00,12	A2
00,13	F8
00,14	08
00,15	B2
00,16	F8
00,17	00
00,18	52

This sequence places the address 08,00 into register pair number two and then it places the value 00 into the memory location addressed by register two. In other words, memory location 08,00 is filled with the value 00.

00,19	12
00,1A	82
00,1B	FD
00,1C	63
00,1D	32
00,1E	21
00,1F	30
00,20	16

This group increments the number contained in register pair two by one count. Next it checks the low order byte to see if it is equal to 63 (63 is not a base ten number). If equal to 63, then the program jumps to 00,21; otherwise it returns to 00,16 at which it will zero out another memory location and increment pair two again.

00,21	F8
00,22	00
00,23	A2
00,24	C4
00,25	C4
00,26	C4
00,27	7A

The contents of the low order byte of register pair number two are set to 00. The Q flip-flop is set to zero.

00,28	F8
00,29	81
00,2A	A6
00,2B	F8
00,2C	00
00,2D	B6
00,2E	E6
00,2F	62

The contents of memory location 00,81 are output, the result being 01 on the output lines. This causes one LED to be illuminated.

00,30	34
00,31	38
00,32	35
00,33	38
00,34	36
00,35	38
00,36	30
00,37	30

These instructions test the input lines from the three frequency fillers. If sound is present on any of the lines, the program will progress to location 00,38; otherwise it will run a loop from 00,30 to 00,37 until a sound is detected.

234

00,38	F8
00,39	82
00,3A	A6
00,3B	F8
00,3C	00
00,3D	B6
00,3E	E6
00,3F	62

These instructions cause the memory byte at location 00,83 to be output. 11 is output, indicating that word number one is being trained.

00,40	C4
00,41	C4
00,42	C4
00,43	C4
00,44	C4
00,45	F8
00,46	54
00,47	A3
00,48	F8
00,49	00
00,4A	B3

00,54 is placed in register pair number three. This is set up as a return address if the soon to be attempted subroutine is successful in detecting a word.

00,4B	F8
00,4C	10
00,4D	A4
00,4E	F8
00,4F	00
00,50	B4

00,10 is set in register pair number four as a return address if the soon to be attempted subroutine is unsuccessful.

00,51	C0
00,52	01
00,53	2C

This jumps to the subroutine which stores the word "picture" in memory.

00,54	F8
00,55	64
00,56	A2
00,57	F8
00,58	08
00,59	B2

This sets 08,64 as the address which will define the starting point for the block of memory used to store word number two's "picture."

00,5A	F8
00,5B	00
00,5C	52
00,5D	12
00,5E	82
00,5F	FD
00,60	C7
00,61	32
00,62	65
00,63	30
00,64	5A
00,65	F8
00,66	64
00,67	A2
00,68	C4
00,69	7A

These instructions place 00 in the memory locations to be used for word number two storage. They also assure that the Q flip-flop is in the low state.

00,6A	F8	This block of instructions causes 02 to be output. 02 is only one line, thus one LED will be illuminated.
00,6B	83	
00,6C	A6	
00,6D	F8	
00,6E	00	
00,6F	B6	
00,70	E6	
00,71	62	

00,72	34	This is a loop from which escape is possible only if sound is detected. Upon detection of sound, the program jumps to 00,A1.
00,73	A1	
00,74	35	
00,75	A1	
00,76	36	
00,77	A1	
00,78	30	
00,79	72	

00,7A	00	These bytes are mere "filler" and will never be executed; therefore it matters not what information they contain.
00,7B	00	
00,7C	00	
00,7D	00	
00,7E	00	
00,7F	08	

00,80	00	These are "data" bytes used for output. When an output is required, one of these locations is selected for output.
00,81	01	
00,82	11	
00,83	02	
00,84	12	
00,85	04	
00,86	14	
00,87	08	
00,88	18	
00,89	10	
00,8A	15	
00,8B	1F	

00,8C	FF	This is unused memory space upon which this program will never operate.
00,8D	FF	
00,8E	FF	
00,8F	FF	

00,90	C0	If the learn-run switch is in the run mode (00,0E); the program jumps here. This is a long jump, moving to 02,BC.
00,91	02	
00,92	BC	

00,93	FF	These bytes are "fillers." Nothing happens here because this area is always jumped over.
00,94	FF	
00,95	FF	
00,96	FF	
00,97	FF	
00,98	FF	
00,99	FF	
00,9A	FF	
00,9B	FF	

00,9C	FF
00,9D	FF
00,9E	FF
00,9F	FF
00,A0	FF

00,A1	F8
00,A2	84
00,A3	A6
00,A4	F8
00,A5	00
00,A6	B6
00,A7	E6
00,A8	62
00,A9	C4
00,AA	C4
00,AB	C4

This block of instructions causes 12 to be output. 12 causes two lines to be active.

00,AC	F8
00,AD	BB
00,AE	A3
00,AF	F8
00,B0	00
00,B1	B3

This sets the successful return address for the 01,2C subroutine.

00,B2	F8
00,B3	54
00,B4	A4
00,B5	F8
00,B6	00
00,B7	B4

This sets the address for an unsuccessful return from the 01,2C subroutine.

00,B8	C0
00,B9	01
00,BA	2C

This jumps to the subroutine which stores the word "picture" in memory.

00,BB	F8
00,BC	C8
00,BD	A2
00,BE	F8
00,BF	08
00,C0	B2

This sets 08,C8 as the address which will define the starting point for the block of memory used to store word number three's picture.

00,C1	F8
00,C2	00
00,C3	52
00,C4	12
00,C5	82
00,C6	FD
00,C7	2B

These instructions place 00 in the memory locations to be used for word number three storage. They also assure that the Q flip-flop is in the low state.

00,C8	32
00,C9	CC
00,CA	30
00,CB	C1
00,CC	F8

00,CD	C8	
00,CE	A2	
00,CF	7A	
00,D0	F8	This block of instructions causes 04 to be output. 04 is only one line, thus one LED will be illuminated.
00,D1	85	
00,D2	A6	
00,D3	F8	
00,D4	00	
00,D5	B6	
00,D6	E6	
00,D7	62	
00,D8	34	This is a loop from which escape is possible only if sound is detected. Upon detection of sound, the program jumps to 00,E0.
00,D9	E0	
00,DA	35	
00,DB	E0	
00,DC	36	
00,DD	E0	
00.DE	30	
00,DF	D8	
00,E0	F8	This block of instructions causes 14 to be output. 14 causes two lines to be active.
00,E1	86	
00,E2	A6	
00,E3	F8	
00,E4	00	
00,E5	B6	
00,E6	E6	
00,E7	62	
00,E8	F8	This group assures that the contents of high order register of pair number two contains the value 08.
00,E9	08	
00,EA	B2	
00,EB	F8	This sets the successful return address for the 01,2C subroutine.
00,EC	FA	
00,ED	A3	
00,EE	F8	
00,EF	00	
00,F0	B3	
00,F1	F8	This sets the address for an unsuccessful return from the 01,2C subroutine.
00,F2	BB	
00,F3	A4	
00,F4	F8	
00,F5	00	
00,F6	B4	
00,F7	C0	This jumps to the subroutine which stores the word picture in memory.
00,F8	01	
00,F9	2C	
00,FA	F8	This sets 09,2C as the address which will define the starting point for the block of memory used to store word number four's picture.
00,FB	2C	
00.FC	A2	

00,FD	F8
00,FE	09
00,FF	B2

01,00	F8	These instructions place 00 in the memory locations to be used for word number four storage. They also assure that the Q flip-flop is in the low state.
01,01	00	
01,02	52	
01,03	12	
01,04	82	
01,05	FD	

01,06	8F
01,07	32
01,08	0B
01,09	30
01,0A	00
01,0B	F8
01,0C	2C
01,0D	A2
01,0E	7A

01,0F	F8	This block of instructions causes 08 to be output. 08 is only one line, thus one LED will be illuminated.
01,10	87	
01,11	A6	
01,12	F8	
01,13	00	
01,14	B6	
01,15	E6	
01,16	62	

01,17	34	This is a loop from which escape is possible only if sound is detected. Upon detection of sound, the program jumps to 01,1F.
01,18	1F	
01,19	35	
01,1A	1F	
01,1B	36	
01,1C	1F	
01,1D	30	
01,1E	17	

01,1F	F8	18 is output by these commands. 18 causes two lines to be active.
01,20	88	
01,21	A6	
01,22	F8	
01,23	00	
01,24	B6	
01,25	E6	
01,26	62	

01,27	C0	This causes program control to jump to 03,70 and is the result of hand assembly, not good programming techniques.
01,28	03	
01,29	70	

01,2A	FF	These locations are unused.
01,2B	FF	

01,2C	F8	This marks the starting point of a subroutine.
01,2D	00	This routine fills the block of memory which is pointed to

01,2E	A8	by register pair number two. A representation of the fre-
01,2F	C4	quencies present is stored by these instructions within that
		memory. This routine also tests the length of time that
		sound is heard; if it is too long to store in the alotted
		memory, the sequence is considered to be unsuccessful
		and program control is returned to the address defined by
		the contents of register pair number four. If successful,
		program control is returned to the address defined by the
		contents of register pair number three. The four instruc-
		tions listed here; 01,2C through 01,2F merely place 00 into
		the low order byte of register pair number eight.

01,30	F8	All contents of register pair number five are set to zero.
01,31	00	
01,32	A5	
01,33	F8	
01,34	00	
01,35	B5	

01,36	F8	A number 4F is set in register pair seven. This number
01,37	4F	defines the number of attempts to detect sound which will
01,38	A7	be made for each memory location.
01,39	F8	
01,3A	00	
01,3B	B7	

01,3C	34	These instructions test the input lines to determine if
01,3D	59	sound is present. If present, the program jumps to a sub-
01,3E	35	routine at 01,59 or 01,61 or 01,69. Each of these sub-
01,3F	61	routines return control to this loop. Each pass through this
01,40	36	loop decrements the number stored in register pair seven.
01,41	69	When the low order byte contains the value 00, escape is
01,42	27	made to 01,48.
01,43	87	
01,44	32	
01,45	48	
01,46	30	
01,47	3C	

01,48	12	These instructions increment registers two and eight.
01,49	18	Register two addresses the memory location being filled.
		Register eight is used to store a number which represents
		the length of the sound heard thus far.

| 01,4A | 39 | This tests to see if the Q flip-flop is low. |

01,4B	71	If low, then no sound was detected during the 01,3C to
		01,47 loop. If no sound was detected, then control of the
		program moves to a short subroutine at 01,71.

01,4C	85	These instructions take the contents of the low order byte
01,4D	FD	of register pair number five and subtract that number from
01,4E	10	10. If the results are zero, then program control goes to
01,4F	32	01,74. Contents of register five indicate the number of
01,50	74	times that no sound has been detected by the loop 01,3C to

01,47. Moving to 01,74 is the only way to escape this subroutine successfully. This test determines that a sufficient period of silence has passed (the 1 0 in 01,4E) to indicate that the spoken word has ended.

01,51	88	This tests the contents of low order register eight. If the loop has been passed too many times (loop starting at 01,3C) then the word is too long and the program jumps to 01,95.
01,52	FD	
01,53	63	
01,54	32	
01,55	95	

01,56	7A	If the tests above have failed (not enough silence to end or not so much sound as to force an end) then the Q flip-flop is set to a low value and the program returns to 01,36.
01,57	30	
01,58	36	

01,59	7B	This subroutine can only be reached from 01,3D. It sets a high value into the Q flip-flop. It forces the least significant bit in a memory location to contain the value 1. The memory location affected is the one addressed by the contents of register pair number two. Control is returned to 01,3E.
01,5A	F8	
01,5B	01	
01,5C	E2	
01,5D	F1	
01,5E	52	
01,5F	30	
01,60	3E	

01,61	7B	This subroutine can only be reached from 01,3F. It sets a high value into the Q flip-flop. It forces the second bit from the right in a memory location to contain the value 1. The memory location affected is the one addressed by the contents of register pair number two. Control is returned to 01,40.
01,62	F8	
01,63	02	
01,64	E2	
01,65	F1	
01,66	52	
01,67	30	
01,68	40	

01,69	7B	This subroutine can only be reached from 01,41. It sets a high value into the Q flip-flop. It forces the third bit from the right in a memory location to contain the value 1. The memory location affected is the one addressed by the contents of register pair number two. Control is returned to 01,42.
01,6A	F8	
01,6B	04	
01,6C	E2	
01,6D	F1	
01,6E	52	
01,6F	30	
01,70	4C	

01,71	15	This subroutine can be reached from 01,4B. It increments the value held in register pair number five when no sound has been detected in the loop 01,3C to 01,47.
01,72	30	
01,73	4C	

01,74	F8	These instructions place 01,80 in register pair number nine. Pair number nine then becomes the program counter, thus the program jumps to 01,80 at the end of this block of instructions. This point in the program is reached by jumping from 01,50.
01,75	80	
01,76	A9	
01,77	F8	
01,78	01	
01,79	B9	
01,7A	D9	

01,7B	00	This is an unused block of memory which this program will never operate upon.
01,7C	00	
01,7D	00	
01,7E	00	
01,7F	00	

01,80	83	This moves the contents of register pair number three (address for a successful return) into register pair number zero. Register pair number zero is then made the program counter, thus the program jumps to the address which corresponds to the number which is held in pairs zero and three.
01,81	A0	
01,82	93	
01,83	B0	
01,84	D0	

01,85	F8	This block of instructions is reached from 01,9E, a timing loop. This block changes the program counter from register zero to register nine after the address 01,90 has been placed in register pair number nine. The program jumps to 01,90.
01,86	90	
01,87	A9	
01,88	F8	
01,89	01	
01,8A	B9	
01,8B	D9	

01,8C	FF	This is an unused block of memory which this program will never execute.
01,8D	FF	
01,8E	FF	
01,8F	FF	

01,90	84	This moves the contents of register pair four into register pair zero. Register pair four, one may recall, contains the address for an unsuccessful subroutine return. The program will jump to whatever address is represented by the contents of register pair number four, which now is also the contents of pair zero, the program counter again.
01,91	A0	
01,92	94	
01,93	B0	
01,94	D0	

01,95	F8	This timing loop, reached from 01,55 is used to generate a delay after a sound has proven to be too long to store in memory. This is used to keep the program from taking the last portion of a long sound and storing it as if it were a complete word.
01,96	FF	
01,97	AF	
01,98	F8	
01,99	FF	
01,9A	BF	
01,9B	2F	
01,9C	9F	
01,9D	32	
01,9E	85	
01,9F	30	
01,A0	9B	

01,A1	00	Unused memory; developing a program by hand often results in such gaps as this.
to	00	
01,F3	00	

01,F4	F8	These instructions insure tha the value contained by register pair number five is now equal to 00,00. This block of instructions marks the beginning of the subroutine which compares the unknown sound against known sounds.
01,F5	00	
01,F6	A5	
01,F7	F8	

01,F8	00	
01,F9	B5	

01,FA	F8	These instructions place the value 09,F4 into the B register pair. 09,F4 is the starting address for the memory block which contains the unknown word (word being recognized).
01,FB	F4	
01,FC	AB	
01,FD	F8	
01,FE	09	
01,FF	BB	

02,00	4B	This instruction takes a type of information from the memory location addressed by register pair B and places that information into the D register. The value contained in the B register pair (address) is incremented by one count.

02,01	EA	These instructions compare one byte of the known word (found in register pair A) to the byte in register D (unknown word).
02,02	F3	

02,03	32	After the above comparison, register D will either contain zero (an exact match) or some other value (meaning the bytes compared were different). If an exact match was found, then the program jumps to location 02,0D; otherwise it continues to 02,05.
02,04	0D	

02,05	1A	These instructions increment the count in register pair A (address of memory of known word). They also test the value found in the B register. If the low order byte of B is found to contain 57, then all bytes have been compared and the program jumps to 02,14.
02,06	83	
02,07	FD	
02,08	57	
02,09	32	
02,0A	14	

02,0B	30	This causes the program to jump back to 02,00 where the loop will be run again.
02,0C	00	

02,0D	15	This point is reached by a jump from 02,04. These instructions increment the count contained in register pair number five (this count is equal to the number of matching memory bytes found during the test). The program then jumps to 02,05.
02,0E	30	
02,0F	05	

02,10	C4	These bytes of memory are unused by this program.
02,11	C4	
02,12	C4	
02,13	C4	

02,14	85	These instructions compare the number of matching bytes found to the validity parameter, 57 found at location 02,16. Decreasing 57 would result in more matches but less accuracy. Increasing 57 (up to the limit of 63) would increase accuracy but decrease the number of successful
02,15	FD	
02,16	57	
02,17	3B	
02,18	30	

finds. If this comparison is deemed successful, then the program jumps to 02,30; otherwise is continues to the next byte in sequence.

02,19	F8	These instructions cause the program to jump to 02,23. They also cause register pair nine to be the program counter rather than pair zero.
02,1A	23	
02,1B	A9	
02,1C	F8	
02,1D	02	
02,1E	B9	
02,1F	D9	
02,20	FF	These locations are unused by this program.
02,21	FF	
02,22	FF	
02,23	8D	Contents of the D register (address for an unsuccessful return from this subroutine) are placed in the zero register pair and the zero pair is again made the program counter.
02,24	A0	
02,25	9D	
02,26	B0	
02,27	D0	
02,28	FF	These locations are unused by this program.
to	FF	
02,2F	FF	
02,30	F8	This location is reached by a jump from 02,18 upon determination that the sound heard matches the sound being compared from memory. These bytes cause the program to jump to 02,40 and they case register pair nine to be the program counter.
02,31	40	
02,32	A9	
02,33	F8	
02,34	02	
02,35	B9	
02,36	D9	
02,37	FF	These bytes are unused by this program.
to	FF	
02,3F	FF	
02,40	8C	The address for a successful return, contained in the C register pair, is loaded into the zero register pair and then the program jumps to that location because the zero register is again made program counter.
02,41	A0	
02,42	9C	
02,43	B0	
02,44	D0	
02,45	FF	These locations are unused by this program.
to	FF	
02,BB	FF	
02,BC	F8	Reached from 00,92; this group of instructions causes 00 to be output (all LEDs off). This mark the start of the RUN section of the program.
02,BD	80	
02,BE	A6	
02,BF	F8	
02,C0	00	
02,C1	B6	
02,C2	E6	
02,C3	62	

02,C4	F8	This places the starting address for the unknown word into
02,C5	F4	register pair two.
02,C6	A2	
02,C7	F8	
02,C8	09	
02,C9	B2	

02,CA	F8	The block of memory to be used for storage of the unknown
02,CB	00	word is filled with the value 00.
02,CC	52	
02,CD	12	
02,CE	82	
02,CF	FD	
02,D0	57	
02,D1	32	
02,D2	D5	
02,D3	30	
02,D4	CA	

02,D5	34	This loop tests for sound and jumps to 02,DD whenever a
02,D6	DD	sound is detected.
02,D7	35	
02,D8	DD	
02,D9	36	
02,DA	DD	
02,DB	30	
02,DC	D5	

02,DD	C4	This block of instructions is used to set register pair three
02,DE	C4	with an address which will be used for successful return
02,DF	C4	from a subroutine.
02,E0	C4	
02,E1	C4	
02,E2	C4	
02,E3	F8	
02,E4	FB	
02,E5	A3	
02,E6	F8	
02,E7	02	
02,E8	B3	

02,E9	F8	This sets an address in register pair four which will be used
02,EA	BC	for an unsuccessful return from a subroutine.
02,EB	A4	
02,EC	F8	
02,ED	02	
02,EE	B4	

02,EF	F8	This sets the address of a memory location which will be
02,F0	F4	filled by the upcoming subroutine.
02,F1	A2	
02,F2	F8	
02,F3	09	
02,F4	B2	

| 02,F5 | C4 | This causes a jump to the subroutine at 01,2C. This sub- |

02,F6	C4	routine will fill a memory block with a sound picture, unless the sound is too long. It will return to either the successful or unsuccessful location.
02,F7	C4	
02,F8	C0	
02,F9	01	
02,FA	2C	
02,FB	F8	Reached by a successful return from the 01,2C subroutine, arriving at this point means that an unknown sound has been placed into memory. Whether or not that sound is one of the learned words remains to be determined.
02,FC	00	
02,FD	AA	
02,FE	F8	
02,FF	08	
03,00	BA	These instructions place 08,00 into the A register pair.
03,01	F8	The D register is filled with the address for an unsuccessful return from the next subroutine.
03,02	10	
03,03	AD	
03,04	F8	
03,05	03	
03,06	BD	
03,07	F8	Register pair C is filled with an address which will be used for a successful return from the next subroutine encountered.
03,08	00	
03,09	AC	
03,0A	F8	
03,0B	05	
03,0C	BC	
03,0D	C0	This jumps to the subroutine which compares the unknown sound with a known sound.
03,0E	01	
03,0F	F4	
03,10	F8	This sets a starting address in register A which will be used for comparison in an upcoming subroutine.
03,11	64	
03,12	AA	
03,13	F8	
03,14	08	
03,15	BA	
03,16	F8	This fills the D register with 03,25 for an unsuccessful subroutine return.
03,17	25	
03,18	AD	
03,19	F8	
03,1A	03	
03,1B	BD	
03,1C	F8	This places 05,20 in the C register for a successful return from the upcoming subroutine.
03,1D	20	
03,1E	AC	
03,1F	F8	
03,20	05	
03,21	BC	
03,22	C0	This jumps to 01,F4, the location of the comparison subroutine.
03,23	01	

03,24	F4	
03,25	F8	This places 08,C8 into the A register pair.
03,26	C8	
03,27	AA	
03,28	F8	
03,29	08	
03,2A	BA	
03,2B	F8	This places 03,3A into the D register pair.
03,2C	3A	
03,2D	AD	
03,2E	F8	
03,2F	03	
03,30	BD	
03,31	F8	This places 05,40 into the C register pair.
03,32	40	
03,33	AC	
03,34	F8	
03,35	05	
03,36	BC	
03,37	C0	This jumps to 01,C4, the comparison subroutine.
03,38	01	
03,39	F4	
03,3A	F8	This places 09,2C into the A register pair.
03,3B	2C	
03,3C	AA	
03,3D	F8	
03,3E	09	
03,3F	BA	
03,40	F8	This places 03,4F into the D register pair.
03,41	4F	
03,42	AD	
03,43	F8	
03,44	03	
03,45	BD	
03,46	F8	This places 05,60 into the C register pair.
03,47	60	
03,48	AC	
03,49	F8	
03,4A	05	
03,4B	BC	
03,4C	C0	This jumps to 01,F4, the comparison subroutine.
03,4D	01	
03,4E	F4	
03,4F	F8	This places 09,90 into the A register pair.
03,50	90	
03,51	AA	
03,52	F8	

03,53	09	
03,54	BA	
03,55	F8	This places 04,00 into the D register pair.
03,56	00	
03,57	AD	
03,58	F8	
03,59	04	
03,5A	BD	
03,5B	F8	This places 05,80 into the C register pair.
03,5C	80	
03,5D	AC	
03,5E	F8	
03,5F	05	
03,60	BC	
03,61	C0	This jumps to 01,F4, the comparison subroutine.
03,62	01	
03,63	F4	
03,64	00	These locations are not used by this program.
to	00	
03,6F	00	
03,70	C4	This sets the address for a successful return from the 01,2C subroutine.
03,71	C4	
03,72	C4	
03,73	F8	
03,74	82	
03,75	A3	
03,76	F8	
03,77	03	
03,78	B3	
03,79	F8	This places 00,FA in the number four register pair.
03,7A	FA	
03,7B	A4	
03,7C	F8	
03,7D	00	
03,7E	B4	
03,7F	C0	This jumps to 01,2C, the subroutine which stores the word "picture" in memory.
03,80	01	
03,81	2C	
03,82	F8	This places 09.90 in the number two register pair.
03,83	90	
03,84	A2	
03,85	F8	
03,86	09	
03,87	B2	
03,88	F8	These instructions place 00 in the block of memory addressed by the contents of general register pair number two. This is the space used for word number five storage. They also assure that the Q flip-flop is in the low state.
03,89	00	
03,8A	52	

03,8B	12	
03,8C	82	
03,8D	FD	
03,8E	F3	
03,8F	32	
03,90	93	
03,91	30	
03,92	88	
03,93	F8	
03,94	90	
03,95	A2	
03,96	7A	
03,97	F8	These instructions cause 10 to be output. 10 represents one line, thus one LED will be illuminated.
03,98	89	
03,99	A6	
03,9A	F8	
03,9B	00	
03,9C	B6	
03,9D	E6	
03,9E	62	
03,9F	34	This is a loop from which escape is possible only if sound is detected. Upon detection of sound, the program jumps to 03,A7.
03,A0	A7	
03,A1	35	
03,A2	A7	
03,A3	36	
03,A4	A7	
03,A5	30	
03,A6	9F	
03,A7	F8	15 is output by these commands. 15 causes two lines to be active.
03,A8	8A	
03,A9	A6	
03,AA	F8	
03,AB	00	
03,AC	B6	
03,AD	E6	
03,AE	62	
03,AF	C4	This sets 03,C1 in the number three register pair.
03,B0	C4	
03,B1	C4	
03,B2	F8	
03,B3	C1	
03,B4	A3	
03,B5	F8	
03,B6	03	
03,B7	B3	
03,B8	F8	This places 03,93 in general register pair number four.
03,B9	93	
03,BA	A4	
03,BB	F8	
03,BC	03	
03,BD	B4	

03,BE	C0	This causes the program to jump to 01,2C.
03,BF	01	
03,C0	2C	
03,C1	F8	This causes 1F to be output. 1F illuminates five LED's.
03,C2	8B	
03,C3	A6	
03,C4	F8	
03,C5	00	
03,C6	B6	
03,C7	E6	
03,C8	62	
03,C9	30	This marks the end of the learning sequence.
03,CA	C9	The program will remain here, looping until some external activity occurs (reset switch is operated).
03,CB	00	These locations are not used by this program.
to	00	
03,FF	00	
04,00	F8	These instructions form a time delay and they are reached from various places after a successful recognition sequence. The time delay assures that the "recognized" light for the appropriate word will remain lit for a brief time before the unit commences searching for another word.
04,01	0F	
04,02	AE	
04,03	F8	
04,04	FF	
04,05	A1	
04,06	21	
04,07	81	
04,08	32	
04,09	0C	
04,0A	30	
04,0B	06	
04,0C	2E	
04,0D	8E	
04,0E	32	
04,0F	12	
04,10	30	
04,11	03	
04,12	C0	This jumps to 02,C4, the place where the RUN part of the program starts listening.
04,13	02	
04,14	C4	
04,15	00	These locations are not used by this program.
to	00	
04,FF	00	
05,00	F8	This causes 01 to be output then it jumps to 04,00.
05,01	81	
05,02	A6	
05,03	F8	
05,04	00	
05,05	B6	
05,06	E6	

05,07	62	
05,08	C0	
05,09	04	
05,0A	00	
05,0B	00	These locations are unused in this program.
to	00	
05,1F	00	
05,20	F8	This causes 02 to be output and the program jumps to 04,00.
05,21	83	
05,22	A6	
05,23	F8	
05,24	00	
05,25	B6	
05,26	E6	
05,27	62	
05,28	C0	
05,29	04	
05,2A	00	
05,2B	00	These locations are unused in this program.
to	00	
05,3F	00	
05,40	F8	This causes 04 to be output. The program then jumps to 04,00.
05,41	85	
05,42	A6	
05,43	F8	
05,44	00	
05,45	B6	
05,46	E6	
05,47	62	
05,48	C0	
05,49	04	
05,4A	00	
05,4B	00	These locations are unused in this program.
to	00	
05,5F	00	
05,60	F8	This causes 08 to be output. The program then jumps to 04,00.
05,61	87	
05,62	A6	
05,63	F8	
05,64	00	
05,65	B6	
05,66	E6	
05,67	62	
05,68	C0	
05,69	04	
05,6A	00	
05,6B	00	These locations are unused in this program.
to	00	
05,7F	00	

05,80	F8
05,81	89
05,82	A6
05,83	F8
05,84	00
05,85	B6
05,86	E6
05,87	62
05,88	C0
05,89	04
05,8A	00

This causes 10 to be output. The program jumps to 04,00.

Chapter 17
The Z-80 Recognizer

More people are familiar with Z-80-based computers than with processors such as the previously discussed 1802. This chapter illustrates a fully developed and tested microcomputer system for voice recognition utilizing the Z-80 circuit. The computer described here may be easily built by following the detailed assembly instructions given. The input stage does not utilize filters, thus the verbal command must be processed solely upon the basis of a squared-up waveform. Software listed is similar to the Length program for the 1802 and it does not support any learning techniques or pattern comparison. The system shown here does not utilize the Random Access Memory or memory select circuits. Why then, you may ask, should I bother to build them? The emphasis here is upon construction of a working microcomputer for verbal recognition. The input port will accept eight bits of information, though only one is being used. The same filter shown in an earlier chapter could be built to provide three bits of input data; remember that this unit will readily accept up to eight channels of data. More sophisticated software can be written (or purchased; see Table 17-1) to utilize the Random Access Memory provided.

Figure 17-1 illustrates the major functions performed by this unit. Sound comes through a microphone, is amplified by an amplifier, and is sent to an input port of the computer. The computer processes this information according to the instructions received from the memory (software). Under software control, lights are illuminated to represent recognition of a word or phrase.

Table 17-1. Parts List for Z-80 Recognizer.

IC1, IC2, IC3: 7404
IC4: 7402
IC5, IC6: 7400
Microprocessor: Z-80
EPROM: 2716 (EPROM's that will work on this system are available from: Computer Voice Products, P.O. Box 985, Norcross, Ga. 30071)
Input-Output Port: (2) 8212
Memory (RAM): (2) 2114
Voltage Regulator: 7805
Light Emitting Diode: (5) Any variety
Crystal: 2.01 MHz
Capacitor: 47 Pf, 50-Volt
R0: 80 Ohm ½-Watt
R1, R2, R3, R6, R7, R8: 330 ohm ½-watt
R4, R5: 910 ohm, ½-watt
R9, R10, R11, R12, R13: 240 ohm, ½-watt
Switch: Single Pole Double Throw
Perforated Board: 4 inch × 6 inch piece
Amplifier: Radio Shack catalog number 277-1008A
Wire Wrap Sockets:
  40-Pin
  24-Pin
  18-Pin
  14-Pin
Misc: heat sink; nut & bolt (tiny); wire wrap wire; microphone cables (to connect amplifier to computer); 9-volt battery (6 D cells and holder).

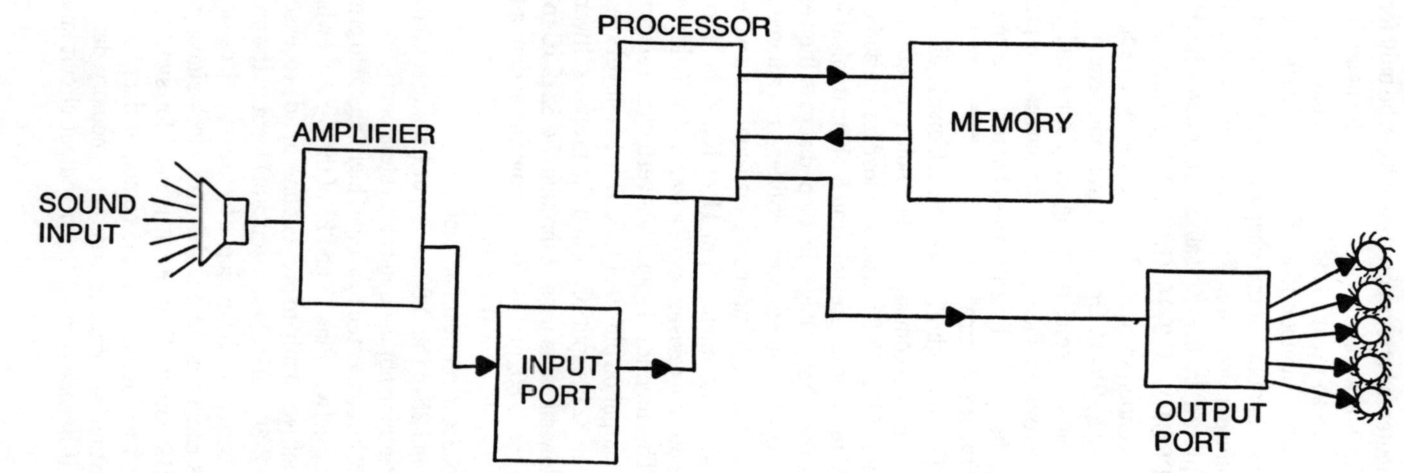

Fig. 17-1. Block diagram of Z-80 recognition system.

This computer is battery powered and can be built for less than $100. With the software provided, it will respond to sound of varying length, the shortest sound being word number one and the longest being word number five. The same hardware (physical device described in detail in this chapter) can have a learn and run mode with different software. Recall that software is the set of instructions placed in the Erasable Programmable Read Only Memory (EPROM). A 2716 (EPROM) purchased from any source will not contain software. *You*, the user *must have the desired program set in the EPROM*. Obtain programming equipment and set the EPROM yourself, send the program listing and EPROM to someone who provides such service, or purchase a programmed EPROM from the source listed in this chapter. The computer will do nothing without software.

Figures 17-2 through 17-5 are the schematic diagrams of the Z-80 based recognition computer. The 80-ohm resistor in the upper left-hand corner of Fig. 17-2 is used as a load for the audio amplifier. The ohmic value must be greater than 8 ohms (typical load for an amplifier) in order that voltage developed across the resistor can achieve logic highs. Do not use an amplifier from a home entertainment system, as this high impedance load could cause the amplifier to damage itself. The input to pin 11 of IC3 is held low (by the ground on the 80 ohm resistor) until a sound of sufficient magnitude is amplified. This high-level sound is inverted (and squared) by IC3 leaving a low output on pin 10 of IC3. This low-level signal goes to pin three of the 8212 input IC. When the proper software request occurs, this low signal is passed through the 8212 IC to pin 4 and ultimately to the Z-80, pin 14. Reviewing this action, a high level sound produces a low level on the D0 data line of the processor when the processor requests an input.

Pins 16 and 25 of the Z-80 are input lines related to interrupt handling (something not used in this system configuration); therefore they must be connected to a logic "high" signal to prevent them from becoming active. Pins 17 and 24 of the Z-80 likewise must be tied to the positive supply to prevent unwanted processor activity. Pin six of the Z-80 is the clock (oscillator) input to the processor. A high speed square wave is developed by the crystal, capacitor, gates and resistors connected to pin six. This clock signal goes to pin 11 of the 8212 output IC where it is used for synchronizing the output information. Recall that the computer data bus can contain input information, software instructions, memory data, or output information; it is necessary to let the output circuit know exactly

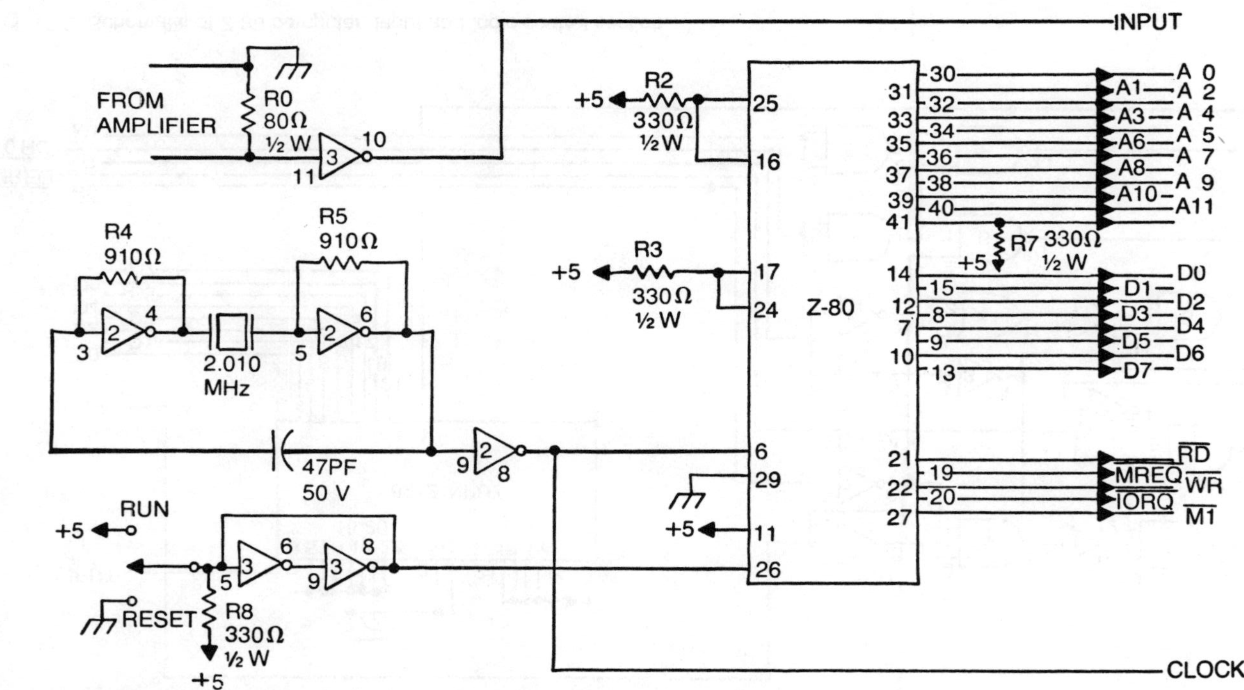

Fig. 17-2. Schematic of Z-80 computer; processor and input section.

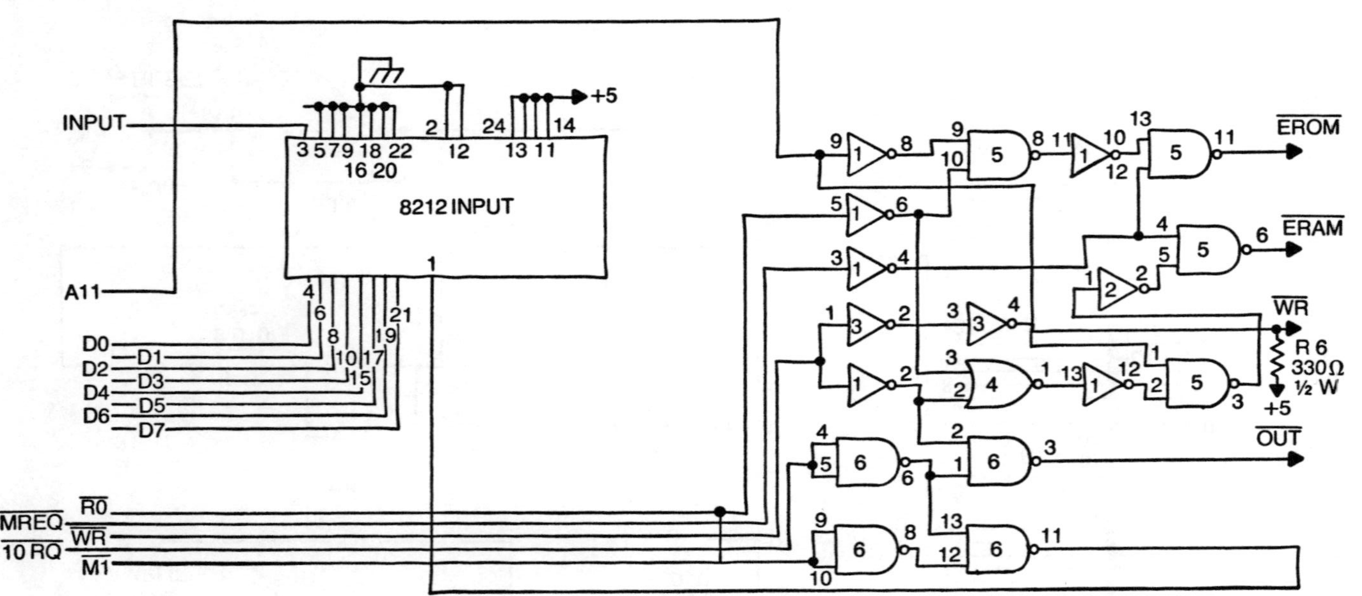

Fig. 17-3. Schematic of Z-80 computer; input and logic control section.

258

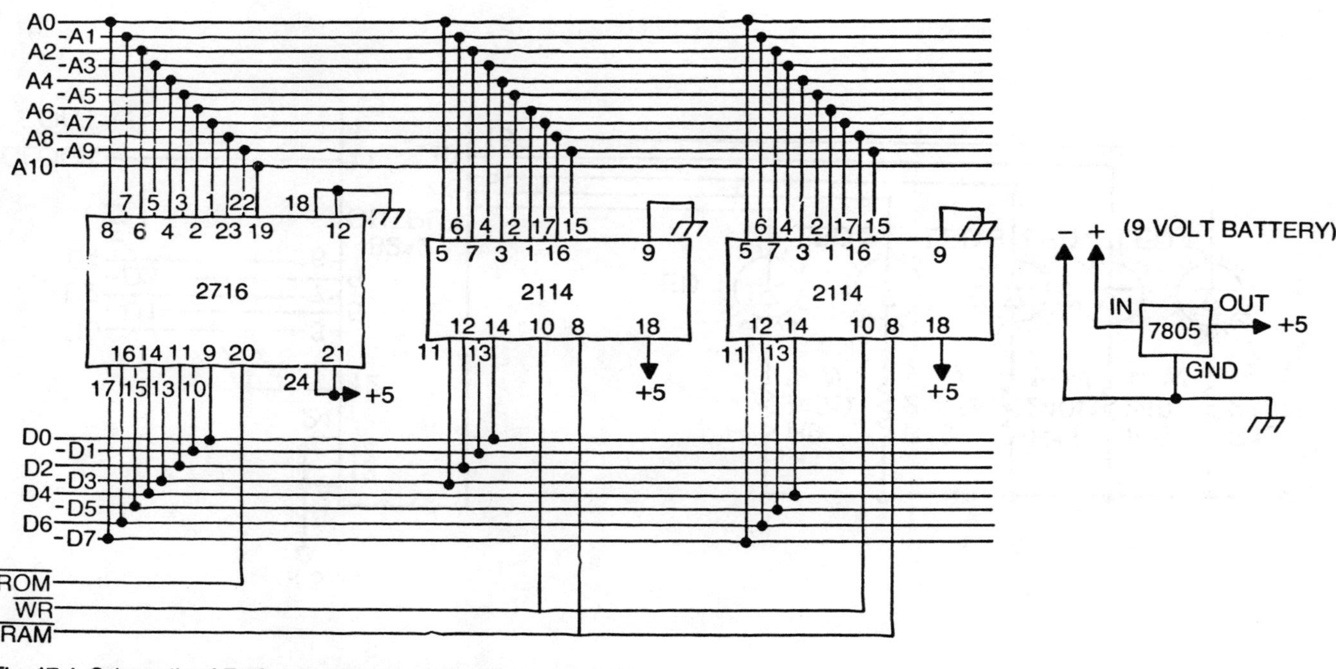

Fig. 17-4. Schematic of Z-80 computer; memory and power supply.

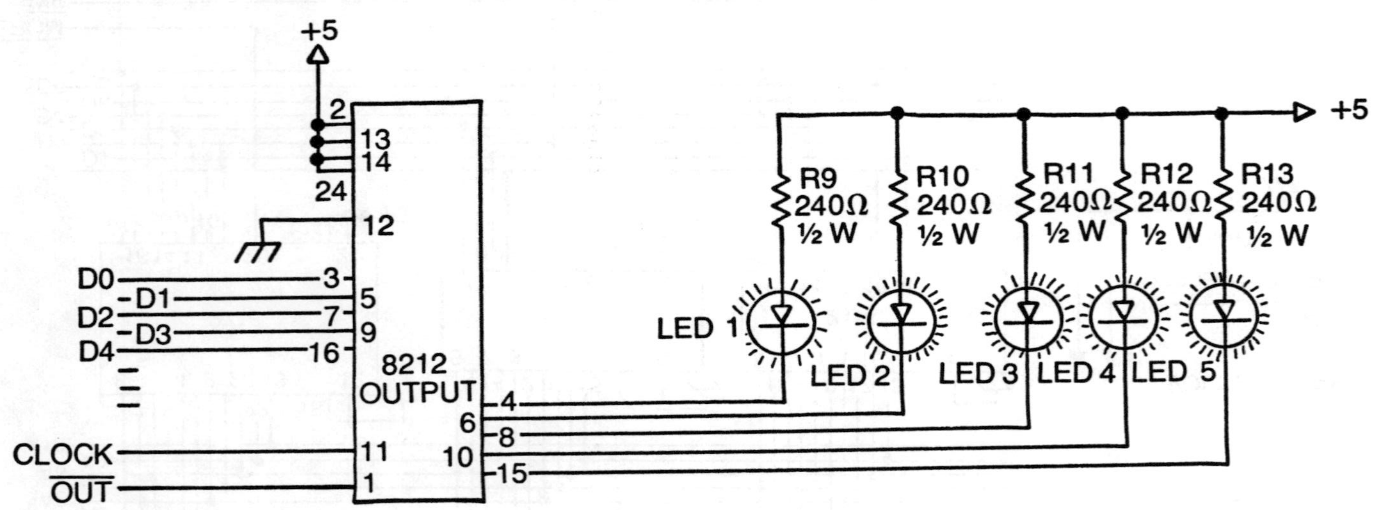

Fig. 17-5. Schematic of Z-80 computer; output port and lights.

when it is to respond lest it output garbage. Pins 29 and 11 are the power supply pins of the Z-80. Pin 26 of the Z-80 is tied to the run-reset switch. A positive voltage applied on this pin will allow the processor to run; a negative voltage will reset it (placing the program counter back to the zero position). Pins five, six, nine, and eight of IC3 are used to debounce the operation of the switch. R8 is used to additionally insure that transients do not occur while the run-reset switch is between positions.

Pins 30 through 40 and pin one of the Z-80 are address lines A0 through A11. These lines determine which memory location is being selected for operation by the processor. (They can be used to select from numerous input output port combinations, though the system is not constructed for such here). Pin one of the Z-80, A11, is used (along with other logic) to select either the EPROM or RAM memory. To expand the memory beyond the level established in this system would require additional logic to insure proper memory selection at all times. R7 is used to aid in this selesion process by assuring that the output of pin one of the Z-80 will always be high unless pulled low by the Z-80.

Pins 14, 15, 12, 8, 7, 9, 10, and 13 of the Z-80 represent the data bus, D0 through D7. Information flows to and from memories and port on this bus.

Pin 27 of the Z-80 is not used in this application and it does not need to be connected to anything. Pins 19 through 22 are control lines used to aid in the establishment of proper timing for various devices in the computer system. An input signal is generated by a combination of RD and IORQ. An output signal is generated by a combination of WR and IORQ. Note that a system with more than one input or more than one output port would require more sophisticated logic because of select information placed on the address lines.

The EPROM (first 2048 bytes of memory) is enabled when A11 is low, RD is high and MREQ is low. The RAM is enabled when A11 is high, MREQ is low and RD or WR are low. The 8212 output IC will drive the light-emitting diodes without the aid of external transistors. R9 through R13 are required in series with the LEDs to prevent high voltage damage to the LEDs. The 7805 regulator circuit provides the proper supply voltage to power the circuitry.

Construction of this computer is not difficult, though it will require eight to ten hours of labor. Acquire all the parts needed and lay them out on the perfboard as shown in Fig. 17-6. This is a top view of the computer; only the regulator circuit will be wired from

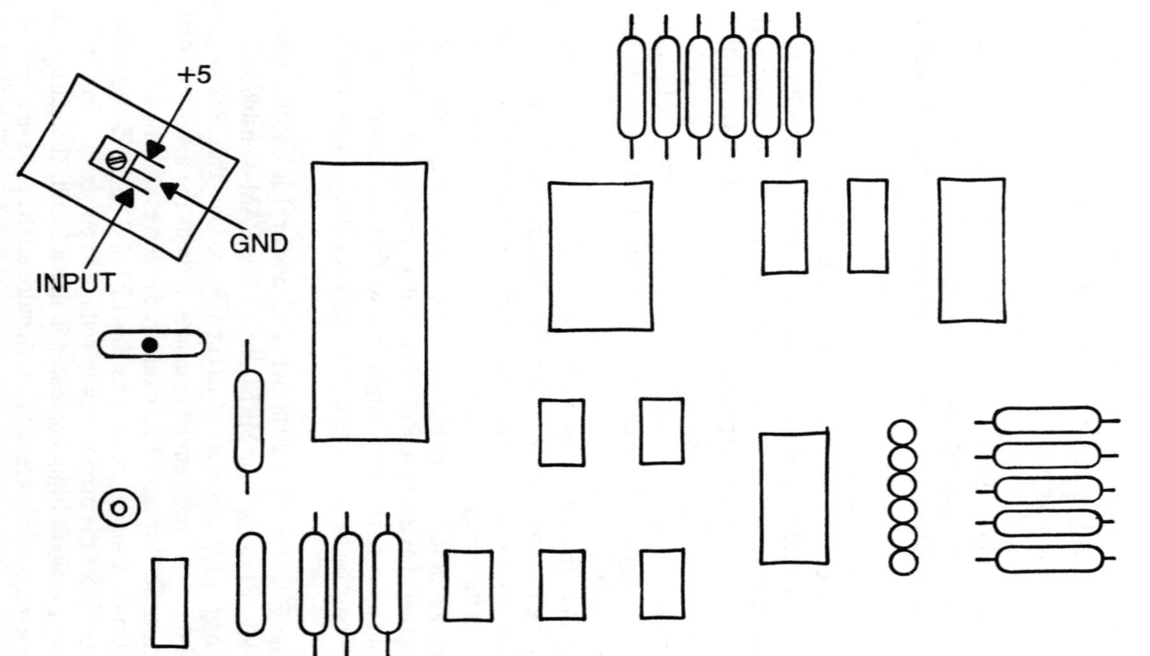

Fig. 17-6. Top view of computer layout. Place legs of 7805 so that they are flush with heat sink. Left leg will be battery positive input. Center leg will be battery negative input (also ground) for computer system. Right leg will be positive 5-volt supply for computer.

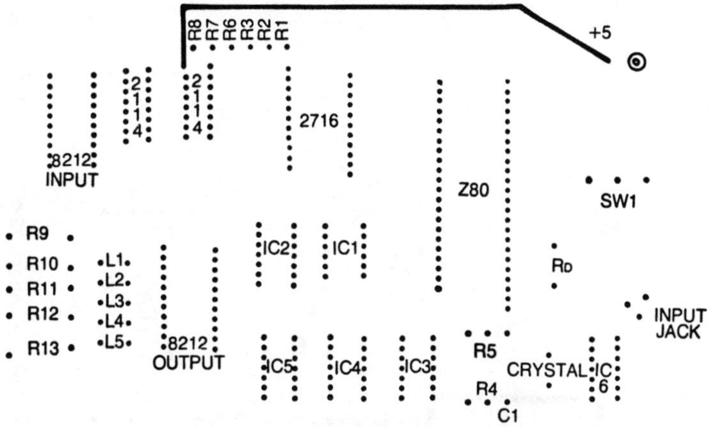

Fig. 17-7. Attach positive 5-volt supply to the top of R1. Connect the top of R1 to the top of R2, the top of R2 to the top of R3, the top of R3 to the top of R6, the top of R6 to the top of R7, the top of R7 to the top of R8, and the top of R8 to pin 18 of the 2114 indicated.

this side. Fasten the regulator through its heatsink to the perfboard with a nut and bolt. Turn the board over. All parts should stay in place (the sockets will stay; the other components may have to be temporarily taped until they are wired). After the components are wired, the wires will hold them down; external methods of securing the devices are not necessary.

Figures 17-7 through 17-46 indicate which wires to place in which location. Each figure shows five or six connections. Make

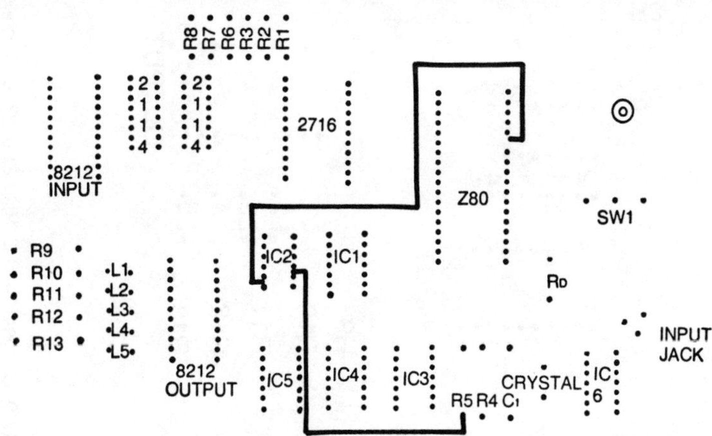

Fig. 17-8. Connect pin 6 of the Z-80 to pin 9 of IC2. Connect 5 of IC2 to the bottom of R5. Connect 5 of IC3 to 9 of IC3.

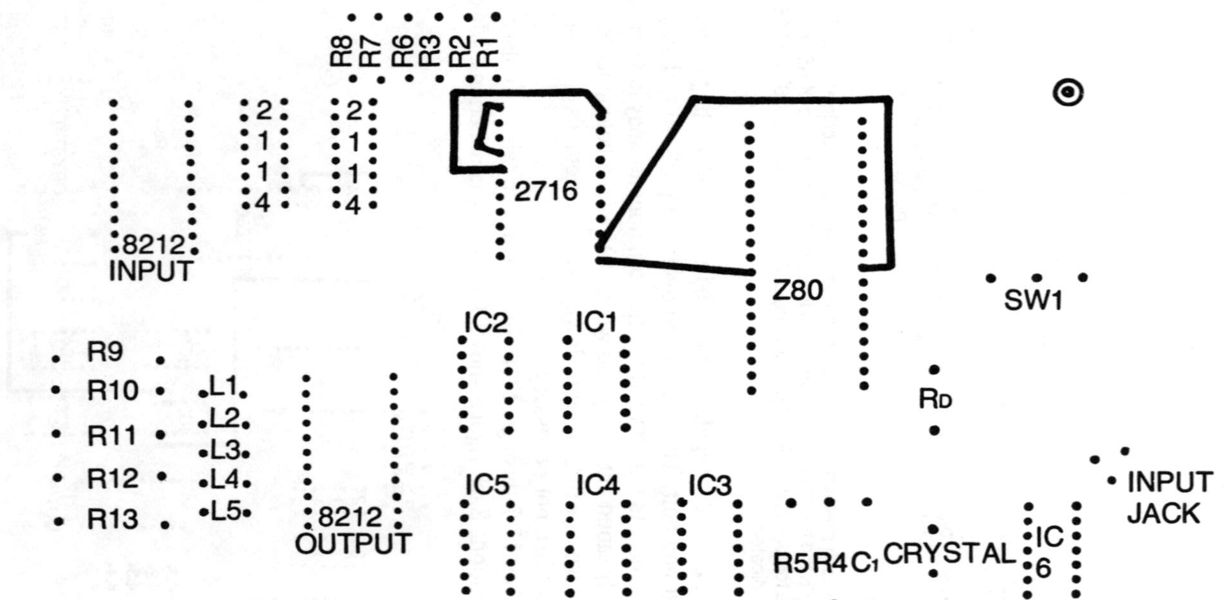

Fig. 17-9. Connect 24 of 2716 to 21 of 2716. Connect 1 of 2716 to 19 of 2716. Attach 11 of 2716 to 12 of Z-80. Attach 12 of 2716 to 29 of Z-80.

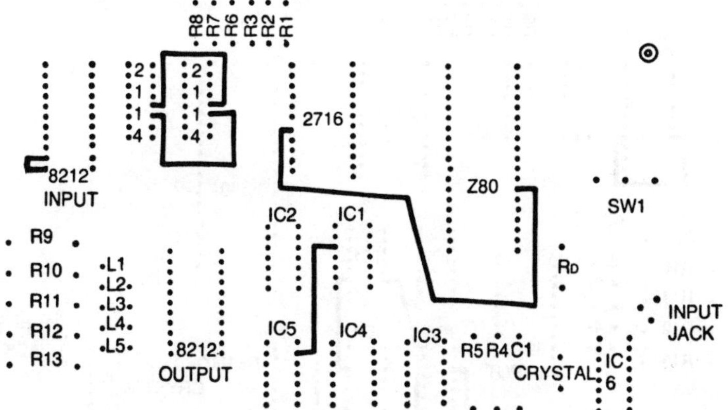

Fig. 17-10. Attach 13 of 8212 Input to 14 of 8212 Input. Connect 5 of 2114 right to 5 of 2114 left. Connect 6 of 2114 right to 6 of 2114 left. Connect 17 of 2716 to 13 of Z-80. Attach 12 of IC1 to 2 of IC5.

these connections and check them carefully. The figures represent the bottom view and indicate exactly where the wires must go. One incorrect connection can cause improper operation of the computer.

A flowchart of the software is given in Fig. 17-47. Initially, all lights are off (after the run-reset switch has been moved from the reset position to the run position). When a sound is detected, the program goes through a delay (half a second) then checks for sound again. Because the processor is very fast and because many highs

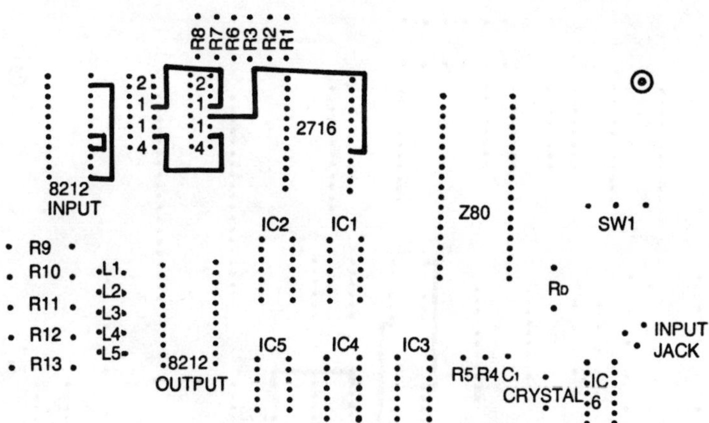

Fig. 17-11. Attach 2 of 8212 Input to 12 of 8212 Input. Connect 7 of 8212 Input to 9 of 8212 Input. Connect 4 of 2114 right to 4 of 2114 left. Connect 7 of 2114 right to 7 of 2114 left. Attach 5 of 2114 right to 8 of 2716.

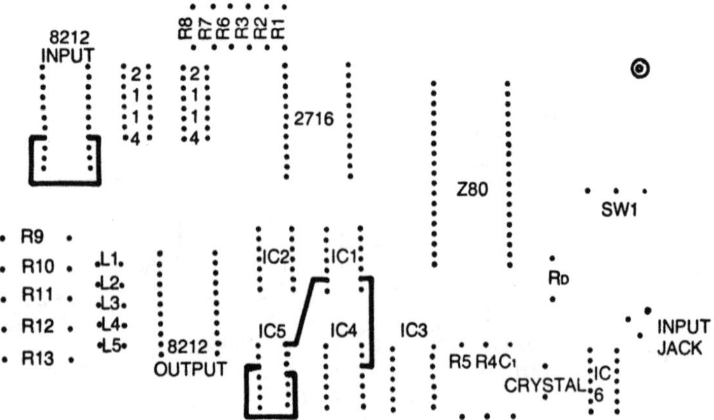

Fig. 17-12. Connect 9 of 8212 Input to 16 of 8212 Input. Connect 6 of IC1 to 3 of IC4. Connect 9 of IC1 to 1 of IC5. Attach 4 of IC5 to 12 of IC5.

and lows occur within a vocalized sound, the computer checks for sound 256 times before declaring that no sound exists. If no sound is found then the position one light is illuminated, a time delay occurs, and the computer awaits the next sound. If sound is detected in this loop, a time delay occurs and the computer checks for sound further down the flowchart. The lights will not go out again unless the computer is reset.

Table 17-2 is an assembly and machine code listing of software for the Z-80 computer.

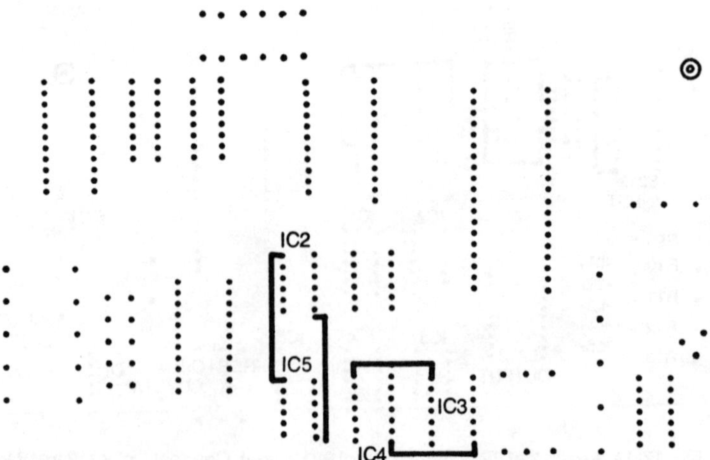

Fig. 17-13. Attach 7 of IC2 to 7 of IC5. Connect 14 of IC2 to 14 of IC5. Attach 14 of IC3 to 14 of IC4. Connect 7 of IC3 to 7 of IC4.

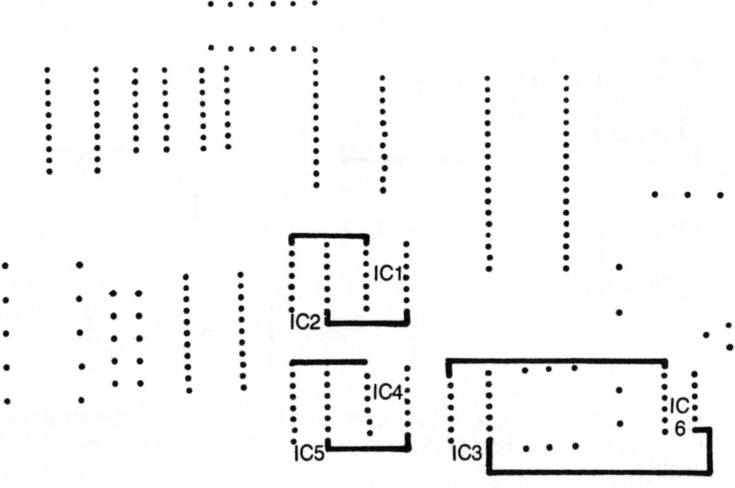

Fig. 17-14. Connect 14 of IC1 to 14 of IC2. Connect 7 of IC1 to 7 of IC2. Attach 7 of IC4 to 7 of IC5. Attach 14 of IC4 to 14 of IC5. Attach 14 of IC6 to 14 of IC3. Attach 7 of IC6 to 7 of IC3.

As in the other recognition devices, proximity of the microphone to the mouth of the speaker is a significant factor in the functioning of the system.

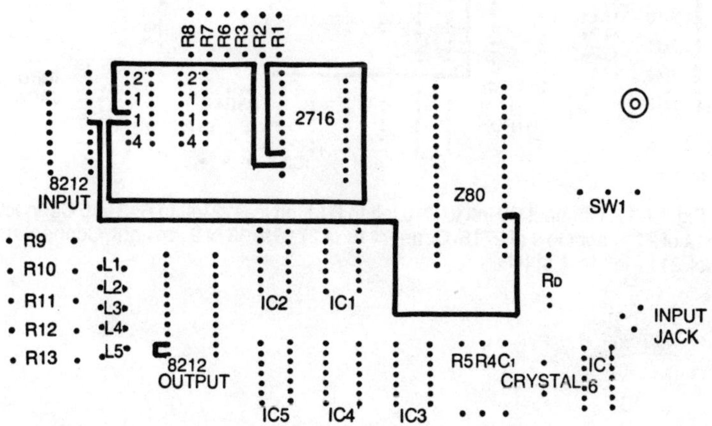

Fig. 17-15. Connect 13 of 8212 Output to 14 of 8212 Output. Connect 6 of 8212 Input to 15 of Z-80. Connect 14 of 2114 left to 14 of 2716. Connect 13 of 2114 left to 15 of 2716.

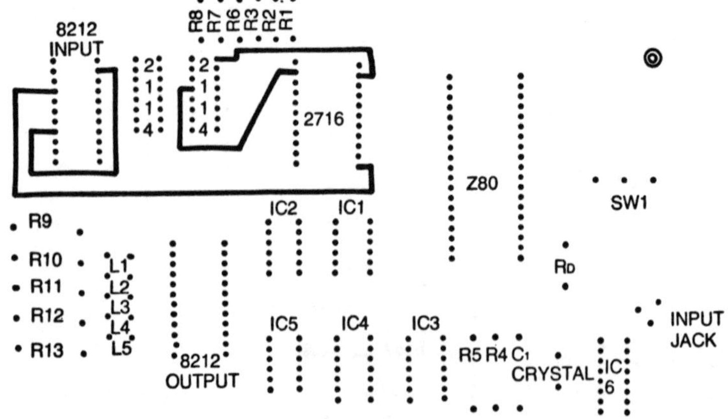

Fig. 17-16. Connect 2 of 8212 Input to 16 of 8212 Input. Connect 20 of 8212 Input to t2 of 2716. Connect 2 of 2716 to 1 of 2114 right. Connect 15 of 2114 right to 22 of 2716.

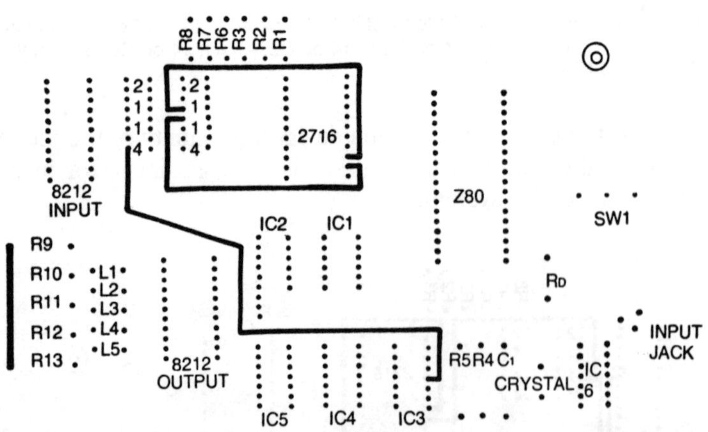

Fig. 17-17. Connect R9 left to R10 left to R11 left to R12 left to R13 left. Connect 14 of 2114 right to 9 of 2716. Connect 10 of 2716 to 13 of 2114 right. Connect 10 of 2114 left to 4 of IC3.

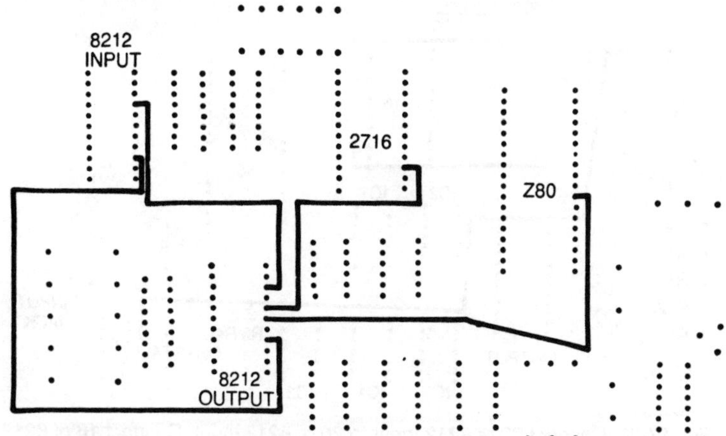

Fig. 17-18. Connect 4 of 8212 Input to 3 of 8212 Output. Connect 10 of 8212 Input to 9 of 8212 Output. Connect 5 of 8212 Output to 10 of 2716. Connect 7 of 8212 Output to 12 of Z-80.

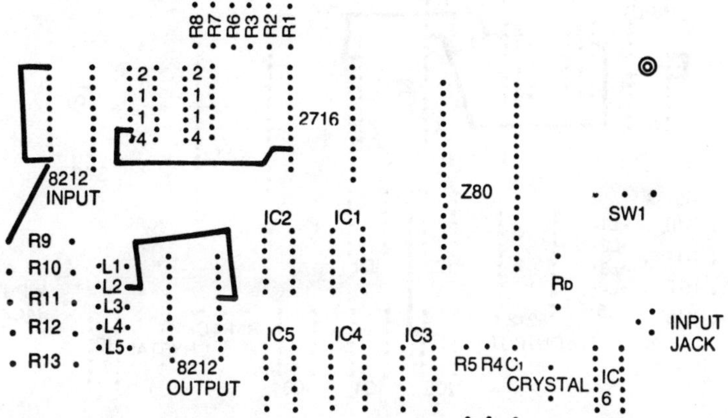

Fig. 17-19. Connect 14 of 8212 Input to 24 of 8212 Input. Connect 13 of 8212 Input to R9 left. Connect 12 of 2114 left to 16 of 2716. Connect cathode of L2 to 6 of 8212 Output.

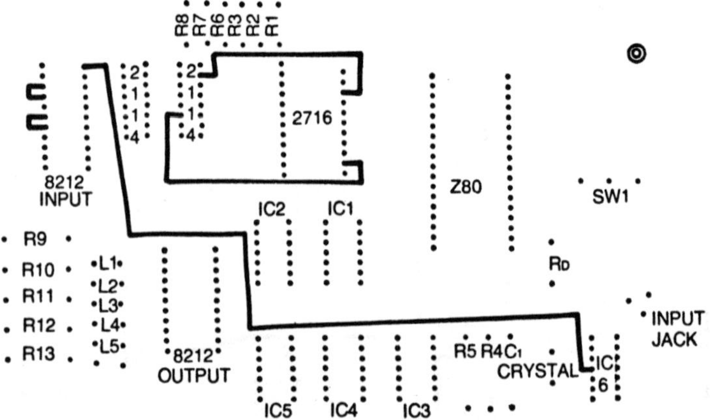

Fig. 17-20. Connect 22 of 8212 Input to 20 of 8212 Input. Connect 16 of 8212 Input to 18 of 8212 Input. Connect 1 of 8212 Input to 11 of IC6. Connect 3 of 2114 right to 4 of 2716. Connect 12 of 2114 right to 11 of 2716.

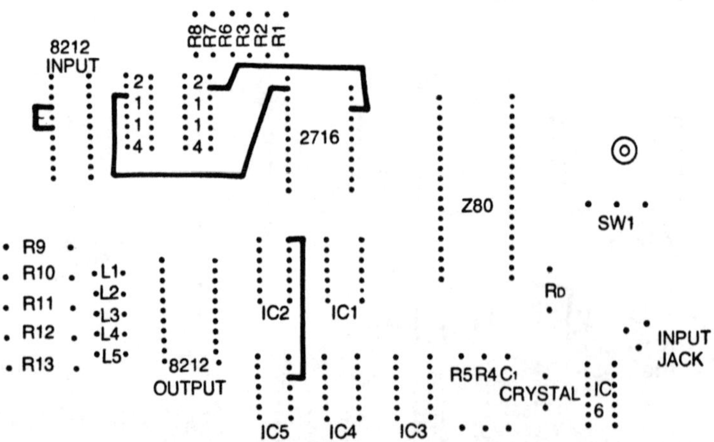

Fig. 17-21. Connect 20 of 8212 Input to 18 of 8212 Input. Connect 16 of 2114 left to 23 of 2716. Connect 2 of 2114 right to 3 of 2716. Connect 1 of IC2 to 3 of IC5.

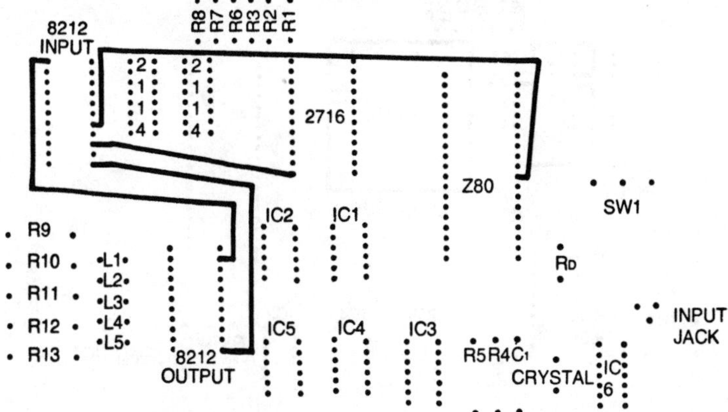

Fig. 17-22. Connect 24 of 8212 Input to 2 of 8212 Output. Connect 12 of 8212 Input to 2 of 8212 Output. Connect 10 of 8212 input to 13 of 2716. Connect 8 of 8212 Input to 12 of Z-80.

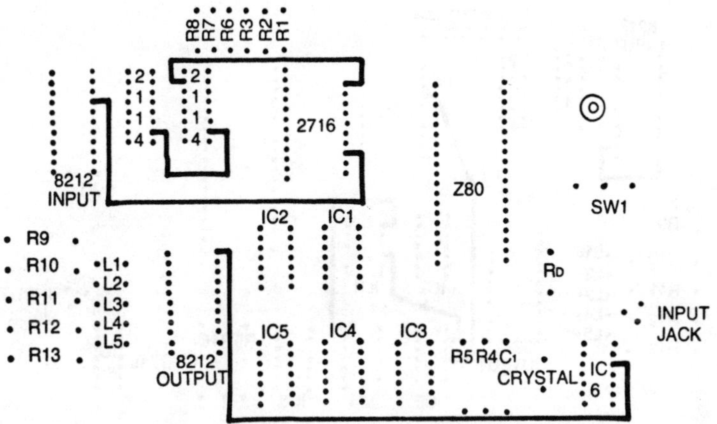

Fig. 17-23. Connect 4 of 8212 Input to 9 of 2716. Connect 17 of 2114 right to 1 of 2716. Connect 8 of 2114 left to 8 of 2114 right. Connect 1 of 8212 Output to 3 of IC6.

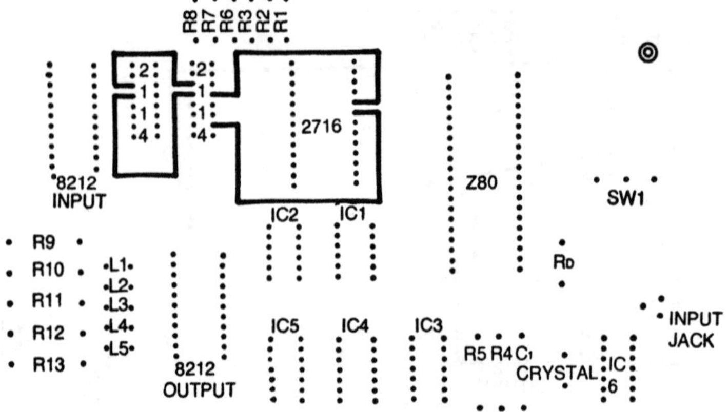

Fig. 17-24. Connect 16 of 2114 left to 16 of 2114 right. Connect 15 of 2114 left to 15 of 2114 right. Connect 4 of 2114 right to 5 of 2716. Connect 7 of 2114 right to 6 of 2716.

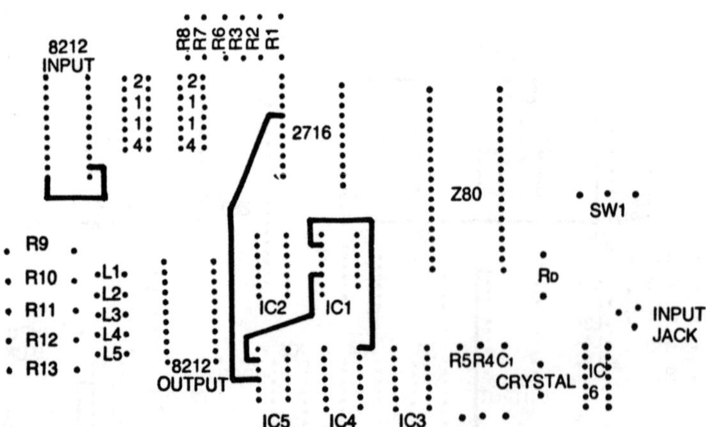

Fig. 17-25. Connect 11 of 8212 Input to 13 of 8212 Input. Connect 20 of 2716 to 11 of IC5. Connect 13 of IC1 to 1 of IC4. Connect 10 of IC1 to 13 of IC5.

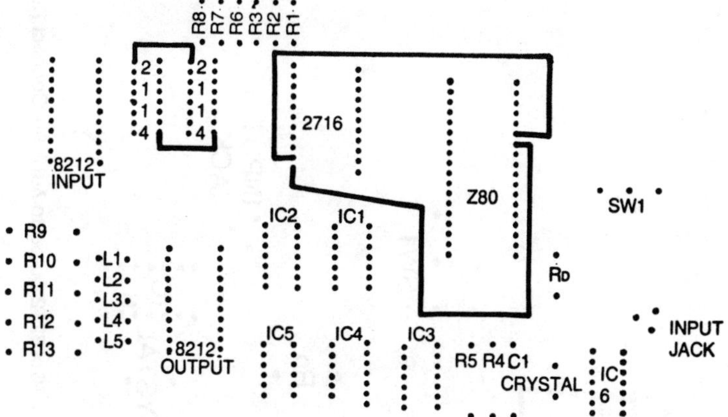

Fig. 17-26. Connect 18 of 2114 left to 18 of 2114 right. Connect 9 of 2114 left to 9 of 2114 right. Connect 14 of 2716 to 7 of Z-80. Connect 13 of 2716 to 8 of Z-80.

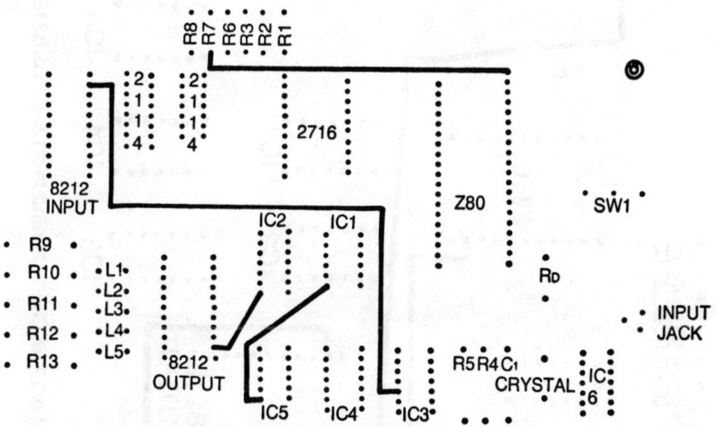

Fig. 17-27. Connect 3 of 8212 Input to 10 of IC3. Connect bottom of R7 to 1 of Z-80. Connect 8 of IC2 to 11 of 8212 Output. Connect 8 of IC1 to 9 of IC5.

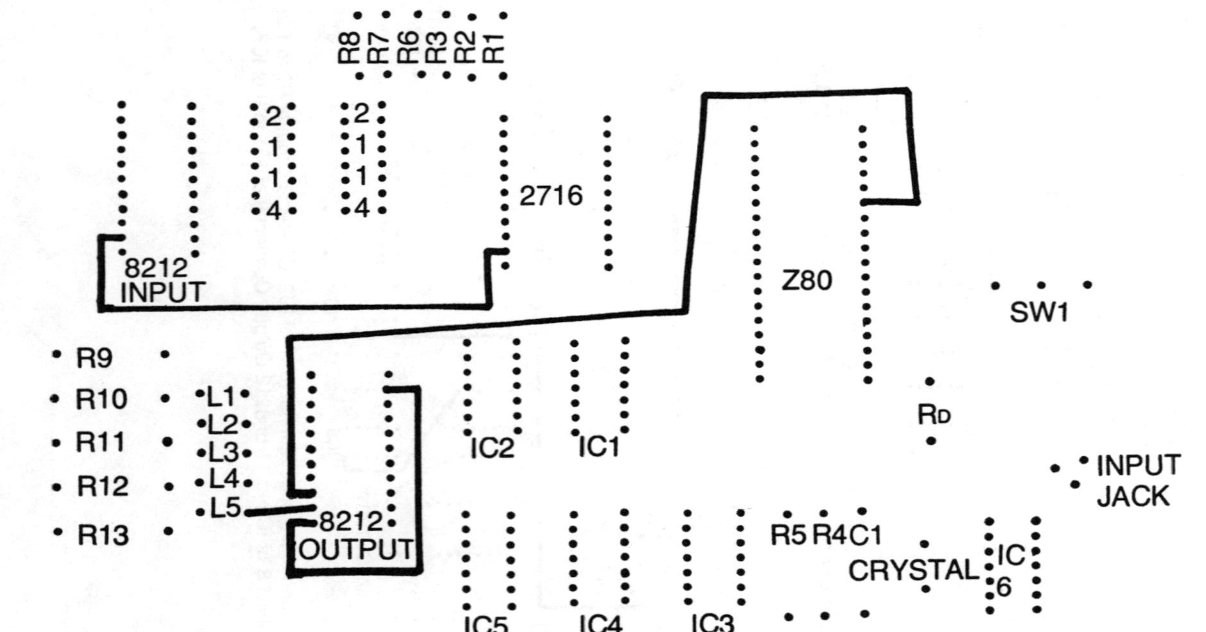

Fig. 17-28. Connect 15 of 8212 Input to 14 of 2716. Connect cathode of L5 to 15 of 8212 Output. Connect 16 of 8212 Output to 7 of Z-80. Connect 13 of 8212 Output to 2 of 8212 Output.

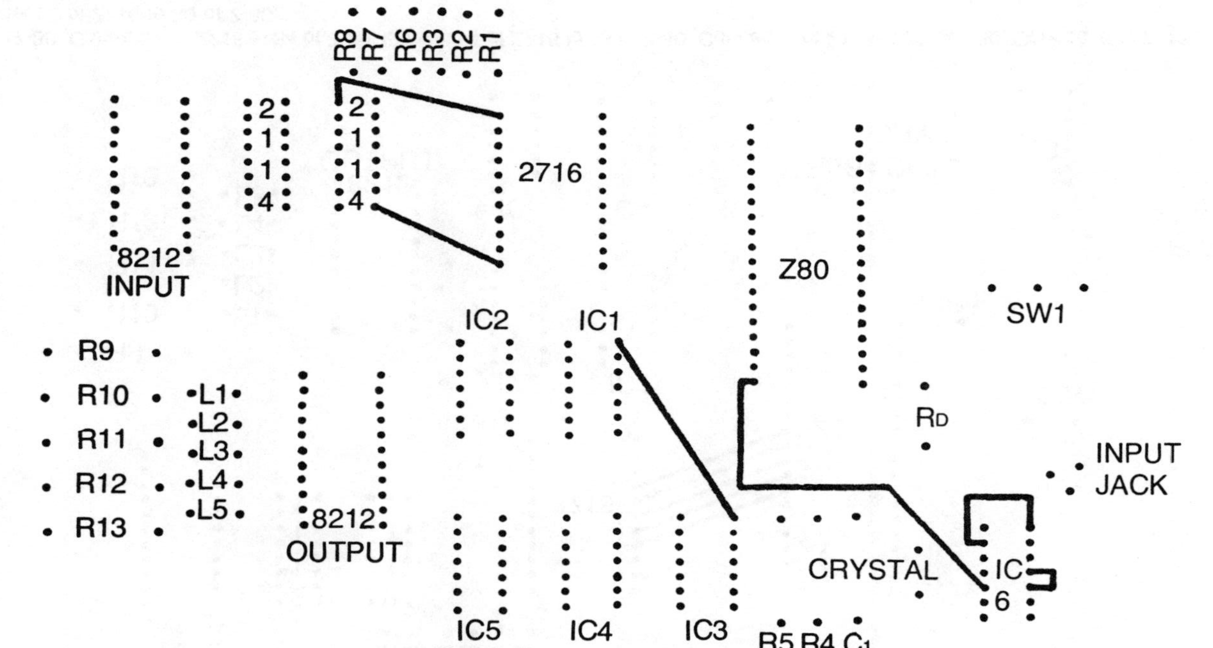

Fig. 17-29. Connect 18 of 2114 right to 24 of 2716. Connect 9 of 2114 right to 13 of 2716. Connect 1 of IC1 to 1 of IC3. Connect 21 of Z-80 to 10 of IC6. Connect 1 of IC6 to 13 of IC6. Connect 4 of IC6 to 5 of IC6.

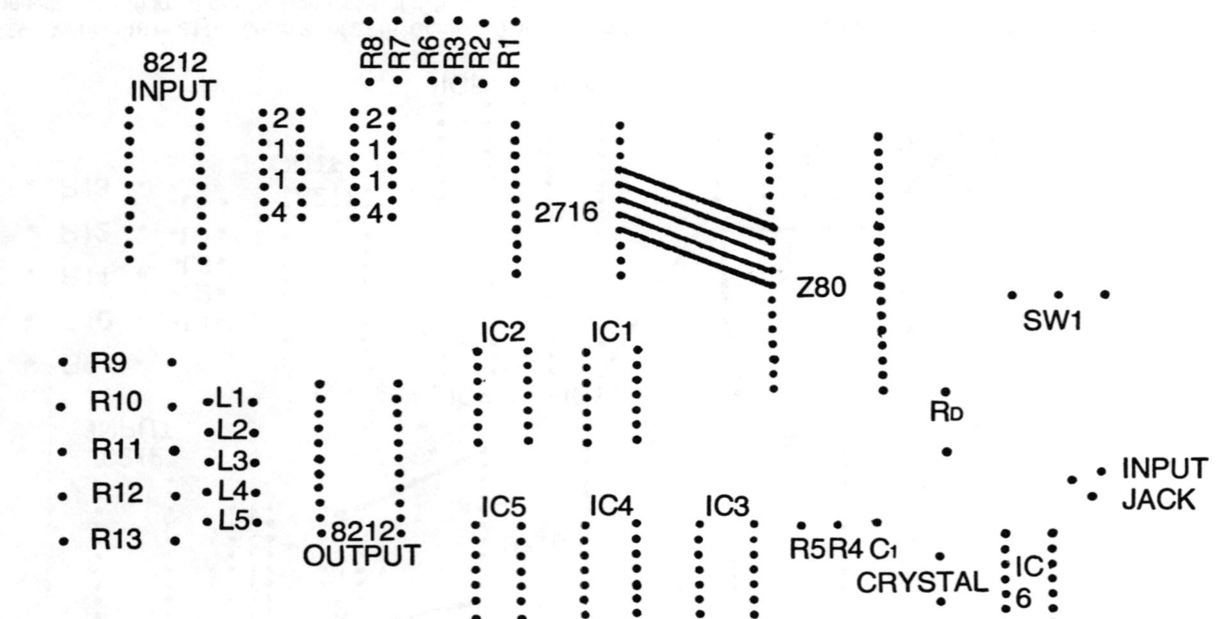

Fig. 17-30. Connect 3 of 2716 to 34 of Z-80. Connect 4 of 2716 to 33 of Z-80. Connect 5 of 2716 to 32 of Z-80. Connect 6 of 2716 to 31 of Z-80. Connect 7 of 2716 to 30 of Z-80.

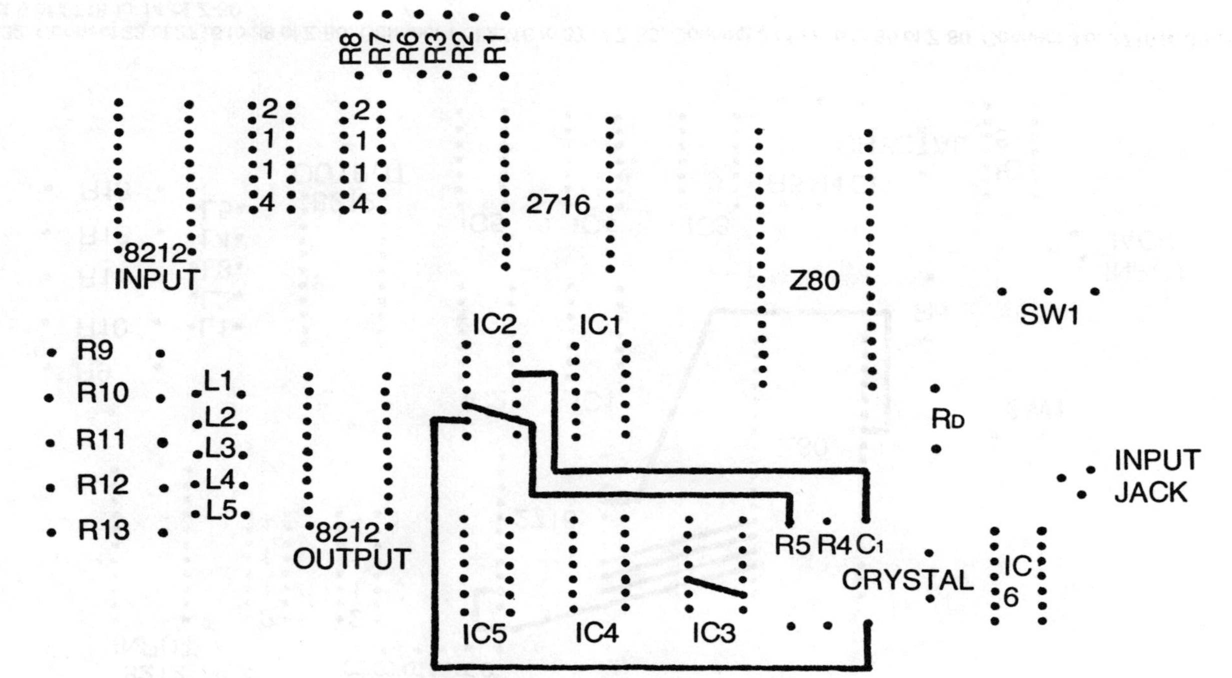

Fig. 17-31. Connect 3 of IC2 to top of C1. Connect 10 of IC2 to top of R5. Connect 9 of IC2 to bottom of C1. Connect 6 of IC3 to 10 of IC3.

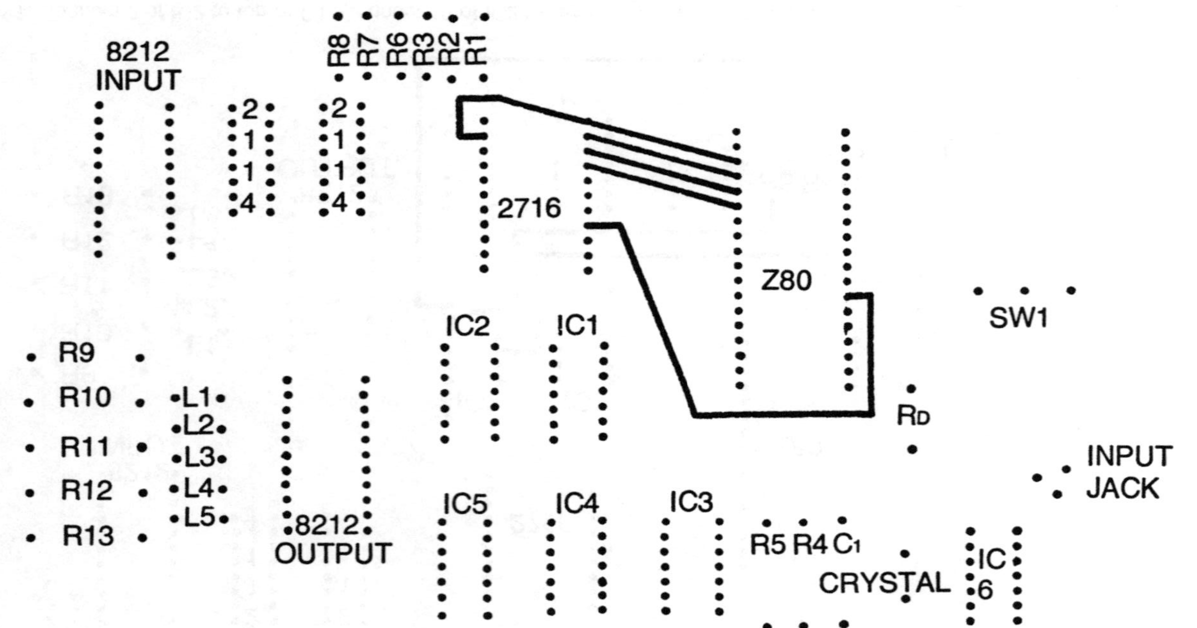

Fig. 17-32. Connect 23 of 2716 to 38 of Z-80. Connect 1 of 2716 to 37 of Z-80. Connect 2 of 2716 to 36 of Z-80. Connect 3 of 2716 to 35 of Z-80. Connect 9 of 2716 to 14 of Z-80.

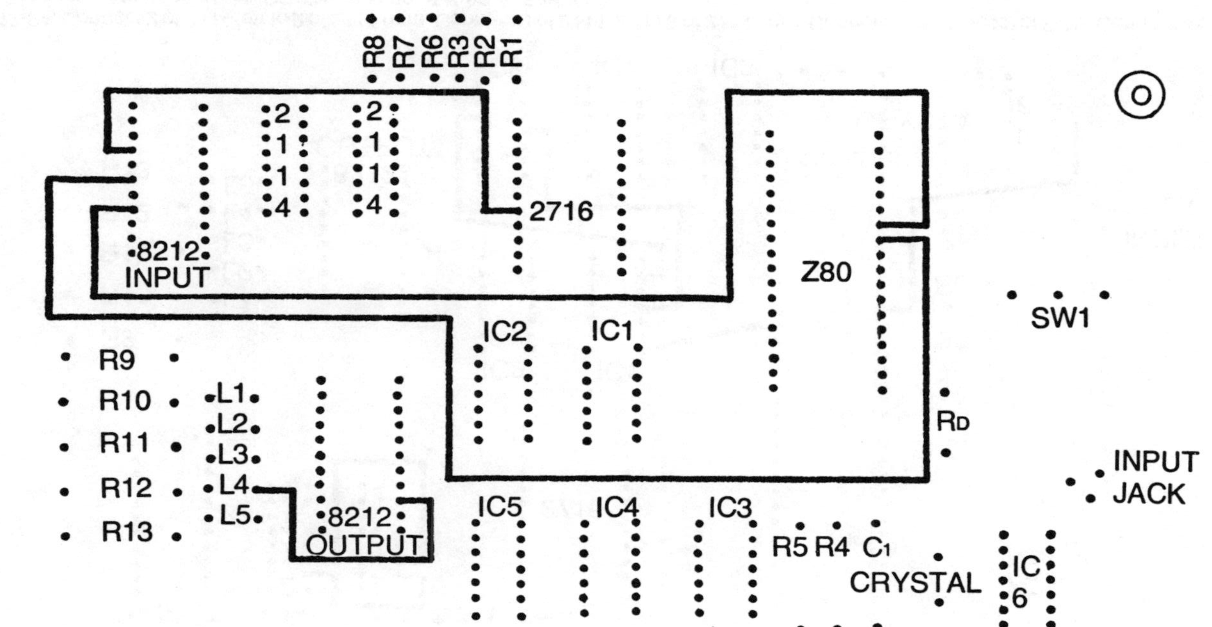

Fig. 17-33. Connect 21 of 8212 Input to 17 of 2716. Connect 19 of 8212 Input to 10 of Z-80. Connect 17 of 8212 Input to 9 of Z-80. Connect cathode of L4 to 10 of 8212 Output.

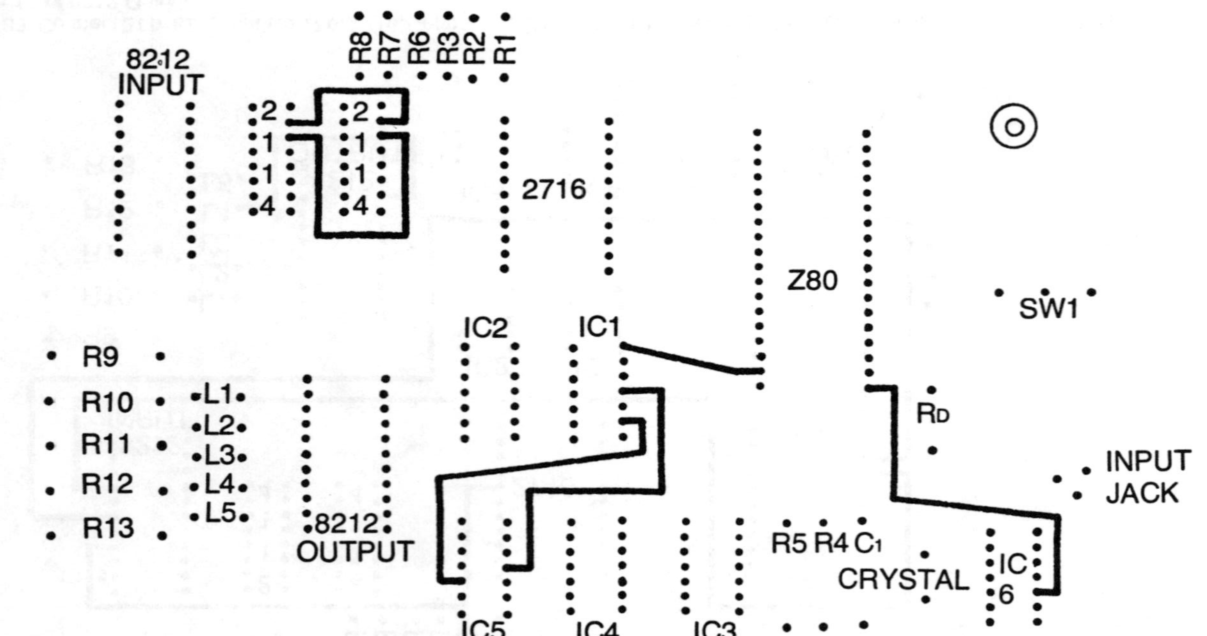

Fig. 17-34. Connect 2 of 2114 left to 2 of 2114 right. Connect 3 of 2114 left to 3 of 2114 right. Connect 1 of IC1 to 22 of Z-80. Connect 4 of IC1 to 4 of IC5. Connect 8 of IC1 to 10 of IC5. Connect 20 of Z-80 to 5 of IC8.

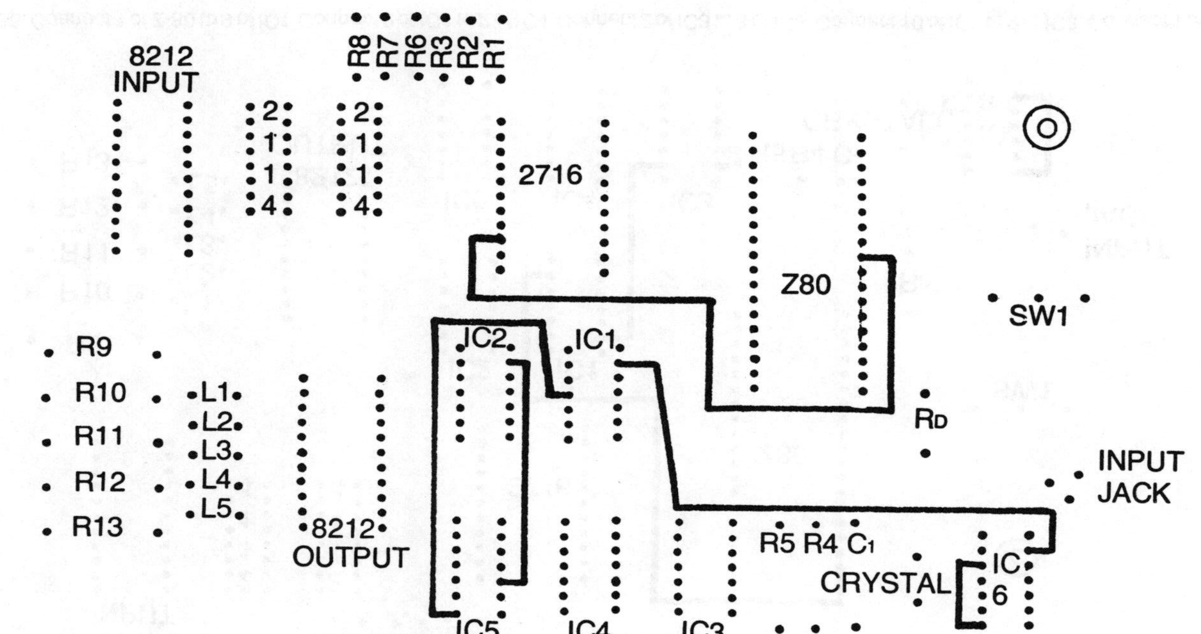

Fig. 17-35. Connect 15 of 2716 to 9 of Z-80. Connect 11 of IC1 to 8 of IC5. Connect 2 of IC1 to 2 of IC6. Connect 2 of IC2 to 5 IC5. Connect 12 of IC6 to 8 of IC6.

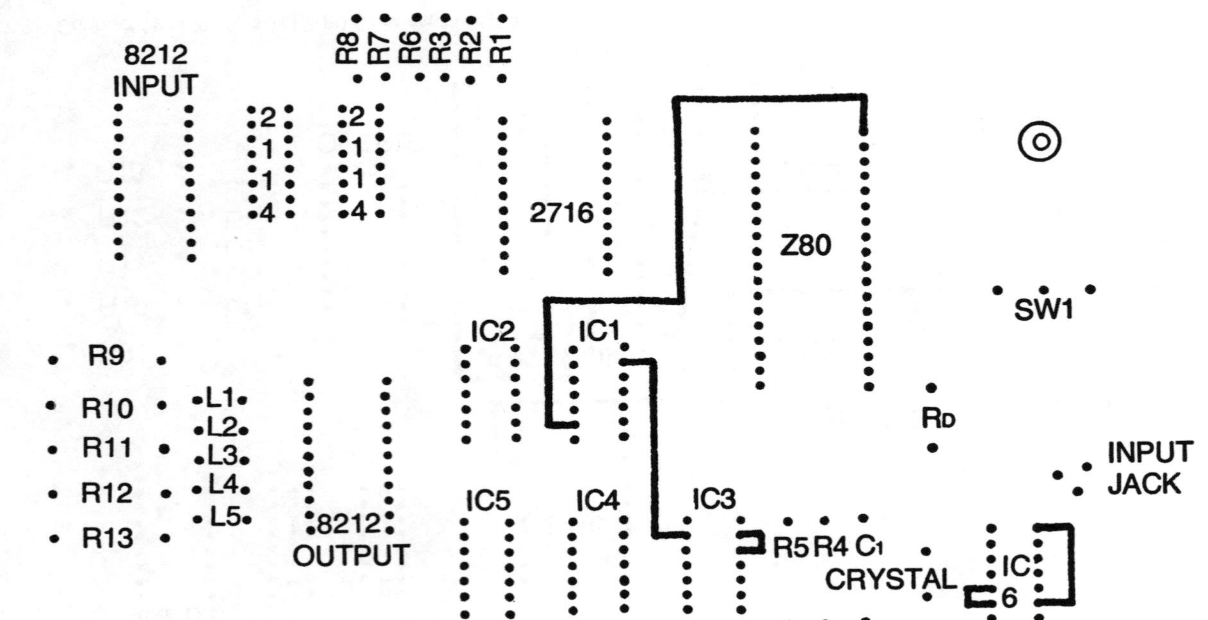

Fig. 17-36. Connect 1 of Z-80 to 9 of IC1. Connect 2 of IC1 to 2 of IC4. Connect 2 of IC3 to 3 of IC3. Connect 10 of IC6 to 9 of IC6. Connect 1 of IC6 to 6 of IC6.

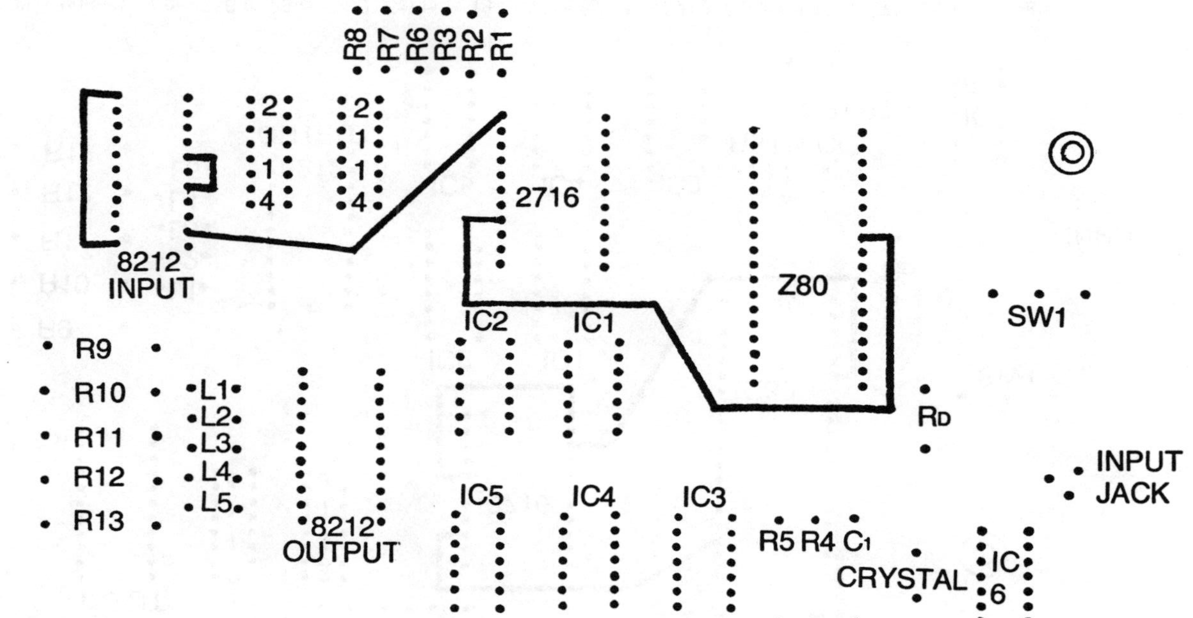

Fig. 17-37. Connect 24 of 8212 Input to 13 of 8212 Input. Connect 5 of 8212 Input to 7 of 8212 Input. Connect 11 of 8212 Input to 24 of 2716. Connect 16 of 2716 to 10 of Z-80.

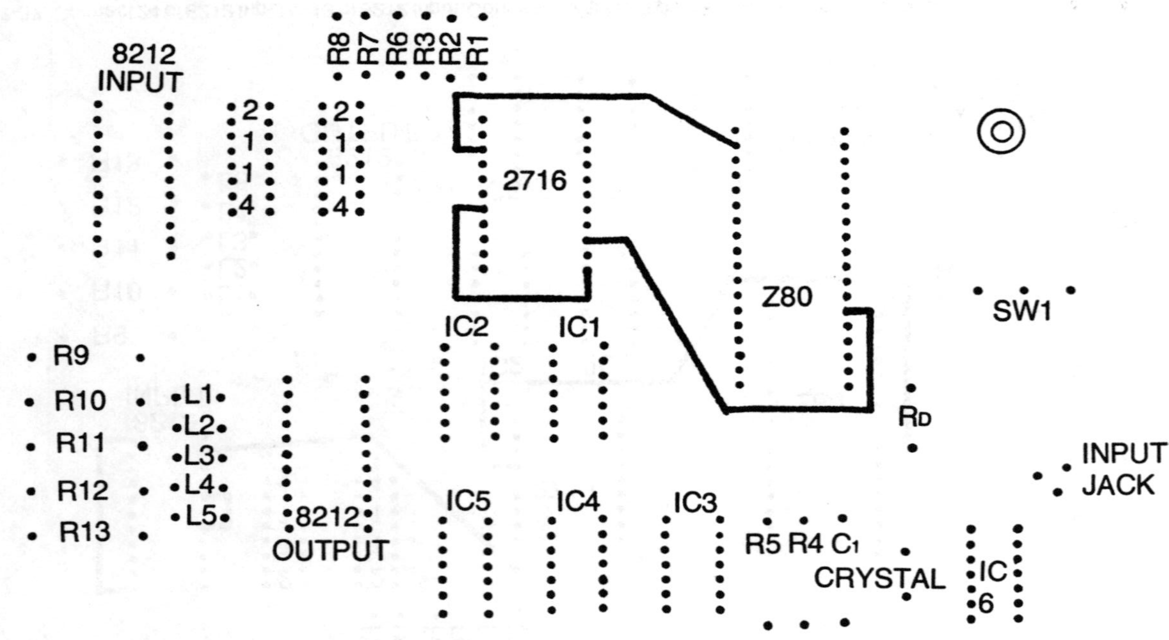

Fig. 17-38. Connect 22 of 2716 to 39 of Z-80. Connect 18 of 2716 to 12 of 2716. Connect 10 of 2716 to 15 of Z-80.

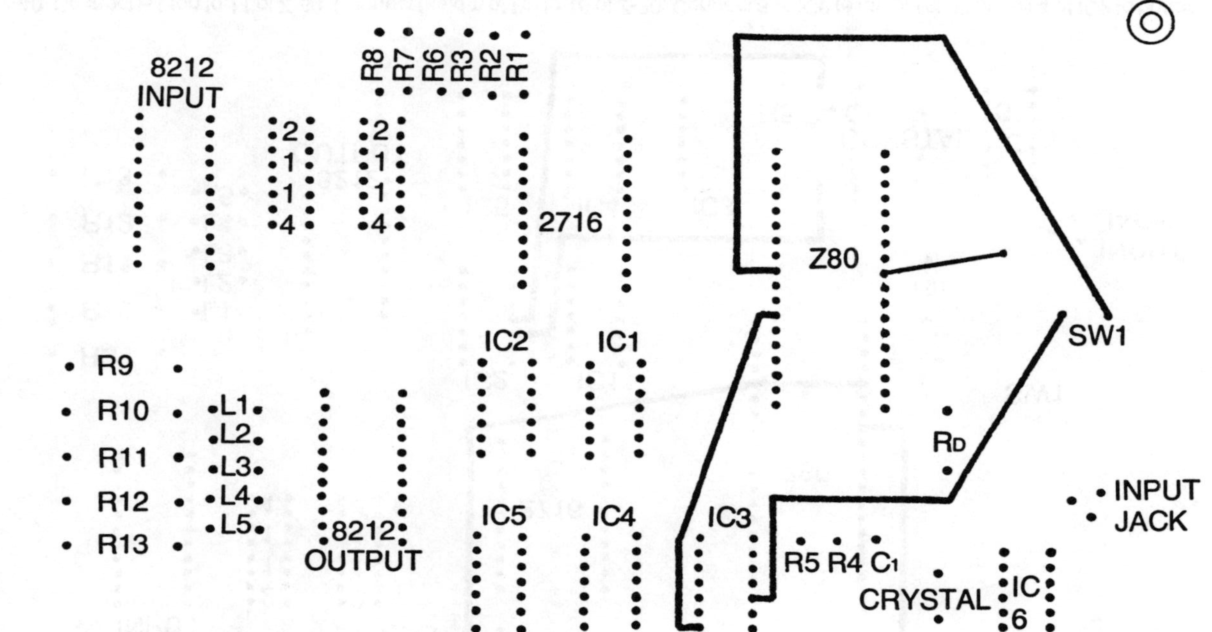

Fig. 17-39. Connect 29 of Z-80 to SW1 right. Connect 11 of Z-80 to SW1 left. Connect 26 of Z-80 to 8 of IC3. Connect 5 of IC3 to SW1 center.

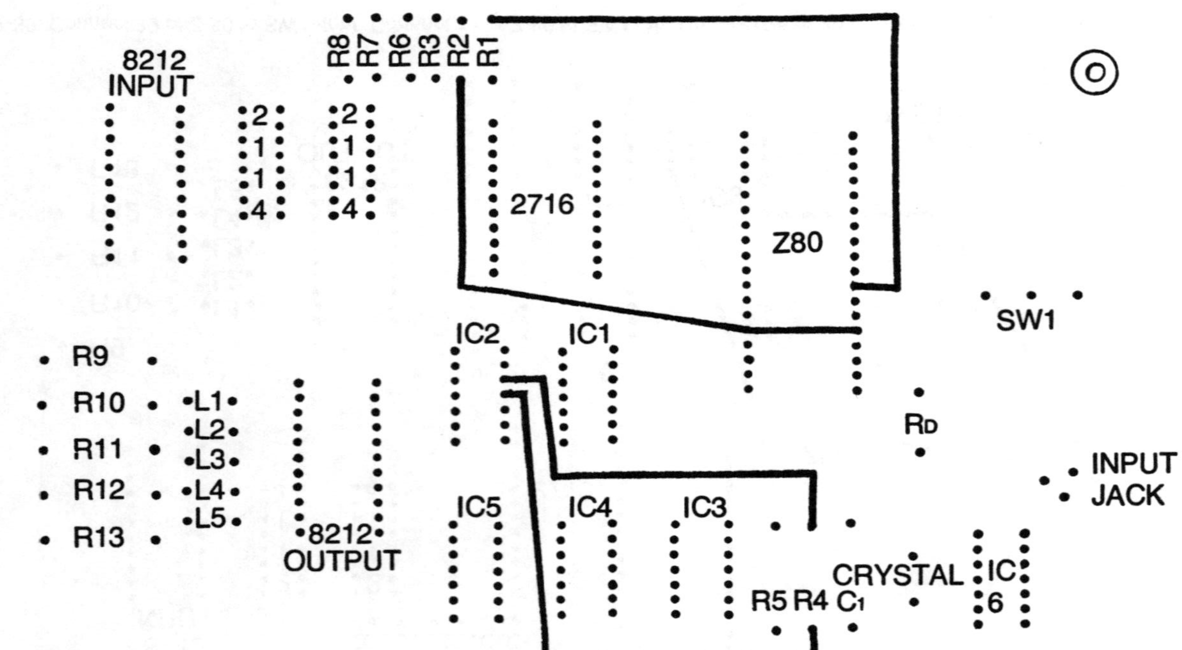

Fig. 17-40. Connect R1 top to 11 of Z-80. Connect bottom of R2 to 16 of Z-80. Connect 3 of IC2 to top of R4. Connect 4 of IC2 to bottom of R4.

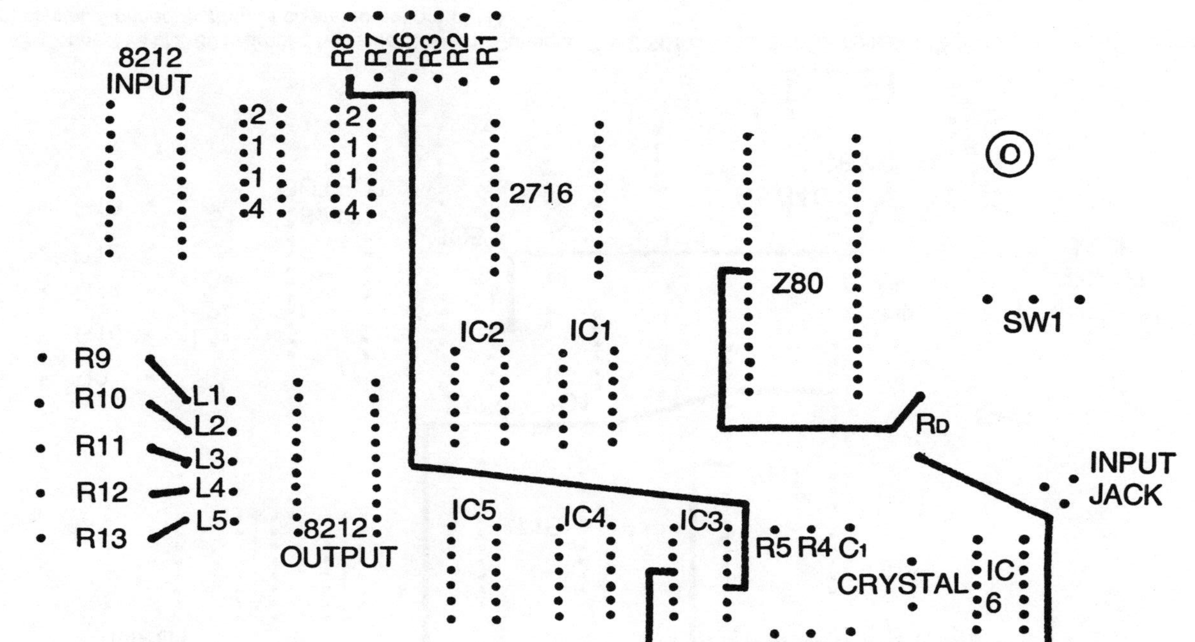

Fig. 17-41. Connect bottom of R8 to 5 of IC3. Connect 29 of Z-80 to top of R0. Connect bottom of R0 to 11 of IC3. Connect right of R9 to anode of L1. Connect right of R10 to anode of L2. Connect right of R11 to anode of L3. Connect right of R12 to anode of L4. Connect right of R13 to anode of L5.

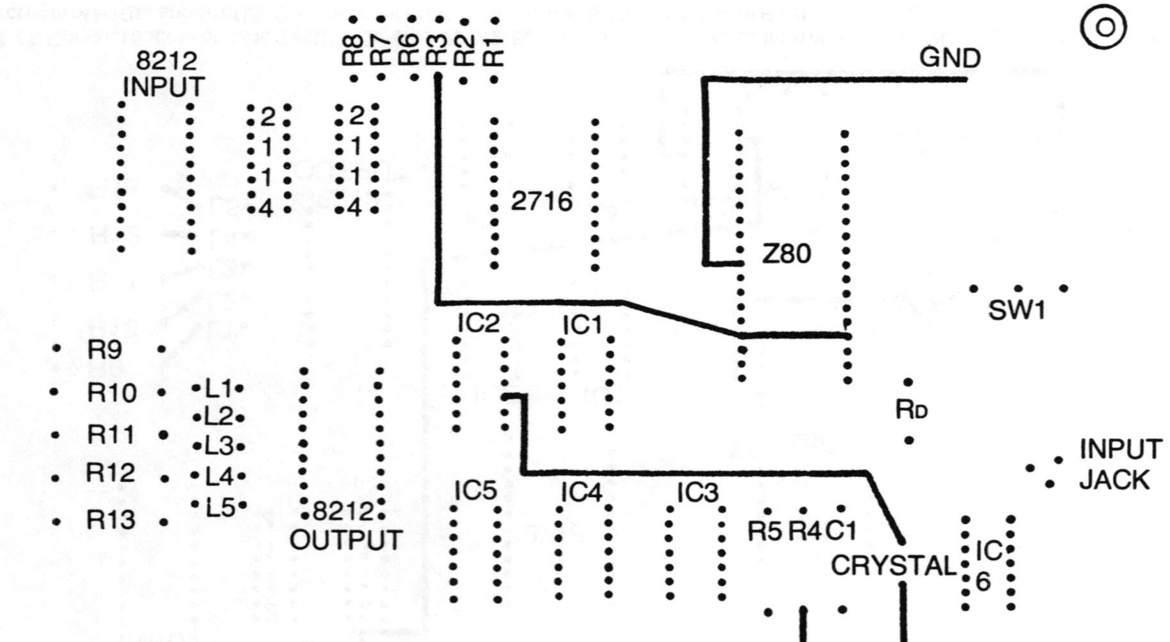

Fig. 17-42. Connect 29 of Z-80 to ground (top side of board). Connect 17 of Z-80 to 24 of Z-80. Connect 24 of Z-80 to bottom of R3. Connect 5 of IC2 to top of crystal. Connect bottom of crystal to bottom of R4.

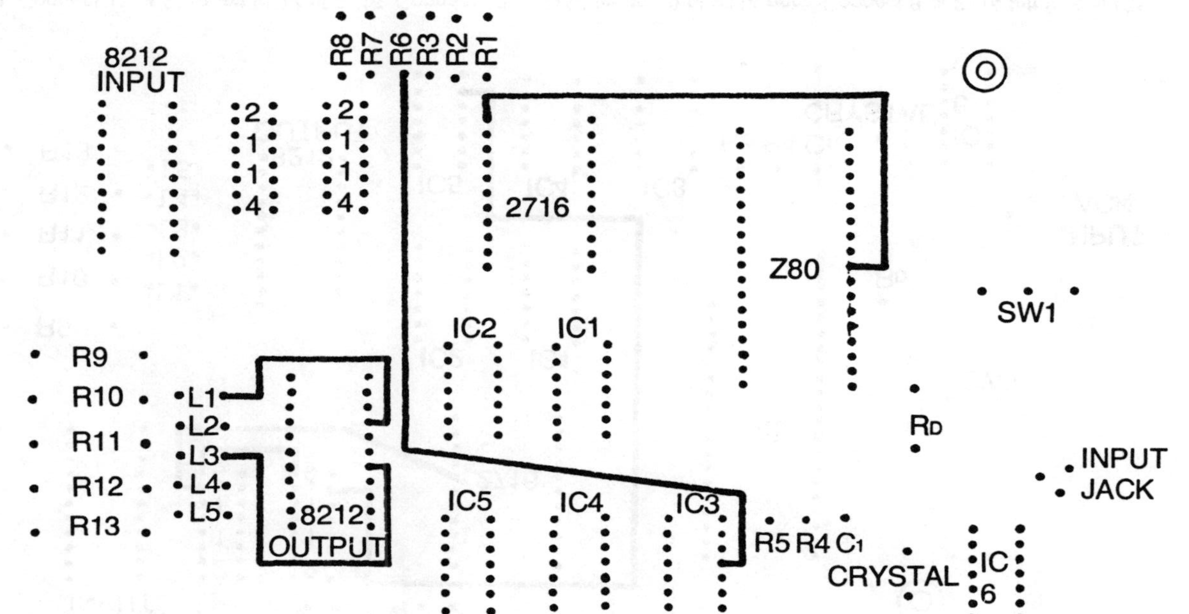

Fig. 17-43. Connect bottom of R6 to 4 of IC3. Connect 24 of 2716 to 11 of Z-80. Connect cathode of L1 to 4 of 8212 Output. Connect cathode of L3 to 8 of 8212 Output.

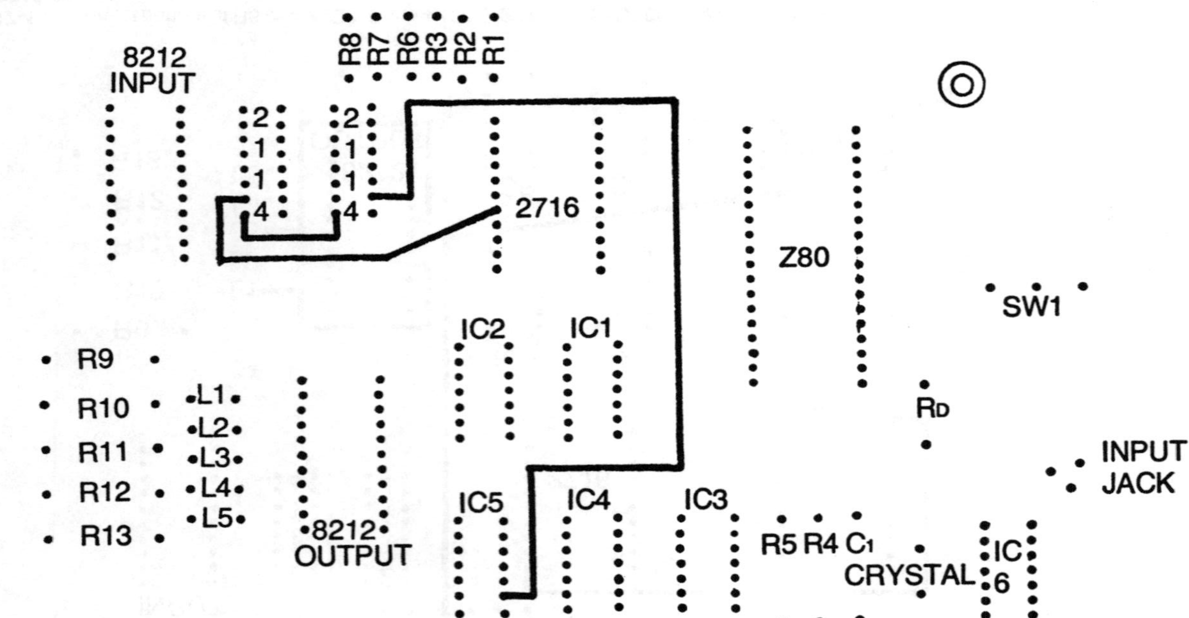

Fig. 17-44. Connect 11 of 2114 left to 17 of 2716. Connect 10 of 2114 left to 10 of 2114 right. Connect 8 of 2114 left to 6 of IC5.

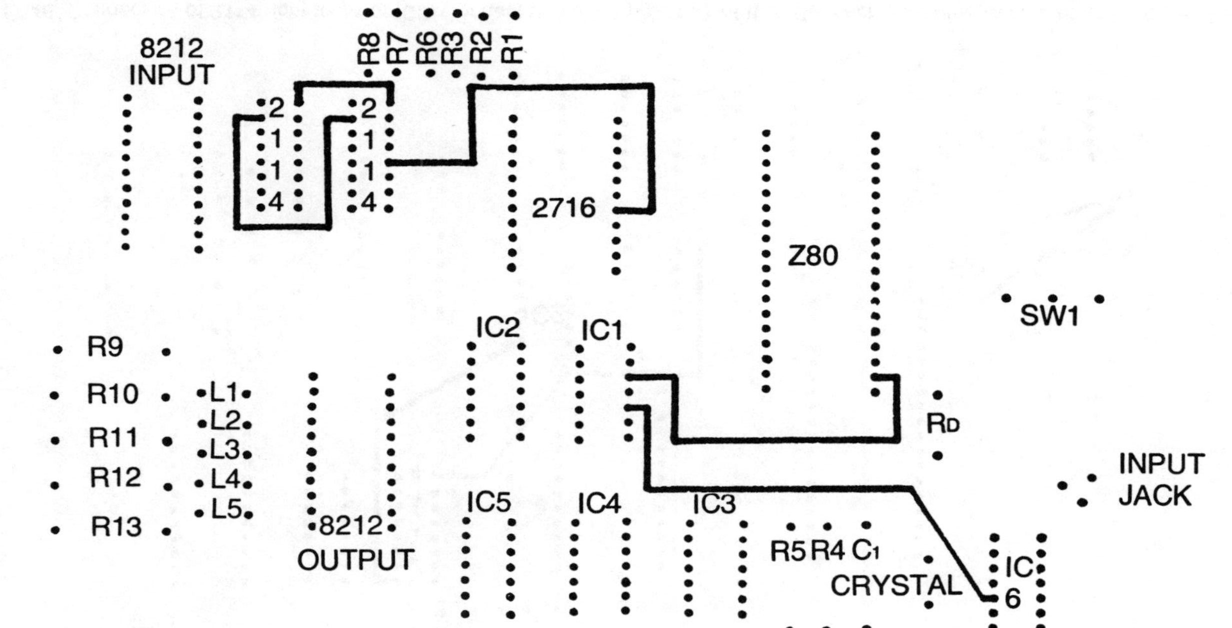

291 Fig. 17-45. Connect 1 of 2114 left to 1 of 2114 right. Connect 17 of 2114 left to 17 of 2114 right. Connect 11 of 2114 right to 13 of 2716. Connect 6 of 2114 right to 7 of 2716. Connect 3 of IC1 to 19 of Z-80. Connect 5 of IC1 to 10 of IC6.

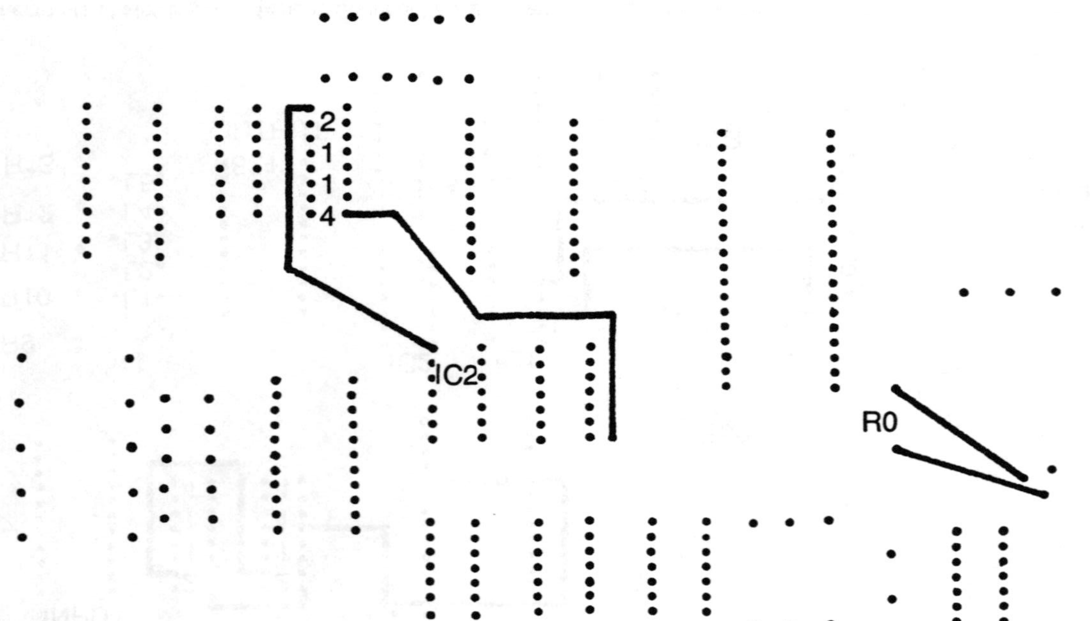

Fig. 17-46. Connect 18 of 2114 right to 14 of IC2. Connect 9 of 2114 right to 7 of IC2. Connect jack wires (output of amplifier) to R0.

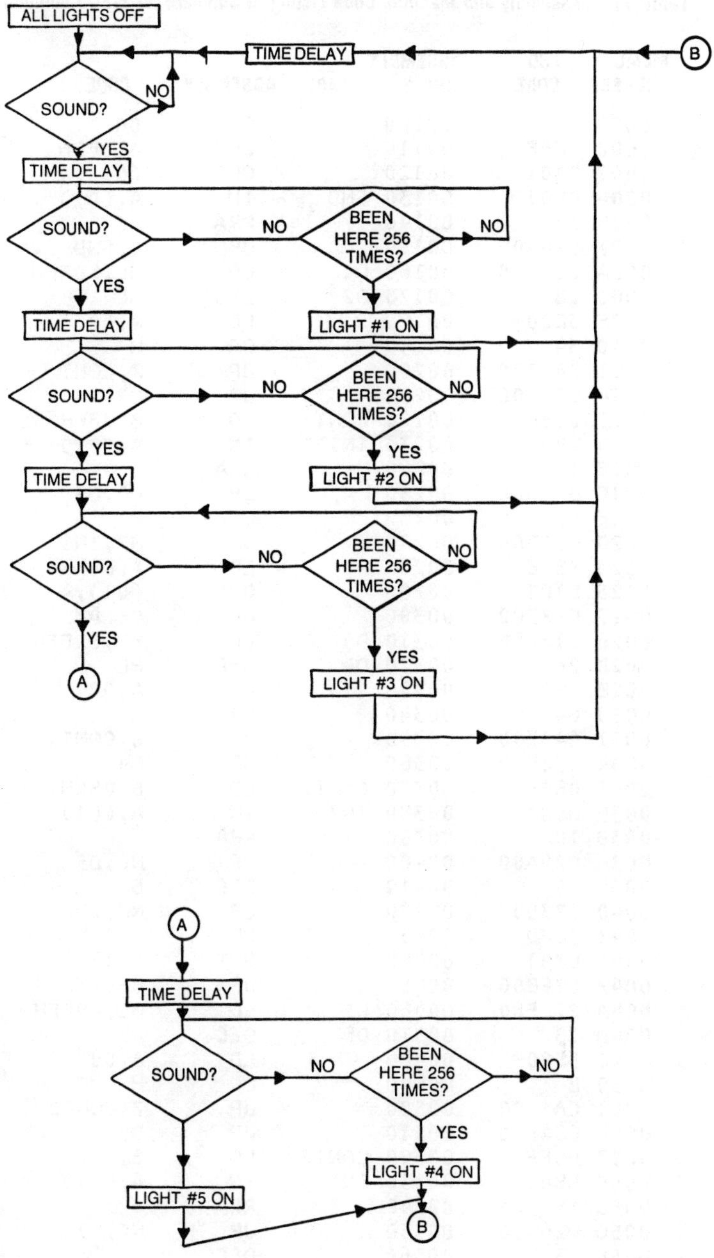

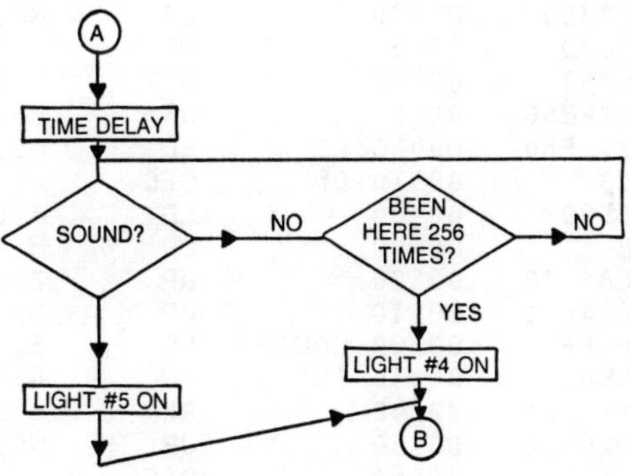

Fig. 17-47. Flow diagram of Length program for Z-80 based computer.

Table 17-2. Assembly and Machine Code Listing of Software for Z-80 Computer.

MEMORY ADDRESS	Z80 CODE	ASSEMBLY LINE #	LABEL	ASSEMBLY	CODE
0000		00100		ORG	00
0000	3EFF	00110		LD	A,0FFH
0002	D301	00120		OUT	(01),A
0004	DB01	00130	SND	IN	A,(01)
0006	1F	00140		RRA	
0007	DA0400	00150		JP	C,SND
000A	21FF60	00160	D1	LD	HL,60FFH
000D	2B	00170	D2	DEC	HL
000E	3E00	00180		LD	A,00
0010	B4	00190		OR	H
0011	CA1700	00200		JP	Z,CONT
0014	C30D00	00210		JP	D2
0017	06FF	00220	CONT	LD	B,0FFH
0019	DB01	00230	IN1	IN	A,(01)
001B	1F	00240		RRA	
001C	D22A00	00250		JP	NC,D3
001F	05	00260		DEC	B
0020	C21900	00270		JP	NZ,IN1
0023	3EFE	00280		LD	A,0FEH
0025	D301	00290		OUT	(01),A
0027	C38E00	00300		JP	DELAY
002A	21FF60	00310	D3	LD	HL,60FFH
002D	2B	00320	D4	DEC	HL
002E	3E00	00330		LD	A,00
0030	B4	00340		OR	H
0031	CA3700	00350		JP	Z,CONT1
0034	C32D00	00360		JP	D4
0037	06FF	00370	CONT1	LD	B,0FFH
0039	DB01	00380	IN2	IN	A,(01)
003B	1F	00390		RRA	
003C	D24A00	00400		JP	NC,D5
003F	05	00410		DEC	B
0040	C23900	00420		JP	NZ,IN2
0043	3EFD	00430		LD	A,0FDH
0045	D301	00440		OUT	(01),A
0047	C38E00	00450		JP	DELAY
004A	21FF60	00460	D5	LD	HL,60FFH
004D	2B	00470	D6	DEC	HL
004E	3E00	00480		LD	A,00
0050	B4	00490		OR	H
0051	CA5700	00500		JP	Z,CONT2
0054	C34D00	00510		JP	D6
0057	06FF	00520	CONT2	LD	B,0FFH
0059	DB01	00530	IN3	IN	A,(01)
005B	1F	00540		RRA	
005C	D26A00	00550		JP	NC,D7
005F	05	00560		DEC	B
0060	C25900	00570		JP	NZ,IN3
0063	3EFB	00580		LD	A,0FBH

MEMORY ADDRESS	Z80 CODE	ASSEMBLY LINE#	LABEL	ASSEMBLY	CODE
0065	D301	00590		OUT	(01),A
0067	C38E00	00600		JP	DELAY
006A	21FF60	00610	D7	LD	HL,60FFH
006D	2B	00620	D8	DEC	HL
006E	3E00	00630		LD	A,00
0070	B4	00640		OR	H
0071	CA7700	00650		JP	Z,CONT3
0074	C36D00	00660		JP	D8
0077	06FF	00670	CONT3	LD	B,0FFH
0079	DB01	00680	IN4	IN	A,(01)
007B	1F	00690		RRA	
007C	D28A00	00700		JP	NC,D9
007F	05	00710		DEC	B
0080	C27900	00720		JP	NZ,IN4
0083	3EF7	00730		LD	A,0F7H
0085	D301	00740		OUT	(01),A
0087	C38E00	00750		JP	DELAY
008A	3EEF	00760	D9	LD	A,0EFH
008C	D301	00770		OUT	(01),A
008E	21FFFF	00780	DELAY	LD	HL,0FFFFH
0091	2B	00790	DELAY1	DEC	HL
0092	3E00	00800		LD	A,00
0094	B4	00810		OR	H
0095	CA0400	00820		JP	Z,SND
0098	C39100	00830		JP	DELAY1
0000		00840		END	

00000 TOTAL ERRORS

```
DELAY1    0091
D9        008A
IN4       0079
CONT3     0077
D8        006D
D7        006A
IN3       0059
CONT2     0057
D6        004D
D5        004A
IN2       0039
CONT1     0037
D4        002D
DELAY     008E
D3        002A
IN1       0019
CONT      0017
D2        000D
D1        000A
SND       0004
```

Chapter 18
The Future

Is it possible to build a typewriter that accepts normal speech and converts it into written words. In my opinion the answer is yes; but today's technology imposes some restrictions. In the system envisioned (Fig. 18-1) the operator must train the system to a selected group of phonemes (sounds), probably about 200. The filter and digital converter section would be more elaborate than any laid out in this book (examine more frequencies, signal strength, etc.). This would involve greater memory and slower operation as the comparisons involve mountains of data possibilities. A single microcomputer would get lost in the onslaught of data. The largest most powerful computer would rapidly fall behind. There are too many comparisons. Parallel processing is the answer. After digitizing the data, a "select" computer would pass about one second worth of speech to an available recognition computer. The recognition computer would attempt to decipher the phonemes used. It and the recognition computer handling "before" and "after" data would often have to get together (via the select computer) to assess overlapping phonemes. Completed phonemes would be passed to the spelling computers where they would be converted into words. Difficult cases would be passed back to the control computer which would take raw data representing the same time period and convert it with different filters and try on the "tough case" recognizers. Successful chunks of data would be passed to the buffer as spelled words. The control computer must keep up the gaps and hold the

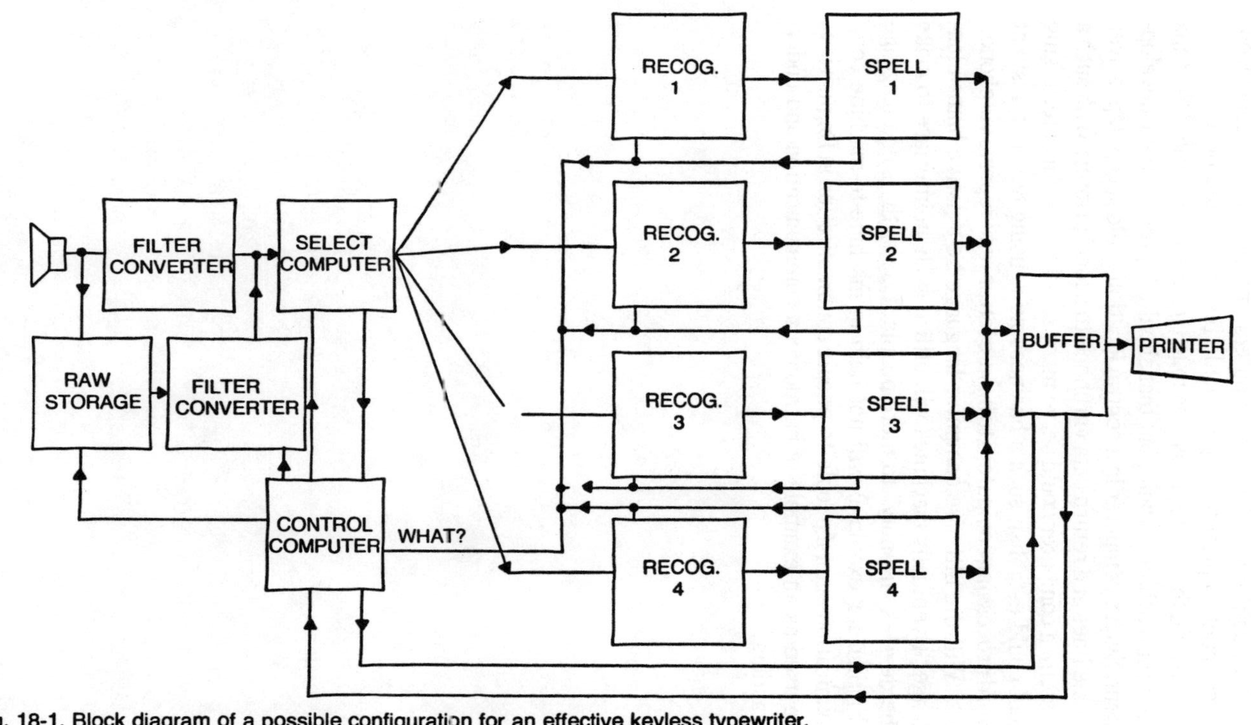

Fig. 18-1. Block diagram of a possible configuration for an effective keyless typewriter.

data from the printer until the long sounds and the tough sounds have been processed.

It might take 40 microcomputers, maybe 60. The delay from voice input to printed output should be one minute or less.

Would this system cost too much for the small office? Perhaps the first machines would, but that shouldn't prevent their development. Such a computer in a central location could accept tapes over phone lines and return data via phone to a local printer. With such a system, a computer could serve many small users. An enterprising soul could establish such a business now, using human typists at word processing computers to handle letters and reports via phone.

Will the ultimate computer language be a native human language? Eventually machines will utilize such an interface to make the devices "friendly" to more people. Use of the same language (English for example) will not help in machine-to-machine communication—not if people-to-people communication in English is to be used as an example of harmonious communication and understanding.

PARTS SUPPLIERS

Advanced Computer Products
P.O. Box 17329
Irvine, CA 92713

Digi-Key Corp.
Highway 32 South
Thief River Falls, MN 56701

Jameco Electronics
1355 Shoreway Road
Belmont, CA 94002

RECOGNITION DEVICES

Audio Signal Processor
Design Solution Inc.
1608 Huntsville Road
Fayetteville, AR 72702
Tel: (501) 521-0281
$99.95 without necessary connecting cable. Works with TRS-80 Model I Level II. Ask Design Solution about Model III. Provides for voice input and output
Cognivox
Voicetek

P.O. Box 388
Goleta, CA 93116

$119.00 to $249.00 depending on unit selected. Works with AIM-65, PET, Apple, Sorcerer, Z-80 based systems. TRS-80 III, 16K. Provides voice input and output 32-word vocabulary.

VET-2
Scott Instruments
815 North Elm
Denton, TX 76201
Tel: (817) 387-9514

$895.00. Requires Apple II, 48K, and at least one disk drive or TRS-80 Model with 32K and two disk drives. 98% accuracy; multiple user capability; 40-word vocabulary with overlay feature allowing for additional groups of 40 words; rapid response time; can be used as substitute keyboard with Apple computer. Handicapped persons are using these units; for details contact Scott Instruments.

ROBOT ARMS

RHINO XR-1, (RS232C interface)
16 ounce lift at extension
$2400.00 in 1981
Sandhu Machine Design, Inc. Sales Dept.
308 South State
Champaign, IL 61820
Tel: (217) 352-8485

THE MICROBOT MINIMOVER-5
8 ounce lift extended
$1695.00 in 1981
Advanced Computer Products
P.O. Box 17239
Irvine, CA 92713
(714) 558-8813

Doring Associates
1744 Route 9
Clifton Park, NY
12065-2497
Tel: (518) 371-9499

Arm complete with interface
$1995.00 in 1981
Sorrento Valley Associates, Inc.

11722 Sorrento Valley Road
San Diego, CA 92121

HIGH TECHNOLOGY MAGAZINES

Robotics Age
P.O. Box 512
Tujunga, CA 91042
Articles and ads related to robots, arms, and sensors; 60 pages of very high quality information.

Radio-Electronics
Subscription Service
Box 2520
Boulder, CO 80322
Articles, projects, ads, equipment reports; 150 pages about electronics and the newest happenings. Recent series included "How to Build a Home Robot" and "How to Build a Home Satellite Receiver." Articles are written very clearly; this is a good place to learn about electronics. Ads include many suppliers of electronic component.

BYTE
P.O. Box 590
Martinsville, NJ 08836
Articles, ads, reviews; 500 pages about various microcomputer topics. Excellent ads, many articles are rather advanced, though the novice can find some things of interest.

80 Microcomputing
P.O. Box 981
Farmingdale, NY 11737
Articles, ads, reviews; 425 pages dedicated to topics relating to Radio Shack computers. Most articles are clear and practical. Although it covers only one manufacturer's product, this is an excellent publication form which to learn what microcomputing is all about.

RECOGNITION LITERATURE

Teaching Your Computer to Talk by Edward R. Teja. Published by TAB Books, Inc., Blue Ridge Summit, PA 17214.

Voice News (newsletter). Published by Stoneridge Technical Services, P.O. Box 1891, Rockville, MD 20850. Tel: (301) 424-0114.

Index